Race and Politics

V

THE HAYMARKET SERIES

Editors: Mike Davis and Michael Sprinker

The Haymarket Series offers original studies in politics, history and culture, with a focus on North America. Representing views across the American left on a wide range of subjects, the series will be of interest to socialists both in the USA and throughout the world. A century after the first May Day, the American left remains in the shadow of those martyrs whom the Haymarket Series honors and commemorates. These studies testify to the living legacy of political activism and commitment for which they gave their lives.

Race and Politics

New Challenges and Responses for
Black Activism

◆

Edited by
JAMES JENNINGS

V
VERSO
London · New York

First published by Verso 1997
© in the collection Jane Jennings 1997
© in individual contributions the relevant author(s) 1997
All rights reserved

The moral rights of the authors have been asserted

Verso
UK: 6 Meard Street, London W1V 3HR
USA: 180 Varick Street, New York NY 10014–4606

Verso is the imprint of New Left Books

ISBN 1–85984–862–1
ISBN 1–85984–198–8 (pbk)

British Library Cataloguing in Publication Data
A catalogue record for this book is available from the British Library

Library of Congress Cataloging-in-Publication Data
A catalog record for this book is available from the Library of Congress

Typeset by Set Systems, Saffron Walden, Essex
Printed in Great Britain by Biddles Ltd, Kings Lynn and Guildford

Contents

PART II: Empowering Black Communities in the United States

Acknowledgements

Several individuals provided important assistance and guidance in the development of this anthology. I wish to thank Michael Sprinker, the North American editor of Verso Press, for his support and encouragement. As I have stated in one of my earlier publications with Verso, Michael Sprinker has played an important role in ensuring that the perspectives and work of scholars and activists dedicated to progressive social change are heard in the United States and abroad. Thanks are due also to Professor John C. Berg and the editors of *New Political Science* for allowing me to reprint one of my articles appearing in the Winter/Spring 1994, no. 28/29 issue, under the title "The Need for a Third Party in U.S. Politics." In slightly revised form, this article appears as chapter 11 in this reader.

I also wish to thank Gemima Remy, who assisted me with the organization and editing of this reader. Gemima Remy also worked closely with the contributors to ensure that their ideas were expressed effectively and with precision. Junette Davids, while a visiting graduate student from South Africa, assisted in initially contacting contributors and producing the early drafts of this reader. Louisa Castner's assistance with the editing and the index was invaluable. Finally, but certainly not least, I wish to thank fellow staff and colleagues for their continual support of my work and the mission of the William Monroe Trotter Institute at the University of Massachusetts Boston.

Preface

James Jennings

This reader has two goals. The first is to highlight some of the political challenges currently facing Black activists and leaders in the United States. Fundamental changes in this nation's demography and economy are creating a new context for Black political activism. Broad demographic and economic conditions, as well as a rapidly growing alienation on the part of many citizens, but especially Black and Latino youth, are transforming the civic boundaries and rules for local and national politics currently in place. The second goal of this reader is to propose strategies and ideas that Black leadership and activists might utilize within this evolving context in pursuing strategies supporting social justice and racial equality in the United States.

The introductory article of this reader gives an overview of the components and nature of racial and urban crisis in the United States and presents a brief description of new challenges facing the Black community and activists. I emphasize three challenges: (1) the need for Black activists to move from Black–White political coalitions exclusively, to broader coalitions involving Black, Latino, and Asian communities; (2) the need to build bridges of activism between communities of color in the United States and those in other places, particularly Europe, the Caribbean, and Central America; and (3) the need for Black activists to build an independent third front, or third party, at the local and national levels. These three themes are discussed in various ways by the contributors.

In the first chapter David Reynolds examines the social and political implications of the transformation of capitalism. He reviews the changing nature of capitalism, and how it is influencing Black political activism and presenting new obstacles – and opportunities – to greater political mobilization on behalf of expanding social welfare. In chapter 2, James Steele reviews recent electoral developments at the national level that point to the need for Black leaders to approach politics differently from strategies used in previous periods. This includes the nation's right-wing shift, as well as significant weakening of the Democratic Party's historical commitment to a civil rights agenda. He ends his essay with a list of questions facing Black leaders and activists as a result of the political ascendancy of right-wing sectors in both U.S. major parties, the Democrats and Republicans.

The next two chapters, by Cynthia Hamilton and Tony Affigne, focus on the failures of local policies and politics to accommodate the social and economic needs of poor and working-class Blacks and Latinos. Both authors suggest a relationship between national developments outlined by Steele and political and economic ramifications at the city level, particularly Los Angeles and Atlanta. Hamilton and Affigne claim that despite some racial and economic progress, poor and working-class sectors in Black and Latino communities in major cities are excluded from influential urban institutions and urban space. These authors suggest that there exists a vacuum of political strategies and activism responding to the needs of poor and working-class sectors in communities of color.

At least one failure of urban United States policies is reflected in the growing political tensions among Black, Latino, and Asian communities. John Betancur and Douglas Gills examine how such policies, as well as structural factors, inhibit the possibilities of political coalitions among these communities of color. The co-authors focus on the Black and Latino coalition that started to emerge in Chicago under the administration of Mayor Harold Washington, but their discussion is applicable to many other cities. Coupled with growing numbers in these communities, the problems of racism and poverty become especially explosive in many urban areas.

The challenges and issues identified by the contributors to this volume are not confined to the United States. The chapters by Louis Kushnick and Clarence Lusane provide a context for examining race and political activism in Britain. These authors show that the kinds of challenges facing the Black community in the United States are similar to an emerging situation in this nation, and perhaps others in Europe. Kushnick presents a historical context for understanding the relationship between race and class and the utilization of race as a political tool in England today. Lusane illustrates remarkable similarities in the relationship between racial politics and the rise of right-wing national strategies in both places. Race relations in both regions reflect the impact of the transformation of national economies, described by Reynolds earlier. Thus, race divisions are a convenient mechanism for managing class conflict and problems arising from such transformations in the international arena. These articles suggest that responses of activists to continuing problems of racism and poverty should not be confined to domestic boundaries. Ultimately, antiracist and antipoverty struggles must be internationalized.

The second section of the reader includes essays that respond to some of the issues and concerns raised in earlier chapters. In chapter 8, William Sales, Jr. and Roderick Bush review some of the obstacles to and reasons for building alliances among Black, Latino, and Asian communities aimed at progressive public and social welfare policies. Their essay indicates that such coalitions can be an important foundation for a renewed movement for social change in many cities in the United States. Sales and Bush believe that grassroots activism, both within and outside the electoral arena, offers the best possibility and most effective examples of Black and Latino coalitions.

The failure of a sector of Black elected and appointed leadership to support change aimed at greater class equality and expanding social welfare has disillusioned so many people in the Black community. This disillusionment, coupled with the structural changes outlined by Reynolds, has resulted in a vacuum of progressive Black political leadership. It is this vacuum that partially explains the rise of Black conservatives reflecting the nation's rightward political movement. In chapter 9, Lewis Randolph analyzes the rise of Black conservatives and summarizes their major ideas. He critiques the theoretical and logical weaknesses in Black neoconservative thought with examples of philosophical and behavioral inconsistencies among this group. Randolph also outlines some of the responses that Black activists should consider in order to mobilize community support within a framework of social change aimed at reducing the effects of class inequality and racism.

One obstacle to the kind of progressive activism advocated by the contributors is the role of the media in creating dialogue aimed at understanding the nature and existence of racism and poverty. The mainstream media generally reflect a sensationalist and exploitive role in encouraging racial and ethnic tensions among Blacks, Latinos, and Asians. Furthermore, the mainstream media play a partnering role with the major United States political parties and their corporate agendas in how social welfarism is conceptualized and defined in this country. This issue is discussed by Farai Chideya in chapter 10. She argues that it is critical for Black people to develop independent news gathering and reporting sources that are predisposed to challenge racism and poverty conditions rather than apologize or justify these problems, as many have done in the nation's leading journals and newspapers. Additionally, Blacks and others must realize that the facilitation of "racialization" of class issues by the media represents a political tool assiduously used by powerful interests to deflect class-based criticism and anger. As pointed out by Steele in chapter 2, however, this characterizes both major United States parties.

In the last article, I argue that supporting a progressive third party effort or some mechanism for asserting independent political power, aimed at redistributing wealth, redefining economic renewal at the national and urban level in terms of the needs of people and neighborhoods, eliminating racism and poverty, and demilitarizing society, is fundamental to resolving the social and economic crisis described by the contributors. This last chapter concludes that the nature of political mobilization in Black and other communities of color should be based on seeking power rather than access to those interests controlling wealth and power. Black leaders and activists are urged, therefore, to adopt the call for a third party as part of the base for creating a progressive politics that builds bridges with other communities of color and supporters. As suggested earlier by some of the contributors, a progressive agenda of social and racial justice is not possible within the current electoral monopoly of national politics on the part of the two major parties in the United States. An independent front, or third party, based on an agenda of eliminating poverty and racism and reducing class inequality, is an alternative that activists should consider for continuing to democratize this society.

Introduction:
New Challenges for Black
Activism in the United States

James Jennings

Several national events have helped to identify issues that are becoming increasingly important for racial politics in the United States. Some of these events include the presidential campaigns of Jesse Jackson in 1984 and 1988, the urban rebellions in Los Angeles and other cities in 1992, the overthrow of apartheid in South Africa, the U.S. invasions of Panama and Iraq, and, most recently, the Million Man March in Washington, D.C., and certainly the O. J. Simpson criminal trial in 1995. Viewed panoramically, these and other events highlight at least three issues that are helping to define and mold Black politics and leadership in this country. These issues are (1) the nature and quality of political relations between Blacks and other communities of color, particularly Latinos and Asians; (2) the impact of international developments on Black life; and (3) the relationship between the Black community and the two major national parties in the United States. How activists and leaders respond to these three issues will fundamentally influence the nature and direction of politics in this country. Although these issues may not be completely new for the Black community, systemic demographic and economic changes, as well as continuing and growing racial divisions across the nation, are raising their saliency.

Demographic patterns in the United States, as well as a national economy characterized by increasing wealth inequalities and including continuing problems of poverty and racism, are forcing upon Blacks a reassessment of the major political issues and potential responses that face this community. The crystallization of ideological debate within the Black community, as illustrated in the struggle between

Rev. Benjamin Chavis and old-guard elements in the NAACP, debates
regarding the purpose and need for the Million Man March on
October 16, 1995, and other events, portends a stage of Black political
activism where traditional agendas and established leadership are
being questioned regarding their viability for the political and economic well-being of the Black community. This period of reassessment
is partially based on a growing disappointment of many with the
ineffectiveness of Black elected and appointed leadership in resolving
social and economic problems.

While the disillusionment of this community grows, Blacks are
increasing in number and concentration in many of the nation's larger
cities. Millions among this group, furthermore, continue to be poverty
stricken, unemployed and jobless, and ill housed. Within this context
the country has yet to adopt effective policies and institutional
practices that facilitate and expand the productive capacities of
Blacks. Instead, as argued sometime ago by Manning Marable in
How Capitalism Underdeveloped Black America and by sociologist
Sidney Wilhelm in his book *Black in White America,* there are
indications that increasing numbers of young Blacks – and Latinos –
are becoming expendable and unnecessary in terms of the needs of
national and local economies.[1]

This period of Black political reassessment is fueled by the fact that
living conditions for the masses of Blacks have not improved significantly and racial divisions remain entrenched in this society. It is
generally acknowledged that in spite of important gains of the Civil
Rights Movement in the 1960s and the growth of a relatively small
and primarily public-sector-based Black middle class in the past
several decades, Blacks have yet to enjoy full social and economic
equality with Whites in the United States. While it is apparent that
other groups of color such as Latinos, Native Americans, and Asians
also suffer greatly from institutional discrimination, the Black community bears a burden that tends to be of a wider magnitude in terms
of absolute numbers, proportion of persons and families impacted in
this community, and concentration than may be found in other
groups.

Concomitant with this situation, there are indications based on
attitudinal surveys and public support for anti-affirmative-action
initiatives that many Whites continue to believe in the inferiority of
Blacks. As reported by political scientist Robert C. Smith, a survey
conducted by the National Opinion Research Center in 1991, for
example, showed that 46.6 percent of all Whites interviewed
responded that "Blacks tend to be lazy," 58.9 percent of all Whites

believe that "Blacks prefer welfare," 53.7 percent of Whites agree that Blacks are prone to violence, and 30.7 percent believe that Blacks are "unintelligent."[2] Smith points out that one recent survey describing White attitudes toward Blacks shows "a much larger proportion of Whites expressing anti-Black stereotypes than in 1978."[3] Perhaps the vituperative reaction to Blacks on the part of some Whites as a result of the not-guilty verdict for O. J. Simpson illustrates the extent of racial division and racism. In fact, some Whites have used the not-guilty verdict to argue that they no longer need to worry or respond to conditions of oppression faced by Blacks. Ku Klux Klan (KKK)-like organizations such as the White Aryan Resistance based in California and the Nationalist Movement in Jackson, Mississippi, have gone further than this and attempted to recruit new members as a result of the O. J. Simpson verdict. Tom Metzger, spokesperson for the White Aryan Resistance, boasted after the trial, "This is a great boost to what we're doing."[4] Despite this kind of brazen statement, commentaries from both liberal and conservative observers on the decision of the jurors in the O. J. Simpson trial indicate that racism in some circles has moved from a KKK version to more subtle apologies and explanations for maintaining racial hierarchy in the United States.

Describing this shift in how racism is expressed and intellectually justified, Marable argues that racism is now reflected in new forms:

> It [is] no longer possible or viable for White elected officials, administrators and corporate executives to attack "niggers" openly. . . . Instead a neoracist strategy was devised which attributed the source of all racial tensions to the actions of people of color. . . . Black college students were attacked as "racists" for advocating the adoption of Black Studies academic programs, or the creation of African American cultural centers. Black workers were accused of racism for supporting special efforts to train people of color in supervisory and administrative positions . . . "racism" had begun to be defined as any behavior by individuals or groups which empowered Latinos, African Americans, or other people of color, or an agenda which took away long-held privileges of White elites.[5]

Another writer notes that "the Black and minority communities of the inner cities are being held responsible for the inequalities and racial tensions from which they suffer. And worse yet, they are being blamed for many of the biggest problems facing American society today, from crime to the government budget deficit."[6] The blaming of Black people for the effects of policies and practices that maintain racial and class hierarchies represents a form of racism different from that reflected in the actions of segregationists in earlier periods, but the consequence of perpetuating social injustice and racial inequality is similar.

Increasing bigotry and prejudice in the United States are accompanied by trends reflecting continuing and widening educational, health, housing problems, as well as economic recession and dislocation in urban places, that impact most negatively on Black people. One observer, Roger Wilkins, argues that this racial situation is so destructive that it is "tearing Black America apart." He adds that "in 1993, 53 percent of Black males in the prime working and family-forming years – the ages 25 to 34 – were jobless or employed with wages too low to raise a family of four out of poverty. The incredible burst of prison construction, the harshness of welfare reform proposals and the unwillingness to put Black economic distress on the national agenda are all evidence of the strength and pervasiveness of racism."[7] Wilkins's concern is reflected in the findings of a recent study of homicides in the Los Angeles county of California revealing that between 1979 and 1994 there were 7,288 homicides reported; 40 percent of these killings involved children and adolescents. A large proportion of these homicides, furthermore, were gang related.[8]

Gangs and prisons, as a matter of fact, are major facets of Black life in the United States as a result of government policies and corporate practices that continue to squeeze resources out of the inner cities of the nation. The lack of ample economic opportunities for jobs and high-wage careers has generated massive social disaffection among Black youth as reflected in the growth of violent gangs competing to control turf for drug-related underground economies in many American cities. But rather than provide economic and educational opportunities for youth in this potentially explosive situation, government leaders respond with calls for law and order, and more costly prisons.

Recently, the United States surpassed South Africa as the country with the highest incarceration rates in the world. The prison population in the United States is disproportionately composed of Black and Latino young men from urban areas. The proportion of Black and Latino men in prisons far exceeds the number and percentage in the total population.[9] Earl Ofari Hutchinson claims in his book *The Mugging of Black America* that by the year 2000 more than half of all young Black males will have served in prison or been placed on probation or parole.[10] Prison is becoming a way of life for masses of young Black and Latino men; prison is now a ritual into adulthood for many young people from these groups. In 1995 the Sentencing

Project in Washington, D.C., reported that an astonishing one-fourth of all Black males between the ages of 20 and 29 are in prison, on parole, or on probation.[11] Thus, there was almost a one-third increase since 1989 in the number of young Black men under a criminal sentence. The figure for Latino young men is 12.3 percent, and for Whites, 6.7 percent. These figures may also reflect racism in that while only 13 percent of all monthly drug users are Black, they compose close to three-quarters (74.0 percent) of all those receiving prison sentences. Other kinds of figures showing discrepancies in the proportion of crime committed by Blacks and the lopsided burden of prison sentencing compared to Whites suggest that policies aimed at putting more Blacks in prison, or under the supervision of the criminal justice system, are part of a grand scenario to control physically movement and activities in the Black community.

The kinds of problems that continue to depress the social and economic well-being of Blacks include continual poverty for significant portions of the community, especially among children; the maintenance of public bureaucracies that are politically unaccountable to poor and working-class neighborhoods; mortgage and insurance redlining practices; increasing crime associated with illegal and legal drugs; law and order policies that effectively condemn many Black and Latino youths to criminal lives and high incarceration rates; inadequate health services, including long waiting lists for drug abuse treatment, and high rates of infant mortality; lack of ample affordable housing stock; and continual loss of jobs that pay decent living wages.

Problems like these and others associated with urban and racial crisis are not confined to the big cities in the United States or to Blacks and Latinos exclusively. Urban and racial crisis is spreading rapidly to the nation's suburbs. As a matter of fact, journalist Jack Beatty proposed recently in *The Atlantic Monthly* that in some ways the white-collar and middle-class sectors may be suffering as much from urban crisis conditions as is the case for other groups.[12] While it is far-fetched to argue that the problems of poor and working-class Blacks are not as bad as, or even comparable to, fellow White citizens, it is true that urban and racial crisis is system-wide, and that it impacts negatively on the lives of many people, albeit not equally. Black unemployment, for instance, continues to be much higher than the White unemployment rate, even when controlling statistically for the level of schooling and training, age, and region of the country. Between 1954 and 1994, the chances of Blacks being unemployed were *consistently* at least twice as great as comparable Whites. According to numbers released by the Bureau of Labor Statistics for

September 1995, 4.8 percent of all White males were unemployed, but the figure for Black males was 11.3 percent – more than twice the White rate. This ratio is repeated for all age categories by race.

In addition to the problem of unemployment, Blacks suffer from joblessness to a much higher degree than Whites. As one writer, Phillip Bowman, observes, "The growing numbers of African Americans who are jobless face difficulties even more severe than the low pay, marginality, and inequity that burden those who hold menial jobs."[13] Bowman adds that "Black workers are more frequently displaced from jobs during economic recession, are jobless for longer periods, become more discouraged in job search, drop out of the labor force more often, and experience greater economic hardship as a result of joblessness."[14]

Blacks continue to experience extraordinarily high rates of poverty. As was the case in 1959, currently at least one-third (33.1 percent) of all Blacks live in households below the official poverty level. This rate compares to 31 percent for Latinos, 15 percent for Asians, and 12 percent for Whites.[15] More than half of all Black children in the United States live in poverty, and many more live in what is now officially referred to by the federal government and social scientists as "near poverty."

In the area of housing Blacks still live in places far removed from the social space of Whites, and in living conditions that are far inferior to those of most Whites. This was recently confirmed by two writers, Douglas Massey and Nancy Denton, in their work *American Apartheid*: "No group in the history of the United States has ever experienced a sustained high level of residential segregation that has been imposed on Blacks in large American cities for the past fifty years."[16] Blacks suffer disproportionately from other housing problems in addition to residential segregation. It is estimated that there are about seven million homeless families in the United States. But African Americans are much more likely to be homeless than any other racial or ethnic group in the United States. In New York City, despite the expenditure of billions of dollars on sheltering the homeless population, this problem has grown to such an extent that during a five-year period, one of every four Black children experienced bouts of homelessness.[17]

Institutional racism in the private sector in the form of inaccessibility to home mortgages and denial of insurance and capital loans for the development of small businesses is a major reason for racial divisions and economic depression in the urban United States. In many cities Blacks are denied access to institutional resources necessary for the social and economic development of their communities. It is the policies and practices of banks, insurance companies, and real estate interests that have been responsible for the emergence and maintenance of ghettos since the turn of the century. Today, these same institutions deny residents the basic tools necessary to strengthen their communities economically.[18]

The Black middle class also feels the impact of racial hierarchy despite legal and political progress in the area of race relations. The Black middle class is economically tenuous and proportionately much smaller than the middle-class sector among White Americans. In terms of households earning more than $50,000 per year, 40 percent of all Black households but 70 percent of all White households comprise the middle-class sector. The Black middle class has far less wealth than the White middle class, or even the White working-class sector, in some instances. Moreover, the Black middle class tends to be based on a "two-paycheck family" and public sector jobs to a larger extent than the White middle class. Public sector jobs that significantly account for the emergence of a Black middle class in the last quarter of this century are now threatened as a result of attacks on affirmative action. Almost 70 percent of all Black professionals and managers work for government agencies in the United States as contrasted with 17 percent of all White professional managers, according to analyst Michael Dawson.[19] Thus, the particular occupational distribution found in the Black community makes its middle-class sector more vulnerable not only to economic downturns but government cutbacks as well. Dawson concludes that the Black middle class "is still an economically marginal class, disproportionately affected by changes in the economic and political environments."[20] These findings help to confirm the existence of this entrenched racial hierarchy with disappointing effects that even upwardly mobile sectors in the Black community cannot escape fully. This conclusion is reiterated in a multitude of studies focusing on race and living conditions of Blacks in the United States.[21]

Accompanying growing social disaffection and increasing economic depression for millions of Black persons is the realization that the American Dream basically bypasses many of them, despite some important breakthroughs in race relations. This disillusionment is not confined to poor or working-class sectors of the Black community. According to a report of a national attitudinal survey by Robert Smith and Richard Seltzer, *Race, Class, and Culture*, alienation is increasing and evident among significant numbers of Black college youth and upwardly mobile sectors in this community. These authors state that a "sense of despair and betrayal about the prospects for new, liberal government initiatives to address pressing social problems probably contributes to and surely reinforces the strain of interpersonal alienation in the Black community."[22] Many Whites also feel increasingly alienated and are bypassed by the American Dream, of course, as is true for individuals in other groups in this society. But, again, based on indicators such as the proportion of poor people and the extent of social and economic problems characterizing relatively large percentages of people, it can be argued that Blacks, as well as some Latino groups, in particular, do not enjoy the social and economic benefits of American citizenship to the same extent as others.

One reason for the failure of the American Dream as far as Blacks and Latinos are concerned is the presence of particular policies pursued by federal and local governments in the area of urban and economic development. Current approaches to economic development have been a failure for poor and working-class people, but especially Blacks and Latinos. Yet politicians – even those representing Black and Latino constituencies – vie for mayoral and local offices on the basis of who can best implement this kind of strategy for urban development or operate as the most effective manager under such a framework. There is an unchallenged assumption inherent in current economic development policies that big is best, neighborhoods do not count as much as downtown, and if we take care of powerful corporations and wealthy individuals, they will take care of other social needs. These beliefs are based on the "supply-side" proposal that the more money, wealth, and resources made available to the upper class and corporate interests, the more resources this sector will control to save and invest in economically productive activities, benefiting everyone.

At the local level the supply-side strategy requires, as pointed out by one social scientist, John Kasarda, that urban space be utilized primarily for the benefit of the corporate sector, its institutional partners, and favored workers.[23] Kasarda and others rationalize that doing this would benefit the poor and working-class because businesses and the middle class would relocate to the cities and thereby increase the tax revenue in these places. But adapting this kind of strategy for economic development, coupled with scarce resources, means that there is not much flexibility, as suggested by political scientist Paul Peterson in his book *City Limits,* for local governments to prioritize redistributive issues related to social justice, resolve racial problems, or favor the needs of neighborhoods over the interests of the corporate sector.[24] Local mayors and legislators, including Black mayors, who accept and implement this kind of public policy rationale have contributed to urban crisis and to worsening living conditions.

Pursuing corporate giveaway schemes and tax breaks and abatements for the rich, in the hope that such will result in benefits trickling down to city fiscal coffers from businesses located in their cities, has not worked and is especially harmful to Black living conditions. Alas, since these strategies are not working in terms of alleviating the problems described earlier, politicians have turned to blaming poor people for the urban and racial crisis that they themselves have perpetuated and made worse. The history and facts about poverty conditions, and the reasons for such, show that the urban version of supply-side economics is the culprit. The strategies and programs utilized over the past several decades and aimed at generating economic development by essentially sacrificing neighborhood agendas, affordable housing availability, and small businesses in order to attract corporations have been ineffective.

Class and wealth inequality in the United States has increased significantly since World War II. Such growing inequality has lowered the standard of living for many Americans, but especially Blacks and other people of color. Based on U.S. Bureau of Census figures, the Associated Press reported in the first week of October 1995 that the top 5 percent of all Americans received 21.2 percent of all the income, while the lowest 20 percent of all Americans acquired but 3.6 percent of all the income generated in 1994.[25] Class inequality has forced poor people, and the working class, to bear the burden of constrictions in the national economy. Despite periodic news of jerky and short-term improvements, the economy as presently structured and managed cannot meet the needs of working-class people. As reported by Ted Halstead of the research group Redefining Progress, "the economy has been declining for 20 years and the rate has been accelerating at an annual rate of 6 percent this decade."[26] This assessment is supported by the widespread job layoffs taking place in the country. During the first week in October 1995 the following companies reported layoffs or impending layoffs: Texaco, a loss of fifteen hundred jobs; Pabst Brewing, four hundred jobs; Kellogg, twelve hundred jobs; Foster Wheeler, five hundred jobs; and IBM, eleven hundred jobs.[27] These are just a few instances indicating how many businesses are being forced to institute layoffs as a result of the economic malaise of the nation. In many places, job retrenchment tends to hurt first the most economically insecure in Black and Latino communities. But, eventually, the economic pain catches up with the White working class as well.

Within a context of increasing social and economic crisis in the
Black community, and greater resentment and resistance on the part
of government and many White citizens toward implementing programs to improve Black living conditions, there are at least three
major political challenges facing Black activists and leadership. One
challenge has to do with the nature of political relations between
Blacks and other communities of color. In many American cities this
issue will gain prominence and become one of the most fundamental
changes in urban politics. Demographic changes are transforming
racial dynamics from relations simply involving Black and White
Americans, to situations involving more complex ethnic and cultural
settings. New groups, as well as groups experiencing growth in
numbers, confronted by race and racism do not fall neatly into the
traditional United States Black–White racial divisions, as outlined in
several national reports on race relations. One task for Black leadership and activists interested in social justice and racial equality,
therefore, is to explore responses to a situation where Black, but also
Latino, Asian, Arab, and Native American people are confronted by
racism and urban crisis.

The issue of race can no longer be defined or approached exclusively
in terms of relations between Blacks and Whites; today, relationships
among Blacks and other people of color have become a significant
factor relevant to the resolution of racism and class exploitation in
the United States. The realization of progressive coalitions among
communities of color, as a matter of fact, could possibly represent the
spark and substance of a new movement for social and economic
change. There have been a few, although short-lived, instances of
emerging coalitions, including the election of Harold Washington as
mayor of Chicago in 1983 and the Jesse Jackson presidential campaigns, that reflect this political possibility. Despite reports of racial
and ethnic tensions among these groups, there are also many localized
instances of collaboration among communities of color.[28] These
episodic examples, however, are laying a foundation for the possibility
of broader coalitions among communities of color that could have a
major impact on national politics. The formation of progressive
coalitions among Blacks and other communities of color could be an
important political glue in support of the expansion of redistributive
public policies. Instead of these kinds of coalitions, however, the
nation can possibly witness conflict, which means that poor and
working-class sectors in these communities would be pitted against
each other. Indeed, the major parties protecting corporate interests
could seek to use communities of color as counterweights to each

other in order to produce a divide-and-conquer strategy for maintaining power and influence.

A second challenge is emerging because of immigration patterns in the United States and increasing racial and ethnic problems in Europe. Blacks in the United States may find themselves increasingly drawn to, and influenced by, international political developments. Issues related to racial crisis in the United States, for example, are becoming dramatically visible in European nations. Perhaps these kinds of problems have been there for a while, but they are beginning to emerge more visibly. As sociologist Jewelle Taylor Gibbs has observed, "In contrast to other post-World War I immigrant groups, Afro-Caribbeans in Britain have less education, lower family incomes, higher rates of unemployment, and are concentrated in deteriorating inner-city neighborhoods. After four decades in Britain, 71 percent of Black males are still in low-income, blue collar jobs." Gibbs continues: "As with Black youth in the United States, Afro-Caribbeans in Britain are more likely than Whites to receive harsh disciplinary measure in schools, less likely to finish college, more likely to be unemployed or to be employed in low-wage jobs, more likely to be arrested for criminal offenses and drug violations and more likely to be harassed and treated unfairly by the police and the criminal justice system."[29] Another observer writes: "Citizens of African-Caribbean origin continue to occupy subordinate positions in the labor market, tend to earn less than White indigenous workers, and are more vulnerable to the risk of unemployment, especially in times of economic recession."[30] The scenarios described here are remarkably similar to racial conditions in the United States. Also similar, as indicated by Clarence Lusane's chapter in this book, are the standard political and policy responses on the part of government in the United States and Britain.

The continuing urban crisis, coupled with broad economic and demographic changes, gives rise to a third major political challenge facing Black leadership and activists today. This is the nature of Black leaders' relationship to the two major United States national parties. As described earlier, problems facing residents of urban areas, but especially Blacks, have been intensified as a result of federal policies and reforms supported by both major parties in this country. Urban policies reflecting class bias in favor of the rich and corporate sectors are not confined to conservatives or the Republican Party. In fact, Ronald Reagan's and George Bush's supply-side and military policies in the 1980s represented merely an extreme version of the class bias also reflected in Democratic Party and liberal administrations. As Kenneth M. Dolbeare noted in his book *Democracy at Risk*,

Reaganism represented the "cowboy" style or version of traditional
Yankee capitalism, as practiced by some Democratic Party-controlled
administrations.[31]

While in recent times the Democratic Party has been more reformist
than the Republican Party in the areas of abortion and sexual
discrimination, its policies are still limited and defined by the interests
of the well-off and corporate sectors. Neither Democrats nor Republicans have responded fully, or comprehensively, to the needs of poor
people, particularly poor people who are not White. As journalists
Ken Silverstein and Alexander Cockburn wrote more than a year
before the past election year, "It's the summer solstice and liberals are
now starting to rally enthusiasm for Clinton in 1996, but the raw
truth is that the political agendas of the president's Democrats and
Newt-led Republicans overlap to such an extent that in almost all
areas of policy-making the differences are imperceptible."[32] Both
parties, furthermore, have exploited race to keep poor and working-
class people divided and thereby neutralize calls for an expansion of
social welfarism, instead pursuing the expansion of military and
corporate welfarism. Black activists must question and propose
political alternatives to longtime loyalty to the Democratic Party other
than supporting the right-wing tendencies of the Republican Party.

In many instances over the past several decades Blacks have been
urged to support national parties on the basis of the lesser-of-two-
evils approach. But this approach has not improved living conditions
for the masses of Blacks who are poor, near-poor, or struggling to
maintain tenuous working-class (or even middle-class) status. Only
when Blacks can command political respect will it be possible to
advocate and implement policies that are aimed at ameliorating poor
living conditions. If Blacks decide to support a third-party effort in
significant numbers, then an immediate effect might be a further
weakening of the Democratic Party. While this might strengthen the
Republican Party and its dominant right wing in the short run, it
would also crystallize ideological politics in this country and make
clearer the political influence of the Black community. Despite possible
victories for the Republican Party, however, it would become clearer
that any winning party or leader has to govern a political situation
and manage an economy where millions of alienated citizens, mostly
Black, will have become serious, and independent, political players in
this country.

Conclusion

The above describes briefly at least three challenges and related issues that are emerging and confronting Black leadership and activists interested in expanding progressive social welfare and economic development policies. These challenges are analyzed in various ways by the contributors to this anthology. These challenges demand that Black leadership seek alternative political responses to intensifying economic crisis and racism. As called by Manning Marable, "we must launch the protracted process of building an alternative political apparatus, with people of color at its core, which is fully committed to participatory democracy and full equality, in both the political and economic senses of the term. The old political ideologies, strategies and organizations no longer can advance the boundaries of progressive change, within the African-American community."[33] This suggests, as has been the case in earlier periods, that the Black community can play a leading role in responding to continuing urban and racial crisis and provide political alternatives aimed at the strengthening of progressive social and economic agendas. This role is crucial because of the numbers and concentration of Blacks in urban America as well as the history of this community in struggles for social justice. Given the changing demographic and political context described briefly here, the metaphor of labor activist James Boggs may still be relevant for understanding the political potential of the Black community regarding momentum for social change. As he stated almost three decades ago, Blacks represent the bottom step in the nation's social ladder; therefore, if Blacks begin to move or shake the bottom step, the entire ladder is in danger of falling.[34] Thus, despite the fact that Blacks remain socially and economically marginalized, and a racial hierarchy is still intact in United States society, this community continues to have the capacity to alter radically the political landscape in favor of progressive social and economic policies. Much of what will happen politically and socially in the United States in the future will depend on how Black leaders and activists respond to the new challenges described above.

Notes

1. See Manning Marable, *How Capitalism Underdeveloped Black America* (Boston: South End Press, 1983); and Sidney H. Wilhelm, *Black in White America* (Cambridge, MA: Schenkman, 1983).

2. Robert C. Smith, *Racism in the Post-Civil Rights Era* (Albany, NY: State University of New York Press, 1995), p. 39.

3. Ibid., p. 40.

4. Reuters News Service, October 4, 1995.

5. Manning Marable, *The Crisis of Color and Democracy* (Monroe, ME: Common Courage Press, 1992), p. 6.

6. Kofi Buenor Hadjor, *Another America: The Politics of Race and Blame* (Boston: South End Press, 1993), p. 4.

7. Roger Wilkins, "Now or Never for the NAACP," *The New York Times* (October 12, 1994), p. A23.

8. Reuters News Service, October 3, 1995.

9. See *Statistical Abstract of the United States: 1993* (113th ed.) (Washington, D.C.: U.S. Bureau of the Census, 1993), tables 342, 343, and 344.

10. Earl Ofari Hutchinson, *The Mugging of Black America* (Chicago: African-American Images, 1990), p. ix.

11. See *Washington Post*, October 5, 1995; and Jeffrey Abramson, "Making the Law Colorblind," *Boston Globe*, October 16, 1995.

12. Jack Beatty, "Who Speaks for the Middle Class?" *The Atlantic Monthly*, May 1994.

13. Phillip J. Bowman, "Joblessness," in James S. Jackson, ed., *Life in Black America* (Newbury Park, CA: Sage Publications, 1991), p. 156.

14. Ibid.

15. For a profile of poverty in the United States, see James Jennings, *Understanding the Nature of Poverty in Urban America* (Westport, CT: Praeger, 1994).

16. Douglas S. Massey and Nancy A. Denton, *American Apartheid: Segregation and the Making of the Underclass* (Cambridge, MA: Harvard University Press, 1993), p. 2.

17. *Report of the Advisory Committee on Homelessness* (New York: Edna McConnell Clark Foundation, 1995).

18. For an overview of these continuing problems, as well as a revisiting of these findings reported in the Kerner Commission, see "Symposium: The Urban Crisis: The Kerner Commission Report Revisited," *North Carolina Law Review*, vol. 71, no. 5 (1993).

19. Michael Dawson, *Behind the Mule: Race and Class in African-American Politics* (Princeton, NJ: Princeton University Press, 1994), p. 30.

20. Ibid., p. 31.

21. See Gerald D. Jaynes and Robin M. Williams, Jr., *A Common Destiny: Blacks and the American Society* (Washington, D.C.: National Academy Press, 1989); Wornie L. Reed, *Assessment of the Status of African Americans* (Boston: The William Monroe Trotter Institute, University of Massachusetts, 1992); and Andrew Hacker, *Two Nations: Black and White, Separate, Hostile, and Unequal* (New York: Scribner's, 1992).

22. Robert C. Smith and Richard Seltzer, *Race, Class, and Culture* (Albany, NY: State University of New York Press, 1992), p. 149.

23. See John D. Kasarda, "Urban Change and Minority Opportunities," in Paul E. Peterson, ed., *The New Urban Reality* (Washington, D.C.: Brookings Institution, 1985).

24. Paul E. Peterson, *City Limits* (Chicago: University of Chicago Press, 1981).

25. Associated Press, October 5, 1995.

26. Cited by Reuters News Service, October 3, 1995.

27. Ibid.

28. For examples of local coalitions among Black, Latino, and Asian community groups, see James Jennings, "New Demographic and Ethnic Challenges to Racial Hierarchy in the United States," *Sage Race Relations Abstracts*, vol. 19, no. 3 (August 1994).

29. Jewelle Taylor Gibbs, "British Black and Blue," *Focus: Joint Center for Political and Economic Studies*, vol. 21, no. 4 (April 1993), p. 3.

30. Ellis Cashmore et al., *Dictionary of Race and Ethnic Relations*, 3rd ed. (New York: Routledge, 1995), p. 23.

31. Kenneth M. Dolbeare, *Democracy at Risk: The Politics of Economic Renewal* (Chatham, NJ: Chatham House, 1986).

32. Ken Silverstein and Alexander Cockburn, "Bush in 1992, Dole in 1996," *CounterPunch*, vol. 2, no. 12 (June 15, 1995), p. 1.

33. Marable, *The Crisis of Color and Democracy*, p. 12.

34. James Boggs, *Racism and the Class Struggle: Further Pages from a Black Worker's Notebook* (New York: Monthly Review Press, 1970).

PART I

Political Challenges for Black Activism in the United States

1

Race, Politics, and the Transformation of U.S. Capitalism

David B. Reynolds

The election and reelection of Socialist Bernie Sanders to the U.S. House of Representatives; the strong showings by the Green Party in New Mexico, Alaska, and Hawaii; the steady growth of the New Party; and the Labor Party's founding convention in 1996 – these and many other examples are signs of a growing political movement outside of the two major parties in the U.S. Some on the political Left have greeted these developments with enthusiasm. Others, however, remain quite skeptical. This caution is understandable. For most of us who grew up during the postwar period the experience of building an independent political party has been an exercise in futility. However, this chapter suggests that the hope for a strong progressive/left political movement is no longer wishful thinking, but a serious possibility – one that merits debate among left-leaning scholars and activists. I attempt to demonstrate this potential by exploring the political implications of the changing U.S. economy. To put the matter concisely, U.S. capitalism has entered a new era, and with it, the possibility of new and alternative politics.

During the 1980s the Reverend Jesse Jackson's campaigns and the Rainbow Coalition revealed emerging progressive-oriented political possibilities – although both Jackson and the coalition failed to develop them fully. In 1988 this potential was most visible not in the places where most observers were focused (i.e., the candidate's campaign trail, the national media coverage, etc.), but in the diverse political experiences of local communities. Jackson gained more than seven million votes in 1988 not simply as a result of his program or the media attention that he succeeded in gaining, but also because of the intense efforts of tens of thousands of volunteers. The Jackson campaign witnessed a level of grassroots mobilization unprecedented in recent national elections.

This grassroots mobilization had three noteworthy characteristics. First, it was a relatively large movement. Second, the mobilization encompassed a genuine racial, ethnic, and political diversity. The Jackson campaign succeeded in pulling together a wide range of local social activists as well as inspiring those who had never participated in progressive activism before. Finally, Jackson's campaign socialized political newcomers; the majority of participants had little electoral experience – as a matter of fact, many of the participants in this mobilization had earlier viewed the electoral process with distrust and suspicion. To understand the nature of this new progressive politics, and how it emerged, this essay examines the economic and political transformation of the nation.

During the 1950s, 1960s, and 1970s several factors tended to prevent the postwar Left from mounting serious political challenges to the status quo. Three characteristics stand out in particular: a relative isolation from a large population of complacent "main-stream" Americans;[1] a tendency toward fragmentation; and an incli-nation to follow protest strategies exclusively at the expense of electoral forms of struggle. In contrast, the Jackson campaigns and subsequent progressive efforts ran noticeably counter to this picture. In terms of their sheer scale the local campaigns reached out and included people from "mainstream" society. They succeeded in unit-ing large sections of the local activist community around a single political aim. While most of the core leadership and general volunteers shared the postwar Left's relative distance from electoral politics, the Jackson candidacy succeeded in convincing activists to participate in electoral arenas.

This contrast suggests that something major changed in the terrain of social protest in this country. But this change also reflected an evolution and transformation of the U.S. political economy. I offer the following observation: the immediate postwar economy simply did not provide terrain favorable for a strong, unified, and majority-seeking left political movement; by 1988, however, the evolution of U.S. capitalism produced openings to make a national progressive political challenge, such as Jackson's, a greater possibility.

The Contraction and Expansion of the Left's Political Base

The Great Depression and the Second World War were periods of significant unrest for the U.S. Social disillusionment and frustration were widespread and translated into a series of mobilizations reflected in unemployed workers' movements, the labor movement, and sporadic independent political action. The postwar boom, however, fundamentally altered the dynamic of protest in the United States by demobilizing large sectors of working-class America. Sociologist Richard Flacks provides a framework for understanding this change. As Flacks argues, most people's political actions are based upon a commitment to their everyday lives. When channels for the individual construction of a fulfilling private life become available, people will pursue these opportunities. In such situations individuals expend their time and energy on personal and apolitical pursuits rather than collective social and political action. However, individuals become receptive to collective mobilization when such personal space is not available or is threatened by outside forces, or when a better alternative becomes a realistic possibility.[2]

When viewed in light of Flacks's framework, postwar U.S. capitalism provided many Americans the option for individual pursuit of a fulfilling all-American, all-White, Leave It To Beaver life. For those who participated in the postwar prosperity, growing incomes, job security, and the availability of leisure time enabled a fulfilling private life in the hours between work. Flacks proposes that, in effect, a large number of American workers tolerated dull jobs and management rule in return for the freedom and ability to enjoy life outside of the workplace. Postwar capitalism did suffer contradictions, however, as well as inconsistencies sinceall Americans did not participate in state-generated prosperity. Those left out included a disproportionate number of minorities and women. In addition, some among those born into material prosperity found the rampant consumerism and suburban lifestyle unfulfilling, if not outright stultifying. These contradictions of the middle-class society produced major social movements among African Americans, Latinos, women, youth, and poor Whites.

The End of the Dream

The postwar dream and reality of limited prosperity for some, however, have come to an end. The current crisis of U.S. capitalism has spelled an end to material prosperity for millions of "mainstream," and predominantly White, Americans.[3] The signs of spreading crisis can be seen across the social landscape. The corporate offensive against organized labor had succeeded in lowering the standard of living for unionized and nonunionized workers alike. Overall, between 1977 and 1991 the median family experienced an income loss of 4.4 percent.[4] Conditions within the workplace have deteriorated as corporate strategies of downsizing the workforce and speeding up the work pace have produced unemployment for some and more working hours, greater work stress, and exploding rates of work-related accidents for the rest.[5]

Corporate restructuring has altered the economic outlook for millions of Americans. Communities that relied upon a single or a few companies are now in a situation where, if they find work after downsizing, they must settle for jobs that pay lower wages. According to statistics compiled by Lawrence Mishel and David Frankel, two-thirds of an almost 10 percent drop in average hourly compensation between 1980 and 1989 was due to shifts toward jobs in low-paying industries.[6] Despite an increase in two-income households, by the 1990s real weekly family income had fallen 19 percent below the 1973 level. In 1991, one out of every four households had experienced at least one person out of work during the previous twelve months.[7] At the same time, the percentage of unemployed individuals who received some form of unemployment insurance payments had dropped from 43 percent in 1967 to 34 percent by 1989.[8] Involuntary part-time employment had increased from 2.6 percent of the workforce in 1969 to 4.7 percent by 1988.[9] Many young people entering the job market found that they would not be able to maintain the kind of lifestyle enjoyed by their parents. For example, in 1987 a male high school graduate with one to five years of work experience earned 18 percent less than his counterpart in 1979.[10] In the 1980s, 80 percent of families who depended almost exclusively on wage earnings saw their real income fall while their taxes increased.[11]

The downward shift of the U.S. economy was especially pronounced among minorities, especially Latinos. Many of the same conditions that had fostered the ghetto riots of the 1960s had only become worse by the 1980s. Black urban poverty grew from 21 percent in 1969 to 34 percent by 1992. Today, a Black male resident of Harlem or the South Bronx has a lower life expectancy than if he moved to Bangladesh. Three percent of the Black male population live behind bars. African Americans make up 44 percent of the U.S. prison population – a reflection of desperate social conditions and a racist judicial system.[12] The poor have gotten poorer. In 1979, 32.9

percent of those below the poverty level lived at less than one-half the poverty income threshold. By 1988, this number had increased to 38 percent.[13] The ratio of male to female income wages has been the major cause of the shift.[14] According to official government statistics, in 1987, 33.6 percent of persons in female-headed families lived below the poverty level. Some analysts have placed the actual number as high as 49.8 percent.[15]

United States capitalism has helped to dismantle the political complacency, based on the prosperity, that a previous generation of left activists had found so frustrating. An October 1991 CBS/*New York Times* poll found that only 29 percent approved of the way Congress was "doing its job." An April 14, 1992 ABC poll found that number had dropped to only 17 percent of respondents. When Jackson ran for office, he appealed to a progressive political base potentially far larger than anything available during the decades of unprecedented boom. As one local activist commented, "In this country there is a need. Someone has to arise to the occasion." In 1988, Jackson received seven million votes, including 20 percent of the total white vote. He did so by placing the economic question at the center of his agenda. As he routinely emphasized, "economic violence is the critical issue of our day." While the Jackson campaign encompassed a wide range of progressive concerns, the basis of his appeal lay in his ability to speak to people's sense that their material well-being and standard of living were becoming increasingly insecure and under attack.

It would be a mistake to assume that falling standards of living necessarily push people automatically in a politically progressive direction. Groups and individuals such as the Christian Coalition, the militia movement, David Duke, and Pat Buchanan demonstrate the reactionary potential of falling living standards. These movements and leaders have made some significant roads into White working-class areas and suburbs. Because the media publicize right-wing activity much more readily than liberal or left activism, one could get the false impression that the conservative drift is the only thing happening. The Republican electoral victories of 1994 were built on a small margin of voters, with the majority of the population staying home. Moreover, the Republican Party win signified more the bank-ruptcy of so-called moderate and liberal Democrats who refused to attack the corporate agenda. Despite the nation's right-wing shift, Democrats who stuck to more left-leaning messages did far better in 1994, while a host of progressive organizations both inside and out-side the party continued to pick up steam. More progressive-minded independents were elected to local, state, and national offices in 1994 than at any time in previous decades. In short, the transformation of the political economy establishes a political potential that we have to organize before the Right does.

The Left's Alienation from Electoral Politics

The postwar Left's relative fragmentation and insulation from "mainstream" America have undermined the potential for a strong progressive political movement. This, in turn, helped to create a legacy of distrust for electoral forms of struggle as social activists found protest strategies far more effective than electoral campaigns. Many activist groups learned to view support for more "mainstream" political candidates as a risk to their independence while, at the same time, independent left electoral campaigns seemed like exercises in futility. The Jackson core groups reflected this experience. The largest percentage of Jackson activists were those who had no prior electoral experience. Some had helped out as general volunteers in past campaigns. Very few had ever organized a grassroots electoral campaign prior to Jackson's. Such a legacy was not accidental. The nation's corporate class reluctantly agreed to the New Deal, in part, to ward off renewed and powerful mass challenges to the two-party system that served as a buffer to political threats to this class's wealth and influence. Under interest-group liberalism, the state held out to progressive activists ample channels for making changes without having to resort to electoral politics.

During the era of the New Deal, as well as the following decades into the 1970s, protest strategies – civil disobedience, lobbying, mass protests, urban uprisings, demonstrations – were able to force some form of state response to worker conditions and problems associated with social injustice. While activists may have often criticized state actions as partial, problematic, and even repressive, nevertheless, protest strategies could and did deliver real benefits for many ordinary people. This dynamic was made possible because the economic conditions of the boom period permitted the state to support capital accumulation while being able to respond, at least in part, to social demands. In other words, postwar economic conditions allowed for the relative avoidance of a zero-sum game between the need of capital and the demands of popular protest. In some instances the requirements of capital accumulation and social need could even prove complementary. Thus, during the 1950s and 1960s the state could at least partially respond to the protest strategies of the Civil Rights Movement while at the same time maintaining capital accumulation.

Clearly, the Civil Rights Movement's social mobilization placed serious pressure on the national government to intervene against southern apartheid. Within the context of the postwar economy, however, U.S. capital had much less incentive to maintain ties to the old southern ruling interests. To an important degree, southern segregation had become economically counterproductive. This is not to argue that federal intervention would have occurred without popular protest. However, by the postwar period, U.S. capitalism had evolved to a point in which the protest strategies of southern Blacks could yield a partially positive state response without having to face the full-fledged opposition of corporate America. When the Civil Rights Movement spread northward and addressed broad economic questions, the potential conflict between it and U.S. capitalism became more apparent. Nevertheless, although the state engaged in sub-stantial repression of African-American groups, the postwar New Deal regime permitted political and economic space in which protest activities could win substantial (although not entirely unproblematic) expansions in the safety net.[16] A similar, relatively favorable dynamic aided the protest strategies of many of the post-material movements. Because of the New Deal framework and relative economic boom, popular protest mobilizations and advocacy work could win a range of new government regulations and interventions in such areas as affirmative action, environmental protection, and consumer safety – in effect, broadening and expanding the New Deal state. In short, social activists could afford the luxury of approaching the political system from the outside because the postwar political economy allowed for at least a partially positive reaction from the state. They did pay a price, however; liberal interest-group politics encouraged groups to narrow their vision around immediate and specific issues. With no party or electoral agenda to bring groups together, the U.S. Left basically fragmented into scattered single-issue activism.

Undergirded by the postwar boom, interest-group liberalism allowed the Democratic Party to develop a significant mass base among the Left's "natural" constituencies. Although both parties operated within the context of the New Deal system, the Democratic Party emerged from the Depression as the party of the New Deal coalition. It also became the party of the Civil Rights laws and the Great Society programs. As long as it could serve as the party of New Deal liberalism, the Democrats proved an obstacle to independent political action. On the one hand, many activists could view the election efforts of the Democratic Party in some kind of positive light – either as an ally or at least the lesser of two evils. For many of these people, the Democratic Party possessed a strong enough "left wing" and sufficient electoral dominance to merit some form of active or passive support. On the other hand, of those who saw less progressive potential within the Democratic Party, its relatively successful ability to pose as the liberal champion of ordinary citizens gave it enough of a claim to loyalties among the Left's potential constituencies that independent political action seemed futile.

New Political Conditions for the Left

Interest-group politics, with its Democratic Party dominance and diminished Left electoral hopes, could only exist within a context of economic expansion and growth. During the 1950s through the early 1970s U.S. capitalism enjoyed enough record prosperity that the country could both support Corporate America and meet many popular demands. This balancing act fell apart when the postwar boom turned into crisis. The right-wing agenda that had emerged sought to return to the nineteenth-century era of minimal government by dismantling much of the New Deal state and, with it, interest-group liberalism. As a result, grassroots activists are finding that playing politics in the old interest-group ways is no longer a viable option. Building coalitions, for example, has become a necessity. The Jackson campaign pulled together many progressive organizations and interests. But while Jackson certainly deserves credit for his skills in bringing different groups together, changes in the U.S. political economy also helped facilitate his Rainbow Coalition.

While the postwar boom tended to divide the progressive community, the crisis of postwar capitalism and the right-wing solution have helped to push groups closer together politically and ideologically. This can be seen in a number of ways. As described earlier the evolution of U.S. capitalism has not simply caused increasing pain and misery. Its negative effects have reached broad sections of the U.S. population – blue collar and white collar, professional and unskilled, White, Black, and brown, male and female, young and old. That the 1984 and 1988 Rainbow mobilizations originated in the African-American community is not a new development. People of color are not only among those hardest hit by economic transformation, but in comparison to other currents of social protest the struggles of African Americans developed relatively active and independent currents of electoral politics by the early 1980s.[17]

During the mass mobilization of the 1950s and 1960s issues such as poverty, homelessness, quality education, adequate wages, unemployment, affordable health care, and hunger could be characterized, at least in the minds of many who were experiencing the postwar prosperity, as "minority issues" or "poor people's issues." By the 1980s, however, many of these same issues had become, in kind if not in degree, concerns and demands of "mainstream" America as well. Jackson could thus take major elements of a "Black" agenda and use them to construct a multiracial and ethnic coalition.[18] In other words, the transformation of U.S. capitalism enabled someone like Jackson to encapsulate, in a single framework, the concrete difficulties experienced by a diverse array of people.

Although the evolution of American capitalism produced a widely felt social crisis, it also transformed many past social movement issues in ways that had fostered a greater potential for bringing groups together.[19] For example, the right-wing budget program highlighted the trade-off between domestic and military spending. Groups concerned with either U.S. intervention abroad or the prospect of nuclear annihilation share increasingly common ground with those suffering the transfer of state resources away from domestic spending and into the military buildup. These groups are potentially joined by increasing numbers of U.S. workers affected by the government's protection of a favorable investment climate overseas, which has aided capital flight at home. Similarly, right-wing deregulation has also increased the potential for bringing groups together. Workers who find it increasingly difficult to protect themselves against unsafe and unhealthy working conditions due to a lack of governmental protection can find potential common ground with environmental groups concerned with the effects of industry on the environment. These people are joined by minority groups who experience "environmental racism." One of the major changes in the U.S. economy in the past few decades has been the accelerating entrance of women into the workforce. By relying increasingly upon female labor, U.S. corporations have created the objective conditions for mobilization of individuals whose life experiences cut across dimensions of class and gender – thus offering the possibility of combining traditional concerns of the labor and women's movements. A similar dynamic is occurring around race as the workforce and population generally become increasingly diverse.[20]

The right-wing agenda also helped push social activists toward greater common ground by providing a shared enemy. Not only did the government become less sympathetic to the concerns of progressive groups, but it often became actively hostile as many right-wing policies sought to dismantle gains made through half a century or more of social movement mobilization. Culturally, corporate and governmental shaping of public opinion sought to reformulate American culture around values of social intolerance and conformity, suspicion and hostility toward "the other," antiradicalism, and obedience and respect for authority. Whether at a policy or cultural level, right-wing policies have affected all elements of progressive activism. The existence of a common enemy helped foster a sense of shared opposition expressed by local Jackson activists.

Finally, the right-wing attack has placed groups that simply pursue single-issue politics in a very weak and vulnerable position. For example, having to defend welfare spending places activists on the defensive, protecting programs that they feel are inadequate and that are perceived by the public as benefiting others – i.e., "those people." In the long run, the only way to throw back the right-wing agenda is to take the offensive by countering the Right with a comprehensive agenda of our own. Simply getting together and drawing up a laundry list of our single concerns is not adequate. Rather, more and more activists are seeking out a process that is going to produce a more integrated and holistic left agenda. Electoral politics is the one arena that allows activists to gather to develop such a comprehensive alternative.

The Jackson campaign took a notable step in this regard. Although he championed many progressive policy initiatives, most activists supported him not only because of the details of his platform, but because he spoke with a comprehensive vision that provided an alternative to politics as usual. Unlike moderate and even liberal Democrats, Jackson unabashedly defended the positive role of an activist government intent on social change. Fundamentally, Jackson saw the political debate as a question of basic morality. Countering the Right's claim to moral virtue, Jackson attacked the right-wing agenda for being spiritually bankrupt and morally hypocritical. Jackson called for values that placed identification with the oppressed above that of the interest of the wealthy, social justice above political expediency, and embracing diversity over individualizing fears and suspicion. By basing his campaign on a moral logic, Jackson was able to appeal to a diverse area of activists. Despite their individual differences in social and political analysis and their contrasting visions of an alternative politics, activists involved in the Jackson campaign could all agree on the fundamental values that he articulated.

Jackson was also able to pull together his Rainbow Coalition because of his deliberate and extensive efforts to participate in and support a diverse array of progressive struggles. Well before the 1988 campaign Jackson had stood outside plants' gates with striking workers. He had talked with members of inner-city gangs. He had visited the Rust Belt, the Farm Belt, and the Sun Belt. He had met the nation's young generations in schools across the country. He had spoken at rallies for abortion choice, for "Jobs, Peace and Justice," for civil rights, and for gay and lesbian rights. He had been inside the nation's homeless shelters, welfare lines, and prisons. In 1983, he witnessed Harold Washington's construction of a rainbow coalition strong enough to defeat the Democratic Party machine and win the mayoral office.[21] These personal experiences, coupled with his extensive contacts with progressive activists and organizations, provided Jackson the breadth of experience necessary to conceive and implement a political challenge based upon a diverse Rainbow Coalition of social activists. In doing so, his campaign momentarily revealed the human building blocks of further left/progressive political movements. Nationally, the contemporary Left appears weak. However, it maintains an active local presence – one that, if brought together, can produce considerable energy.

At the same time, the transformation of U.S. capitalism has altered the Left's relationship to electoral politics. It has placed the Democratic Party's liberal image in jeopardy while simultaneously pushing more progressive activists into electoral politics. While the Republican Party became the banner carrier of right-wing solutions, both parties have realigned around the new right-wing agenda. Thomas Ferguson and Joel Rogers have documented how the dominant forces in the Democratic Party have abandoned New Deal liberalism.[22] Indeed, many of the policies that observers would later associate with Reaganism actually began in the later years of the Carter presidency.[23] In addition, although commonly viewed in terms of presidential initiatives, the Reagan policies were enacted by a Democratic Congress. In 1988, Michael Dukakis's notable unwillingness to utilize New Deal ideals to attack Republican policies reflected his party's drift from the postwar compromise.[24] The Democrats' flight from New Deal liberalism reveals the reality that, with the end of the postwar boom, the material ability of the state to respond to progressive activism with liberal reforms has greatly contracted. Indeed, popular reforms within today's political economy require an agenda that moves the New Deal far more to the left – something that corporate-dominated Democrats are unwilling to do. This contradiction between

reform politics and the state's rightward drift has helped to spur a
growing sense among progressives that they can ill afford simply to
push the state from the outside. Engaging directly in elections to place
allies in office has become more and more of a necessity for moving
progressive politics forward.

The shift to the right by the Democratic Party influenced progressive
activists in two ways. At one end of the spectrum, for those activists
who had viewed the party in some kind of positive light, it seemed
less and less an effective vehicle for election allies. On the one hand,
until 1992 the party proved remarkably unable to reclaim the White
House. In the eyes of local activists, the party's complicity in the
right-wing agenda left it unable to mount the kind of populist attack
on Republican policies that these activists saw as the key to winning
office. Dukakis's rallying cry of "competence" was simply not effective. The 1994 Republican victory in the Congress has only further
underlined the inability of centrist Democrats to appeal to people's
frustrations or stave off reactionary antiestablishmentism.

On the other hand, even when many Democrats won office, they
often did not speak or act differently from their Republican
opponents. In the experience of many local activists, the Democrats
proved just as unresponsive, if not outright hostile, to social movement concerns as did the party of Reagan. In short, by 1988 many
activists had begun to conclude that the Democratic Party no longer
served their interests, even partially. In response, local activists who
had previously looked toward Democratic victories increasingly
viewed running and supporting their own candidates as the only
political option. In their eyes, only genuinely progressive candidates
could both win mass support and respond to the concerns and
demands of the activist community once in office.

At the other end of the spectrum, for those Jackson activists who
had never placed much faith in the Democratic Party, its rightward
shift signaled not so much a need as an opportunity. While both
parties had realigned around the right-wing agenda, the public had
not. As Ferguson and Rogers have documented, the poll data show
that the majority of Americans still favored specific New Deal
programs.[25] By surrendering the terrain of populism, the dominant
forces in the Democratic Party had left the electoral playing field open
for an unrivaled progressive critique of the status quo. With voter
alienation and frustration climbing, the possibilities for a progressive
political challenge seemed credible.

The Jackson campaign was an attempt to steer the Democratic
Party in a progressive direction. His campaigns occurred at a time in

which the debates within the party over how to respond to Reaganism were not yet over. Jackson's defeat in 1988, the way in which his supporters were dismissively treated at the party's national convention that year, and the nomination of Bill Clinton in 1992 all signified a resolution to that struggle. The "mainstream" of the party adopted Reaganism and would try to steal away Republican voters rather than mobilize the vast section of the electorate that generally does not vote at all.

Many grassroots Jackson activists had few illusions about the ultimate direction of the party. They joined the Jackson campaign because it existed outside the Democratic Party in everything but their candidate's party label. Many hoped that the Rainbow Coalition would turn into an outright third party. Locally, the Jackson campaigns had little to do with activists from the mainstream of the party. In some places they were able to get along with liberal Democratic activists; in others, open hostility existed between the two camps. In short, many Jackson activists were already moving toward independent politics. The continued drift of the Democrats rightward has pushed even more people in this direction.

Today, the United States encompasses political, economic, and social dynamics different from those found two decades ago. The political economy of the prosperous "middle-class" "liberalism" society has evaporated into social, economic, and political crisis. Although the new conditions have brought pain and frustration, they have also brought new opportunities. Many ordinary Americans, and among them many social activists, may look back on the immediate postwar years with nostalgia for the so-called good old days. However, although many people may have benefited from prosperity and New Deal liberalism, these same forces also posed major obstacles to independent left political action. A strong progressive political movement – one that sought to unite a majority of Americans around a common political project – did not develop during these years, in part because the political economy did not favor such a movement. Yet today the transformation of U.S. capitalism around the right-wing project has begun to dismantle some of these obstacles and to create objective conditions necessary for a progressive political challenge.

This process continues today. During interviews that I conducted across the country in 1995, activists engaged in independent politics commented on the growing interest of both the general population and the activist community in what they are doing. Bill Clinton's continuation and even activist promotion of most elements of the right-wing agenda, coupled with his ready retreat away from the few

progressive elements of his campaign platform, have simply heightened people's sense of the Democratic Party's bankruptcy. The 1994
Republican congressional victory has also motivated the building of
progressive third parties. The Contract with America has underlined
the weakness of single-issue activism and progressive noninvolvement
in electoral politics. It has also left both activists and many sections
of the population running scared and with a renewed sense of urgency.

The Current Status of Progressive Political Organizing

The failure of the Rainbow Coalition retarded briefly some of the
momentum toward a progressive and independent politics. Today,
however, there is a rich growth of grassroots groups and organizations
pursuing a variety of strategies. Some use a party-within-a-party
strategy similar to the Rainbow Coalition. In Connecticut, the Legislative Electoral Action Program (LEAP), a labor–community coalition,
recruits and promotes progressive activists for state office by entering
Democratic primaries. Founded in 1980, LEAP has built a solid
contingent in the Connecticut legislature. In 1994, twenty-five of the
coalition's thirty-five candidates won elections. LEAP is not simply an
electoral vehicle; it also pulls together progressive groups for cooperative lobbying and public political actions in the state capital. The
coalition building and ties that LEAP has fostered among progressive
groups are in many ways as important as its electoral victories.

Many more activists, however, have chosen to break away from the
Democratic Party outright. Progressive organizing has the growing
potential of displacing the Democratic Party as the effective force
balancing the right wing. For example, when Bernie Sanders came
within a hairsbreadth of winning Vermont's seat in the House of
Representatives in 1988, he completely wiped out the Democratic
candidate, who received only a few percentage points of the vote.
When elected in 1990 and reelected in 1992 and 1994, Sanders faced,
in effect, a two-way race against the Republicans. Similarly, ever since
he won the 1981 mayoral race in Burlington, the local Progressive
Coalition has rapidly displaced the Democrats in all central areas of
the city, rendering them to a third-place status. New Party organizers
in places such as Wisconsin speak of similarly taking over the role of
opposition from the Democrats in many local communities in which
the party of moderation has become completely moribund.

Locally based campaigns and newly formed political organizations
have sprung up in communities across the country. For example, in

1994 Mike Ferner ran as an independent for mayor of Toledo, Ohio. Pulling together a rainbow coalition of progressive groups and individuals, he came within a few hundred votes out of ninety-two thousand of winning. In Pittsburgh, Pennsylvania, the Independent Political Actions Network has brought together grassroots activists to begin building local progressive political power. They have run progressive independents for the city's community advisory boards and for the city council. A National Independent Politics Summit in Pittsburgh during the summer of 1995 included groups as geographically diverse as the California Peace and Freedom Party, Houston's New Democracy Party, and the New Jersey Independents.

In addition to many local efforts, there are several new national organizations that aim at building progressive political parties. Some, such as the 21st Century Party launched a few years ago by the National Organization of Women, never really got off the ground. Many others have, however. The Greens are the oldest of these currents. The party was inspired by the example of the German Green Party, which has proved instrumental in transforming that country's Left – infusing it with the ideals of the environmental, peace, and women's movements. Highly decentralized, the U.S. Greens operate largely as a federation of local Green Party groups built by combining electoral and nonelectoral activism. In New Mexico, the Green candidate for governor, former Democratic Lieutenant Governor Roberto Mondragon, won 11 percent of the vote in 1994, with the Green candidate for state treasurer gaining 33 percent. Local Green groups within the state have run candidates for school boards and city councils, winning some of those positions and having strong showings in others. In Hawaii that same year Keiko Bonk-Abramson went on to win reelection to the Hawaiian Council, soundly defeating the Democratic challenger 60 percent to 40 percent. More than 75 Greens hold local offices across the nation and as many as 450 local Green chapters exist throughout the country. Today, Green activism continues to expand, although questions concerning a national structure and plan and the balance between electoral and nonelectoral politics have caused at times vigorous debates among different chapters. While the Greens' principles have potentially broad applications, their activist core remains highly identified with the New Left milieu of environmental, women's, and peace movements. Thus, internally, they remain distinct, although their holistic principles lead many Green groups to build broader alliances with other parts of the community such as people of color. Indeed, where Greens have done the best may have been in building such coalitions.

Formed in 1991, Labor Party Advocates (LPA) has worked to build support for the idea of a labor party within the ranks of organized labor. Supported nationally by the Oil, Chemical and Atomic Workers Union, the Brotherhood of Maintenance of Way Employees, and the United Electrical Workers, Labor Party Advocates has also gained endorsements of a growing number of local unions and regional federations. In the summer of 1996, the group held a national founding convention for a labor party in Cleveland, Ohio. After heated debate, the majority of delegates decided to endorse for the next two years a nonelectoral strategy. Preferring to build its strength first, the LPA plans to establish educational work and issue campaigns, such as promoting a living wage, that will spark greater political discussion and organizing among union members. The union movement has by far the greater amount of resources, giving LPA's efforts to strip labor of its dependency on the Democratic Party a great deal of potential. However, the Labor Party is based upon progressive activists within the ranks of organized labor, a base that it will ultimately have to expand to reach into broader communities.

The Campaign for a New Tomorrow (CNT), formed around the 1992 presidential campaign of Ron Daniels, former chair of the Rainbow Coalition, has successfully established active chapters in Washington, D.C., New York City, and Pittsburgh. Reflecting the racially unequal ways in which resources have been distributed in this society, the CNT has been the most resourceful of the major national party-building efforts. The group has attempted to launch a broad, people-of-color-led political coalition or party. A proposed founding of an Independent Progressive Party in late 1995, however, never achieved sufficient momentum to get off the ground.

From the viewpoint of an overall third-party practice, the New Party has developed a strong national strategy. The New Party sees that the key to political power is to build locally a grassroots organization. The New Party emphasizes a flexible and long-term strategy that seeks to build the movement through concrete local victories. New Party chapters, operating on a basis of tactical pragmatism, do not enter races they do not think they can win. They will consider running a progressive using the Democratic Party line if that tactic makes the most strategic sense in building the overall movement (most New Party candidates thus far have entered nonpartisan races). While more structured at the national level than the Greens, local and state New Party chapters operate with a high degree of autonomy and grassroots control.

The organization's strongest chapter is in Wisconsin. In Madison, the local chapter has secured a sizable bloc on the nonpartisan elected city council and several seats on the county board. In Milwaukee, activists have elected several candidates to the county board, gained one on the city council, sent Johnnie Morris-Tatum to the state legislature, and led the fight for control of the Milwaukee School Board – successfully staving off candidates who favored privatization of the city's public schools. Alongside this growing electoral work, Milwaukee New Party organizers have launched an independent coalition, called Sustainable Milwaukee, to develop a community, grassroots-based economic plan for the city of Milwaukee. A year and a half in the making, this plan was unveiled in October 1994 and has picked up clear momentum. It covers not only economic development, pointing to governmental policies that would foster family-supporting jobs and penalize companies who do not do so, but also a progressive alternative to transportation, the environment, suburban development, and public education. The Milwaukee New Party branch has been able to use the plan as a kind of platform for its electoral efforts and as a focal point for its nonelectoral work. In 1995 Milwaukee activists won major victories when their Living Wage campaign secured a $6.90 minimum for workers at companies contracting with the city and $7.70 for thirty-seven hundred public school employees.

In addition to running candidates and engaging in nonelectoral activism, many of these groups are also working to change the rules of the political game. For example, in Minnesota, the Twin Cities New Party succeeded in getting a bill called the Democracy Act introduced into the state legislature. It includes provision on free media, voting of sixteen-year-olds in school board elections, shortened campaign seasons, fusion (allowing two parties to run a single candidate), and more. The LEAP-style groups in New England are working hard for serious campaign-finance reform in their states. In Maine activists succeeded in getting a citation placed on the November 1996 ballot that would establish the basis for complete public financing of the state's elections. The New Party also convinced the U.S. Supreme Court to rule on a lower court ruling that struck down state laws banning fusion. Fusion benefits third parties by allowing them to cross-endorse candidates from other minor and major parties. Most states outlawed fusion after third-party efforts, such as the People's Party, used it effectively to build their organizations.[26] The Center for Voting and Democracy serves as a clearinghouse on voting systems that enhance citizen participation and representation. In November 1995, it held a conference in Massachusetts centered around the goal of bringing proportional representation to this county's major elections. The group also publishes an annual report packed with information on proportional representation as well as other issues such as campaign-finance reform and ballot access.

With all these different groups and organizations, what does this mean for Black activism? Should activists place their energy in an African-American-led, independent, and progressive party, or one of the existing efforts, all of which support racial justice and are open to multiracial membership? The problem with many of the existing groups is that, despite their ideological opposition to racism, they remain largely White organizations. The Greens are mostly White and professionally trained, as are the organizers involved in LEAP. The Labor Party cannot avoid reflecting the White, male-dominant character of leadership within the labor movement. Local activists in all groups are aware of their need to diversify and have undertaken concrete activities to make contacts and support with African-American communities in their areas. These initiatives range from fundraising for community organizations, to cooperating in campaigns against police brutality, to providing training resources for community organizers of color. However, organizations that do not start out as multiracial in their leadership and membership historically have often found it quite difficult to change their composition decisively once they have been established.

Of the national organizations, the New Party stands out for the multiracial character of both its membership and leadership. Half the candidates run by the New Party have been people of color. Roughly one-third of the party's membership is African American and 10 percent is Latino. This did not happen by itself but reflects a great deal of effort and the key support that organizations such as the Association of Community Organization for Reform Now (ACORN) have given to the New Party. While starting off with a multiracial effort may be possible in some areas, in other communities Black-and/or people-of-color-led organizations might prove the best way to begin. In poll after poll, the majority of African Americans have expressed their support for the idea of a Black political party. However, current progressive political organizing already seems fragmented among different local and national efforts. Would not a new political organization only add to the confusion? Yet a new party does not have to cause fragmentation. The movement for a progressive political power in this country is still very young. The first step is to build active local groups – to bring together different progressive activists within our communities, and to begin generating leadership and support among the vast number of Americans who are politically inactive. Given the diversity of this country, the current existence of a variety of third party and independent groups can be as much a blessing as a curse. Each group is free to articulate an agenda and culture that resonate with specific sections of the population. For example, that the Greens and the Labor Party are both based in particular social movements strengthens their ability to mobilize particular groups, although by themselves such constituencies are not sufficient for a national, majority-seeking progressive party.

In the U.S., several groups are dedicated to fostering greater communication and cooperation among progressive independent organizations. The National Committee for Independent Political Action (NCIPA) publishes the Independent Political Action Bulletin as a very good source for keeping abreast of what is going on with various groups across the country. During the summer of 1995 and again in January 1996, a group called Third Parties '96 organized a diverse meeting of political parties, independent organizations, and progressive groups to develop a Common Ground Platform – to be used in a way in which participants could consider a range of options. Also during the summer of 1995, another conference in Pittsburgh brought together grassroots activists to discuss current independent political efforts including proposals for a 1996 presidential campaign, a nationally coordinated slate of local candidates, and a People's Pledge Campaign to collect grassroots signatures in favor of a third party.

After the period of Reaganism, we now face a political situation in which those in power are not simply maintaining the policies of the 1980s but are furthering the right-wing agenda in a manner that is even more blatant, sweeping, and reactionary. The Republican-dominated Congress has also shown the inadequacy of the strategy of voting for the lesser evil. In 1994, supporting "mainstream" Democrats only ensured Republican victories as the Democrats continued to refuse to raise a class-based attack on the right-wing agenda. In more and more areas, running independent progressive candidates and engaging in third-party organizing represents the most effective way of countering the Republican and conservative momentum. Eventually, progressive activists are going to have to achieve a greater degree of unity. In the immediate future, however, activists need to pursue whatever frameworks best work in their own communities. Once we have organized in our own backyards, we can begin planning a more unified national movement representing independent and progressive politics, rather than the current two-party monopoly that continually forces progressives to choose between the lesser of two evils.

Notes

1. On the one hand, the term "mainstream" can describe the large bloc of people who would not consider themselves self-consciously left or radical. On the other hand, however, as used by many political observers, the term often implies that the Left is somehow "extreme" and hence inherently marginalized – that given full exposure to both ways of thinking, people would self-consciously choose a more "moderate" establishment agenda. Since many progressive activists would consider their views to be much more in line with the interests and desires of the vast majority of Americans than with the political establishment, I use the term "mainstream" in quotation marks in order to avoid the second connotation.

2. Richard Flacks, *Making History: The American Left and the American Mind* (New York: Columbia University Press, 1988), see chapters 1–3.

3. Giovanni Arrighi argues that the postwar economic boom separated working-class social power and mass misery between the industrialized nations, on the one hand, and the Third World, on the other; today, however, the two conditions are converging as mass misery spreads back to the core countries while working-class power develops in the periphery. See Giovanni Arrighi, "Marxist Century – American Century: The Making and Remaking of the World Labor Movement," in Samin Amir, Giovanni Arrighi, Ander Gunder Frank, and Immanuel Wallerstein, eds., *Transforming the Revolution: Social Movements and the World-System* (New York: Monthly Review Press, 1990), pp. 54–95.

4. Lawrence Mishel and Jared Bernstein, *The State of Working America* (New York: M. E. Sharpe, 1993).

5. Ibid., chapter 8. Also see Michael Goldfield, *The Decline of Organized Labor in the United States* (Chicago: University of Chicago Press, 1987), pp. 40–48.

6. Lawrence Mishel and David M. Frankel, *The State of Working America* (New York: M. E. Sharpe, 1991), pp. 1, 2. Also see William Goldsmith and Edward Blakely, *Separate Societies* (Philadelphia: Temple University Press, 1992), chapter 3.

7. John Miller, "Silent Depression: Economic Growth and Prosperity Part Company," *Dollars and Sense*, no. 175 (April 1992), p. 6.

8. Mishel and Frankel, *The State of Working America*, p. 130.

9. Chris Tilly, "The Politics of the 'New Inequality,'" *Socialist Review*, vol. 20, no. 1 (January–March 1990), p. 108.

10. Mishel and Frankel, *The State of Working America*, p. xii; also see Goldsmith and Blakely, *Separate Societies*, pp. 67–68.

11. Miller, "Silent Depression," p. 8.

12. Ward Churchill, "The Third World at Home: Political Prisoners in the U.S.," *Z Magazine* (June 1990), pp. 11–15; also see Goldsmith and Blakely, *Separate Societies*, chapter 2.

13. Mishel and Frankel, *The State of Working America*, p. 161.

14. Ibid., p. 81.

15. Tim Wise, "Being Poor Isn't Enough," *Dollars and Sense*, no. 158 (September 1990), pp. 6–7. Also see Goldsmith and Blakely, *Separate Societies*, pp. 35–38.

16. Jack Bloom, *Class, Race, and the Civil Rights Movement* (Bloomington: University of Indiana Press, 1987), pp. 59–87, 155–86.

17. For example, see Rod Bush, ed., *The New Black Vote: Politics and Power in Four American Cities* (San Francisco: Synthesis Publications, 1984). In a recent work, James Jennings argues that Black electoral activism both increased in the 1980s and began to take on a new character. Unlike past efforts that aimed at obtaining a "piece

of the pie," current Black electoral activism, Jennings argues, has acquired a progressive "empowerment activism" that more fundamentally questions the distribution of wealth and power. As he argues, "a new kind of political activism is beginning to emerge, especially at the local level in urban America." See James Jennings, *The Politics of Black Empowerment: The Transformation of Black Activism in Urban America* (Detroit: Wayne State University Press, 1992), p. 10.

18. Many of Jackson's specific 1988 proposals bear a striking similarity to the policy priorities of the famous 1972 "Black Agenda" from Gary, Indiana. On the latter, see Derrick Morrison and Tony Thomas, *Black Liberation and Political Power: The Meaning of the Gary Convention* (New York: Pathfinder, 1972).

19. In addition, there is today a greater appreciation of the existence of different kinds of social movement possibilities. For example, interviews with Jackson activists clearly showed the impact of the New Left. Jackson activists were clearly sensitive to issues of class, race, gender, and sexual orientation.

20. Data reported by the U.S. Bureau of Labor project that by the year 2005, 87.5 percent of the new entrants into the labor force will be minorities and/or women – by then they will make up nearly half of all workers. For a sample of the new ideas emerging within the ranks of labor in response to this emerging reality, see "Building on Diversity: The New Unionism," *Labor Research Review*, vol. 2, no. 1 (Spring/Summer 1993). In responding to the condition of struggle fostered by contemporary U.S. capitalism, organized labor has increasingly sought coalitions with community groups and other social movements; see Jeremy Brecher and Tim Costello, *Building Bridges: The Emerging Grassroots Coalitions of Labor and Community* (New York: Monthly Review Press, 1990).

21. Sheila Collins describes a number of precursors to Jackson's rainbow strategy including the "Stop Rizzo" movement in Philadelphia and the mayoral campaigns of Washington in Chicago and Mel King in Boston; see *The Rainbow Challenge* (New York: Monthly Review Press, 1986), chapter 3.

22. The right-wing shift of the Democratic Party has also been noted by scholars who identify with its more liberal side; see Thomas Ferguson and Joel Rogers, *Right Turn: The Decline of the Democrats and the Future of American Politics* (New York: Hill and Wang, 1986).

23. Ibid., pp. 105–13.

24. Joshua Cohen and Joel Rogers, "Reaganism after Reagan," in Ralph Miliband et al., eds., *Socialist Register 1988* (London: Merlin Press, 1988), pp. 387–424.

25. My own research about the CBS/*New York Times* polls concerning voters' issue priorities that ran throughout the 1988 primary season supports Ferguson and Rogers's findings; see Ferguson and Rogers, *Right Turn*, chapter 1.

26. Some on the Left have misinterpreted the New Party's promotion of fusion and tactical use of the Democratic Party label as sacrificing their commitment to a third party. However, the New Party aims to build an autonomous grassroots movement, not just elect candidates.

2

The Right Wing in
the U.S. Congress:
Challenges for Black Leadership

James Steele

The 1994 midterm elections transferred control of the United States Congress to Republicans representing the right wing of this party. Congressional Republicans changed position from a 178:256:1 minority to a 230:204:1 majority in the House of Representatives (there is one independent), and from a 46:54 minority to a 52:48 majority in the Senate.[1] Together with the demographics of voter turnout and a low rate of voter participation, this election posed an unprecedented set of public policy and political challenges to African-American leadership. Only 37 percent of the eligible electorate took part in the 1994 elections. In numerical terms, about 68 million voters out of an estimated eligible electorate of 193 million citizens actually cast ballots. Nonetheless, it is probably true that this electoral minority did reflect a widespread disgust with government and angst over a deteriorating status quo. The Republican Party was able to play this volatility and restiveness like a fiddle. Republican victories were a product of an agitated electorate on the one hand, and – given the stakes involved – a low level of voter participation, on the other hand.

Traditionally, a sitting president allows a 2-to-3-percentage-point boost to his party's congressional candidates. This time the opposite occurred. The president visited California, Washington, Michigan, Minnesota, Pennsylvania, and New York in the final two weeks of the campaign. Rather than boosting the turnout for Democratic candidates in close races, Clinton's presence – which became a focal point of local Republican mobilization – appears to have sapped votes from hard-pressed Democrats. Key Democratic incumbents who were deemed to have a good chance of pulling out a narrow victory lost by slim margins. Despite the Clinton administration's relatively successful management of the economy on behalf of the corporate sector, there was widespread popular dissatisfaction with the economic performance of the federal government. The public felt insecure about the future and questioned the Democrats' ability to maintain already endangered standards of living. Two years of a Democratic president and Congress, furthermore, had not delivered the health care reform, welfare reform, or the middle-class tax cut promised in the 1992 campaign.

Peculiar to U.S. electoral history, widespread anxiety did not produce a high turnout in 1994. Additionally, a shift, though probably temporary, in party allegiance occurred. Many of the Democrats *and* Republicans who voted for President Clinton in 1992 recused themselves to the Republican column. Core Democratic constituencies stayed home in substantial numbers, which enabled the GOP to consolidate its growing base in the South and the West, as well as in the suburbs of every region. In essence, marginal and independent voters who were disaffected with the Clinton administration and the Democratic Congress formed an electoral alliance with Reagan Democrats, the Christian Right, Southern suburbanites, longtime Republicans, and Ross Perot voters. Yet if the total vote is aggregated nationally (see Table 2.1), this was indeed a close election in terms of the popular vote. The Republican share was 51.3 percent while the Democrats took 46.6 percent; independent and third-party candidates obtained 2.1 percent. If House races won by margins of 6 percent or less are defined as close contests (there were sixty-one such races), rough parity existed between the two major parties in that context. The Democrats actually won thirty-two close races compared to twenty-eight for the Republicans. One of the close seats was taken by the House's lone independent, Bernie Sanders of Vermont.

Table 2.1 Partisan Breakdown of Voter Turnout in the 1994 Congressional Election

Party	Total Votes	Percentage Won	Number of seats Won	Percentage
Republican	33,180,220	51.3	230	52.9
Democratic	30,186,126	46.6	204	46.9
Other	1,375,152	2.1	1	0.2
Total	64,741,498	100.0	435	100.0

Source: Congressional Quarterly, vol. 52, no. 48 (December 10, 1994), p. 3517.

Contrary to the hype regarding the role of redistricting in the Democrats' defeat, only a handful of the outcomes of the tight races can be said to have been affected by voting rights redistricting – perhaps nine at most. In fact, the Democrats won ten of the eighteen close contests in the South (the only region that gained African-American majority congressional districts on the basis of 1991 redistricting). The loss of fifty-two House seats nationwide is inconsistent with the argument that redistricting bears responsibility for the Democrats' debacle. It could be said just as easily that the defeat of a large number of key Democrats suggests dissatisfaction with Democratic leadership as the decisive factor in their trouncing.

The distribution of the voting turnout poses a problem not only for the Democratic Party and interests that have historically pegged their well-being and agendas to Democratic electoral victories. This challenge may also prove to be exceptionally difficult for the African-American community and other racial minorities to overcome. African Americans in particular have been able to achieve breakthroughs in political representation as well as have some of their public policy preferences accommodated as a function of the Democratic Party's capacity to muster cross-class, multiracial, largely urban-based electoral coalitions. The manifest decline and defection of some of the Democratic Party's traditional constituencies may have undermined prospects for fashioning such coalitions in the near future. For instance, 37 percent of union households went Republican. A whopping 44 percent of union members did so in the New York gubernatorial election. As was just indicated, turnout dropped in the big cities, but went up in the suburbs. This is where the Democrats have experienced their greatest difficulty competing against Republicans.

Democrats also competed poorly among White evangelical Christians. This group, constituting 20 percent of the electorate, favored the GOP by a margin of 76 percent to 24 percent. The leadership of the Christian Coalition claims credit for electing twenty-four House candidates by significant margins. It claims to have provided the margin of victory for a majority of seventy religious conservatives who were publicly supported by the Religious Right. Nationwide, conservative Christians composed almost a third of the Republican electorate.[2] The decline in the level of voter participation of traditional allies of the African-American community, as well as of African Americans themselves, amplifies the electoral clout of interests whose policy preferences are antagonistic to this group. An astonishing 120 to 125 million eligible voters stayed home on election day in 1994. It was obvious that most of these inactive voters were neither African American nor

Latino, although both groups continued to abstain from electoral participation in large numbers and thereby undermine their own position within the electorate. Who were the nonvoters? Why did they not vote? Why do they not vote? What are their policy preferences? What will it take to get them to "turn on" and then turn out? The theoretical and practical answers to these questions can shape the character of national governance, the direction of public policy, and the prospects for constructing a progressive political alternative.

The Democrats' poor performance was linked to their inability or unwillingness to fashion a clear, consistent, creative message based on the mutual interests of middle-class and working-class Whites, racial minorities, and poor people in the cities as well as the suburbs. In many respects, Democratic ambiguity with regard to a powerful and mobilizing message is linked to the Democrats' inability or unwilling-ness to address the issue of race. This allowed the Republicans – as they have consistently done since the election of Ronald Reagan in 1980 – to fashion a cross-class, "Whites only" electoral coalition that effectively united the top and the middle-income brackets. Some Democratic Party candidates joined the Republicans – even if less intensely so – in pandering to the racial fears of White suburbanites. Save for conservative Democrats in parts of the South, this has never been a winning strategy for the Democratic Party on the national level. Playing the race card, whether overtly or by implication, foments divisions among the interests and groups whose unity most Demo-cratic candidates, congressional and statewide, need to win.

African-American voter participation was low enough in several other crucial contests to affect the outcome negatively, including the U.S. Senate races in Michigan, Tennessee, and Pennsylvania, and the gubernatorial elections in Alabama, New York, and Texas. Only 28 percent of New York City's African-American voters turned out in the gubernatorial contest, for instance. This contributed to just a 46 percent turnout for New York City as a whole, where Blacks comprise nearly 30 percent of the voting-age population. New York City African Americans account for more than two-thirds of New York State's 1.8 million eligible African-American voters. This low turnout figured prominently in Governor Mario Cuomo's defeat. Despite the low African-American and overall turnout in New York City, Cuomo took the Big Apple by a 2-to-1 margin. However, the election was decided in the metropolitan suburbs (Nassau, Suffolk, Westchester, and Rockland Counties) and upstate where, respectively, 53 percent and 70 percent of the electorate turned out. While Cuomo broke even in the suburbs, he lost two-thirds of the upstate vote.

Racially Divergent Voting Patterns

The future of American politics and democracy hinges on the degree to which voters are able to overcome their racial biases at the ballot box and vote their genuine economic and political interests. It may also rest on the direction and extent to which breakthroughs are made in elevating the political participation of the lower-income brackets. This will probably have to pivot on constructing political, as well as electoral, cross-class, multiracial coalitions of the poor, the working class, and the middle class. The racial segmentation of party support and voter performance poses a challenge that African-American leadership can ill afford to avoid or misunderstand. The point is that if the activation of the pool of nonvoters is not achieved within a context of a progressive coalition, the prospects for overcoming the relative isolation of the African-American community and the marginalization of its policy concerns in the body politic will remain bleak. This is why a special burden must be shouldered by the African-American community and its leadership, especially elected officials, in giving voice to the genuine interests of the broad public, and in overcoming the urban–suburban split that Republican politicians and right-wing political movements have engineered so effectively over the past two decades.

One of the most essential tasks of leadership – as it has been for more than a century – is to prevent the isolation of the African-American community from the heart of the political economy and the marginalization of its interests in the body politic. This necessarily involves influencing the political and electoral behavior of as many Whites as possible. What deserves reflection is why African-American leaders, and the once-vaunted moral authority of the African-American struggle, not only seem to exert so little influence on Whites today but also encounter such enmity from so many of them. It is necessary as well to assess whether there is anything in the conduct of African-American leadership and the character of political discourse emanating from the African-American community that contributes to dynamics detrimental to the interests of this group and its ability to catalyze progressive-oriented, multiracial coalitions.

The Redemption of White Supremacy

Intended or not, the tone of the 1994 Republican campaign, including the tenor of the Republican accession to congressional power and the lyrical demagogy with which Republicans have used the Contract with America to serenade the country, resonates with racially encoded language that harkens back to the redemption of White supremacy in the 1870s – the period of the wholesale disfranchisement and segregation of African Americans reflecting the betrayal and defeat of Reconstruction. While the Reagan and Bush eras dealt a severe blow to the enforcement of existing antidiscrimination statutes, Congress still had a political balance that made possible not only the passage of legislation restoring civil rights protections, but also the enactment of new laws that extended antidiscrimination coverage to women and disabled Americans.

In contrast, the 1994 midterm election signaled an end of a congressional balance of forces capable of preserving the enabling legislation of the "Second Reconstruction" – the Civil Rights Act of 1964, the Voting Rights Act of 1965, and Lyndon Johnson's Great Society entitlement programs. Republican majorities in the House and Senate can now stop the enactment of new or strengthened civil rights statutes. Onslaughts against affirmative action, economic set-asides, minority scholarships, the Equal Employment Opportunity Commission, voting rights, and voting rights redistricting are now on the legislative agenda. The dominance of right-wing ideologues and activists within the GOP House and Senate majorities creates conditions for resuscitating the Conservative Coalition. The Conservative Coalition's growth may make it powerful enough to approach a veto-proof majority. Already in the last Congress there were about thirty-five Democrats who voted with the Republicans on crucial legislation more often than they did with the Democratic leadership. Add that number to 230 Republicans, and throw in a dozen or so additional Democratic defectors and backsliders, and the Conservative Coalition begins to approach the 291 votes needed to override a presidential veto. A parallel situation exists in the Senate.

The Republican majority in the 104th Congress was one of the least representative ever in terms of the total population. Only two of the 230 House Republicans, and none of the 53 Senate Republicans, were African American. The GOP majority was littered with multi-millionaires. Not a single African American or Latin American chaired a committee or subcommittee of the House or Senate. Most House Republicans, furthermore, were antagonistic to the historic policy preferences of the African-American community.

Public Policy Impact and Implications

What were the public policy implications of right-wing Republican control of the 104th Congress? What were the political consequences for African Americans of the legislative agenda of the House and Senate Republican leadership? The Contract with America was not only the definitive policy framework for Republican congressional initiatives; it also created a focal point for right-wing political mobilization nationally. Approached in terms of class, the contract was biased heavily toward the private sector, including the most powerful financial interests and transnational corporations. The contract suggested an unprecedented and continuing shift of wealth from the working class and middle class to the wealthy and to transnational corporate elites, perhaps superseding even that which occurred under the Reagan administration. The implementation of the contract, furthermore, exacerbated racial and social tensions, economic inequality, and gender discrimination.

Speaker of the House Newt Gingrich promised that Republicans would dismantle the Great Society programs of the 1960s. Americans who voted Republican may have believed he was talking about minorities, immigrants, and feminists. But these voters would have been well advised to recall that Lyndon Johnson's Great Society programs not only expanded direct assistance to those living in extreme poverty; they not only created federal antipoverty agencies; they not only involved the enactment of far-reaching civil rights and voting rights legislation; but they also initiated Head Start, Medicare, Medicaid, the student loan program, food stamps; raised the minimum wage and increased Social Security coverage. The Republicans have proposed to take the nation full cycle from the War on Poverty of the 1960s to a war on the poor of the 1990s. Representative Dick Armey, the House Majority Leader, even opposed a federal minimum wage. What Gingrich and company meant by "ending welfare as we know it" amounts to ending the social safety net as we have known it. Insofar as one-third of African Americans and one-half of African-American children live in poverty, a war against the poor is a war against the well-being of the Black community and its children. But the dismantling of these programs would also hurt other groups, including Whites.

The Contract with America's welfare reform proposals were punitive enough in their own right – tossing people off assistance after ninety days, denying benefits to unmarried mothers less than eighteen years of age, demanding forced training for jobs that do not exist –

but they were part of a larger strategy of using the call to balance the budget in seven years, particularly cutbacks in entitlement programs (long a target of Republican enmity), to subsidize tax cuts for the rich. The contract promised to cut capital gains taxes, curtail federal regulation of corporate activity, eliminate unfunded mandates to the states, and enact a balanced budget amendment to the Constitution. During the election campaign, Gingrich counseled Republicans to convey three "resource messages" to corporations, lobbyists, and wealthy individual donors. They should help elect a Republican majority to (1) "get even for the Clinton tax increase" (which mainly affected the highest income brackets); (2) take revenge for the Democrats' effort to restrict lobbying; and (3) "look to the future corporate savings" once Republicans replace Democratic committee and subcommittee chairs.[3] Democratic committee chairs in the 103rd Congress were far more favorable to environmental protection, labor rights, civil rights, and consumer rights than either the GOP or America's business circles would have liked.

The contract's call for an income tax and capital gains tax cut, a balanced budget amendment, massive cuts in social spending, along with merging mandated federal aid into unrestricted block grants to the states has continued to starve the nation's largest cities, where the majority of African Americans live. In this regard, the contract was a reincarnation of Reagan's "New Federalism" under which the federal government passed the buck, but not the bucks, to the states, and the states in turn did the same to the municipalities. Since the municipalities are the last major government link in this system, they have no choice but to raise property and local income taxes to maintain minimum public services, or to adopt austerity budgets, downsized services, privatize assets and functions, and lay off government workers in order to reduce deficits. Either that or have their bond ratings lowered, or face a takeover by a nonelected emergency financial control board. Already Washington, D.C., finds itself in this situation. Of course, the predicament of the District of Columbia is further compromised by its semicolonial status in relation to the federal government. With the Republicans in charge of Congress, which has jurisdictional and oversight responsibilities for the District's budget, finances, and public policy, the people of Washington, D.C., have found themselves effectively without even "home rule." Symbolically as well as substantively, this, too, has been a devastating blow against African-American governance. But again, Washington, D.C., may be but a precursor of the future experiences of other cities.

The Republicans attempted to steamroll a balanced budget

amendment to the Constitution through Congress. GOP congressional leaders also pursued an alternative tactic of using the authorization and appropriation processes to balance the federal budget by the year 2002. After already promising $40 billion per year in tax cuts and $140 billion per year in spending cuts over the next seven years, and a new military buildup while leaving Social Security alone, the Republicans were faced with cutting about $200 billion a year from an annual budget that then stood at $1.6 trillion. This is the equivalent of eliminating an entire year's budget during one of the next seven years, or eliminating one of out every four dollars in federal expenditures over the next seven years.

Interest on the national debt has to be paid out of whatever is left. If Social Security ($350 billion a year), military spending ($280 billion), federal pensions ($70 billion), and Medicare ($200 billion) are not ultimately touched, as the GOP Congress initially promised, only about $450 billion a year will be left, from which an average of $200 billion in annual budget reductions would need to be made to reach the Republican goal of a balanced budget by 2002.[4] This necessitates a wholesale dismantling of much of the federal government, especially aid to cities and states, as well as most programs, services, and regulations. Save for the very wealthy, most of the people the Republicans said would gain from tax cuts have lost much in reduced federal benefits and services.[5]

The dimensions of the cuts have been cleverly concealed in the rhetoric of block grants to the states, "personal responsibility," and the ending of unfunded mandates. There has been no illusion on this score, however. The GOP cannot reach its goal solely by cutting programs for the poor. The new "constitutional" framework the Republicans have tried to erect would force Congress to pull out its knife and slice away at the Social Security Trust Fund, Medicare, and other entitlements. The country faces the all-too-real prospect of being thrown back to pre-New Deal conditions when federally guaranteed social protections and entitlements were nonexistent.

White middle-income Americans seem to be particularly vulnerable to the demagogy surrounding the alleged interconnection between their tax burden, on the one hand, and civil rights, social entitlements, and affirmative action, on the other hand.[6] Racial resentments became heavily embedded in this issue as many White, middle-class, and working-class voters came to reason or were persuaded that "we" are being taxed to pay for programs for "them," then "they" turn around and use affirmative action to take "our" jobs. Taxpayers from all races, regions, and income brackets generally resent the evident imbalance between their tax burden and the services they get in return. The primary reason for this, however, is an increasingly regressive tax structure in which the wealthy and the big corporations do not come close to paying their fair share.

The tax proposals of the Contract with America, already implemented in state after state by Republican governors and Democrats in some instances, as well, have worsened economic inequality. This will only intensify and accelerate economic as well as racial inequality. Citizens for Tax Justice estimates that corporations and wealthy individuals will rake in $100 billion in additional income from capital gains tax cuts (reductions in taxes paid on capital investment), repeal of the 1993 tax increase on Social Security income for upper-bracket individuals, and restoration of IRA tax breaks for higher incomes.[7] The resulting increases in local and state taxes and user fees will increase the overall tax burden of the middle and working classes.

The call for an end to unfunded federal mandates and for a "devolution of power" back to the states has been essentially a scheme to restore the doctrine of "states' rights" – the notoriously antidemocratic doctrine against which African Americans waged a century-long struggle that finally culminated in the 1954 *Brown* decision and the passage of the Civil Rights Act of 1964 and the Voting Rights Act of 1965. Civil rights and voting rights were not mentioned in the ten-point Contract with America. Yet in the aftermath of the 1994 election, it became crystal clear that an all-out offensive against affirmative action, economic set-asides, and voting rights comprised an unstated eleventh point on the GOP agenda. Most of the contenders for the 1996 Republican presidential nomination, including Bob Dole, committed themselves to dismantling affirmative action programs.

The Challenge of Coalition Building

In summary, the 1994 congressional elections initiated a sea change in U.S. politics. Control of the legislative branch of the federal government rests with an activist right-wing coalition bent on undoing historic social and democratic gains. Underneath the Contract with America lay an attempt to impose a new model of the state predicated on survival-of-the-fittest ideology. Led by Newt Gingrich, congressional Republicans effected a historic transfer of power from the executive to the legislative branch, much of which was consolidated in the House speakership. While Senate Republicans used the power to advise and consent to control judicial and senior administrative appointments, House Republicans employed the power of appropriation and the authority to originate revenue to redistribute income upward, dictate public policy without public debate, and undermine the power of the presidency.

Remarkably, this extraordinary undemocratic posture has been justified in the name of freedom – freedom of the fittest, uninhibited by mandates, federal regulations, affirmative action, and the 1960s and 1970s' expansion of democratic rights – to survive and prosper in Newt Gingrich's "opportunity society." As the Speaker has said, "we are a muscular society." While he has insisted that, "it is impossible to maintain a civilization with 12-year-olds having babies, 15-year-olds killing each other, 17-year-olds dying of AIDS, and 18-year-olds getting diplomas they can't read,"[8] the Contract with America has not furnished these young people with an opportunity to free themselves from these social ills. Instead of jobs, better education and health care, or a "muscular" war against AIDS, drugs, and guns, Gingrich would "save American civilization" by depriving these young people of the very things they need most to improve their life choices.

Authoritarian rule, not opportunity, containment of dissent, diversity, and democracy, not civilization or civility, follow logically from right-wing, virtually all-White, nearly all-male, pro-big-business control of the U.S. Congress. The ideological, political, and legislative transformation embedded in the 1994 election results has presented African-American leadership with an unprecedented challenge that cannot be met by going it alone, by rhetorical flourishes lacking in substance, by relying on paradigms whose best days are past, or by playing to the crowd. New political thinking is needed urgently. A new consensus on the political direction and focus of the African-American community must be constructed, new tactics fashioned, and new approaches to coalition and political action undertaken.

Dialogue and debate on basic questions of theory, strategy, and practice will facilitate the political mobilization of African-American constituencies. A key issue centers on how the African-American community – as has been its historical role in social change movements in the U.S. – can help catapult the country in the direction of greater democracy, inclusion, and empowerment. The following are among the tasks involved in meeting this challenge: (a) finding ways to both broaden and accelerate African-American political participation – specifically, preparing the African-American community ideologically to make a maximum contribution to slowing down and eventually derailing the Republican juggernaut. This means, among other things, getting over the comfort level that many African-American elected officials appear to have with low rates of Black voter registration and participation, and with the relative abstention of African-American constituents from crucial, nonelectoral areas of political action, including legislative mobilization; (b) finding ways of getting the country to discuss the persistence of racism and racial discrimination in the contemporary context – especially in relation to the global economy and transnational corporations; (c) developing bold, innovative conceptual approaches and practical initiatives for coalition. Consideration needs to be given to building progressive legislative caucuses and coalitions that link urban and suburban interests, and unite broad segments of the working class, middle class, and the poor around overarching issues like education, regional economic development, infrastructure, a real war on drugs, maintenance of a humane social safety net, environmental justice, and the protection and nurturing of children and youth; (d) unfolding a broad-based conversation among African-American politicians, scholars, activists, policymakers, and voters, aimed at redefining "black politics"; and (e) mobilizing a level of electoral participation sufficient to deal a major blow to right-wing Republicanism in future elections.

The challenge of shaping a new consensus upon which such a mobilization can take place in turn raises fundamental questions, such as whether or not the building of a genuinely progressive wing of the Democratic Party is still a viable strategy and how exercising a third-party option would impact African-American legislative seniority. Will taking this course increase or decrease the marginalization of the African-American community and its political claims in citywide, statewide, and national politics? Are progressive forces large enough, broad enough, strong enough, and flexible enough to justify African Americans opting for a third party? Will enough White and Latino voters come on board and thus ensure that African Americans are not left to "go it alone"? And how can African-American leaders develop a language that enables them to talk with and thus more effectively influence the political behavior of White Americans?

Conclusion

The Republican juggernaut, operating at high speed for the balance of the 104th Congress, rolled over a passive and ideologically inconsistent Democratic opposition. The House enacted all ten provisions of the Contract with America within the first six months. The road was bumpier in the Senate, where the Republicans fell just one vote short of passing a balanced budget amendment to the Constitution. The appropriation process, which specified the exact spending amounts for each department and agency of the federal government, revealed to the public in graphic detail the dimensions of the Republican assault on entitlements and other social programs. And the public responded with outrage, saying in effect that "This is not what we voted for." Negative public opinions on the Republican leadership gave President Clinton the fortitude to veto the GOP budget.

While House Speaker Newt Gingrich and presidential candidate Bob Dole thought that the president had played into their hands and would be blamed for the government shutdown, Republicans had actually fallen into Clinton's. The public blamed Republicans for the impasse. Public outrage intensified when a second Clinton veto was followed by another shutdown. Unable to tell which way the political winds were blowing, the Gingrich crowd threatened to force the country into default on payments on the national debt if Clinton did not assent to their budget demands. The president again stood his ground. Public opinion sided with him and the Democrats in Congress. Gingrich's standing plummeted. By midwinter of 1996 he had become the most unpopular national political figure in the country.

Meanwhile, Bob Dole, on the campaign trail in quest of the Republican presidential nomination (which he eventually won), moved further and further to the right to stave off a spirited challenge from Pat Buchanan and multimillionaire Steve Forbes. The Republican nomination was securely his midway through the primary season. By running on the Right Dole allowed President Clinton to seize the political center, where he co-opted some of the Republican message while also championing popular Democratic stances. This, the fact that the Dole campaign emerged from the primaries nearly broke, and the continuing public disgust with the Gingrich gang positioned the president to achieve what only months before was thought so unachievable: reelection to a second term. By Labor Day, Clinton had restored the double-digit lead that was temporarily narrowed by the bounce that the Republican convention gave the Dole campaign.

Although Clinton's victory in the November 1996 general election precluded right-wing Republican control of all three branches of the federal government, he has already embraced much of the Republican program. Most glaring was his decision to sign draconian welfare "reform" legislation, which had virtually unanimous Republican backing, split congressional Democrats nearly down the middle, and angered liberals and progressives. This episode prompted left-of-center forces to wonder whether their constituencies would continue to lose even after Clinton won reelection.

And the response of African-American leadership? Over the course of the 104th Congress, and the 1996 election cycle, how did it respond to the challenges outlined above? In the space of nine months, from the Million Man March on October 16, 1995, to Stand For Children on June 1, 1996, Black leadership brought at least 1.25 million people to the nation's capital. While in concept and composition those two actions stood in diametrical contrast to each other, they were similar in lack of political focus and failure to enunciate a public policy agenda. Although incredible mobilizations in and of themselves, neither articulated the clarity of vision needed to spawn a political mobilization of the breadth of the African-American community for the elections and the critical policy battles that lay beyond. The march leaders rejected making claims on government, despite the facts that African Americans are citizens, that they serve with distinction in the armed forces, and that they pay tens of billions of dollars in taxes.

To date, the Congressional Black Caucus (CBC) has not provided the leadership for policy or political action. On pivotal questions the CBC has been bogged down with internal differences or diverted by an unfocused message. The annual CBC legislative conferences in 1994 and 1995 were missed opportunities with respect to clarity and mobilization. Like most other black leaders, CBC members protested Clinton's signing of the welfare reform legislation. It does not appear that much was done, however, to prevent the bill from reaching the president's desk; to engineer a coordinated effort with Senate liberals; to pressure Senate Democrats to organize a filibuster; or to mobilize constituents. The CBC seems hamstrung, particularly by indecision in relation to a Democratic administration with which it (or at least some CBC members) has profound differences. This, of course, is attached to the larger problem of the African-American community's relationship to the Democratic Party as such.

It was not expected that the issues of leadership and direction raised above would be answered by election day in 1996. But in an election that on the presidential level could have narrowed and produced a closer contested battle for Electoral College victory and, on the congressional level, possibly have ousted the Republicans from control of the House and Senate, which would among other things give African-American Democrats an unprecedented number of committee and subcommittee chairs, black voters had to make a choice. If they had not, it still would have been a missed opportunity of catastrophic proportions. Under any future scenario, with respect to the outcome of elections, questions about the need for a new consensus, independent political mobilization to defeat and advance historic gains, and a strategic alternative for the African-American community and the nation quickly assert themselves as issues of the nature, composition, and direction of the postelection governing coalitions come into play.

Notes

1. Actually, the Republicans only won fifty-two seats on election day. Senator Richard Shelby of Alabama, arguably one of the most conservative members of the entire U.S. Senate, switched parties the next day. Nine months into the 104th Congress, a total of four Democratic House members had switched to the GOP, giving the Republicans a 234:200 majority in the House of Representatives.

2. Marcia Gelbart, "Religious Right Held Key to Vote in South," *The Hill* (November 10, 1994).

3. See "Gingrich Foresees Corruption Probe by a GOP House," *The Washington Post* (October 1, 1994).

4. "The Contract's Brutal Arithmetic," *The New York Times* editorial (November 14, 1994).

5. See *The New Fiscal Agenda: What Will It Mean and How Will It Be Accomplished?* (Washington, D.C.: Center for Budget Priorities, 1994).

6. See Thomas Byrne and Mary D. Edsall, *Chain Reaction: The Impact of Race, Rights, and Taxes on American Politics* (New York: W.W. Norton, 1991), pp. 130–31, 137–53.

7. Citizens for Tax Justice, "*The GOP's Contract with America*" (December 8, 1994).

8. "Excerpts of Remarks by Gingrich on Victory," *The New York Times* (December 6, 1994).

3

From Streets of Hope
to Landscapes of Despair:
The Case of Los Angeles

Cynthia Hamilton

Land-use planning and zoning are powerful tools for the manipulation of space, and thereby political and social behavior. Decisions about the use of land have retarded social justice and created racial, ethnic, and class conflict in American cities. These decisions have resulted in the deterioration of Black communities through displacement and redevelopment. Historically, Black communities have offered alternative sources of identity and meaning for life in America. These places, as suggested by some observers, were sources of support and assistance for residents and maintained control and order based on shared values. Order has disappeared along with community and the artificial replacement (through the use of police, courts, and prisons) is far too costly for the well-being of communities. This concern is raised by David Harvey in *Social Justice and the City*, even though the focus of his attention is eighteenth-century London:

> If, in the short run, we simply pursue efficiency and ignore the social cost, then those individuals or groups who bear the brunt of that cost are likely to be a source of long run inefficiency either through decline in . . . those intangibles that motivate people to cooperate and participate in the social process of production . . . or through forms of anti-social behavior (crime and drug addiction) which will necessitate the diversion of productive investment towards their correction.[1]

Sadly, this is the situation and dilemma faced by urban government today. Yet it seems that urban policies continue to ignore Harvey's warning.

The Loss of Space

While policymakers and developers speak of growth and redevelopment, we have actually witnessed the continual devastation of Black communities through deindustrialization and disinvestment used as mechanisms for growth. The few remaining enclaves of Black Americans suffer the crisis of underdevelopment, characterized by decay, abandonment, and poverty; simultaneously, large sectors of space that were part of these communities have been consumed by new growth strategies that have displaced residents and swallowed community and cultural institutions in the name of office towers, expansion of central business districts, parking lots, sports arenas – in short, anything that would increase land values for outsiders. A basic part of the history of Black people in the U.S. in the past forty years is how Black communities have been the victims of growth.

Globalization has exacerbated the social and economic problems confronting cities. Plant closures, corporate center development, expansion of the service economy, and corporate expansion in suburban areas have given shape to economic restructuring that has changed the face of city life. Urban households have been restructured during this period and process, and thus we see the displacement of middle- and low-income households, and the rise of female-headed households. This is accompanied by the reshaping of urban space with its residents experiencing the loss of a meaningful sense of "place."

The space/place of community at one time provided a buffer from the abuse and neglect of a racist society. "Place" in this context is clearly more than location. Place is memory; it provides a location for identity and history. For Black people in the U.S., the "place" that we live in has always been a source of refuge and resistance against a consumer culture that either ignored us based on an affirmation of superiority or sought to exploit us in the barest ways. Place is both symbolic and real and has been central to Black culture despite pejorative labels, like slums, leveled by policymakers and social analysts. Place is that space that one can "claim," though not necessarily own (like Harlem or Chicago's Southside in the 1920s and 1930s). These places, once the homes of Black America, are increasingly being reshaped, redefined, consumed by corporate capital – be it by the construction of office towers, hospital expansion, or land clearance. The new use of place/space reflects not only competing philosophies of use and exchange value, but also the political intentions of the new owners to reverse the political unity that came to be centered around these places. Dispersal and displacement have been central elements of reconstruction, redefinition, and control. Public space has increasingly been eliminated through privatization.² Those common areas where children could play and families congregate, where the elders could gather for talk, where women could feel safe from assault have become "private property" – the use to be determined by the one who owns.

Place is essential for social and cultural identity, particularly for the young – it provides their first sense of belonging, sense of community, and safety. The loss of place has robbed poor children of color, in particular, of moments of childhood security. Without an alternative community structure, young Black children have defined themselves in relation to "the other" – White society – as in the stereotyped, racialized notions that dominate urban discourse: crime, drugs, criminals, gangs, war. The alternative is, of course, defined as redevelopment, growth, gentrification – the re-creation of old communities that obliterates all semblance of the past and the historical memory of older residents.

Resisting corporate incursions and accompanying consumer culture is difficult in the current physical environment. Since 1965 the areas in major cities that were the traditional places of the Black community have been redefined and reshaped to fit dominant corporate and civic definitions and uses of urban space. The new use of space has been intentional, designed to reverse the political unity resulting from proximity and density and the shared experience of racism. As Black communities lost their center and residents lost the ability to interact spontaneously and informally in ways that have reinforced alternative cultural style and values, individuals have become unwitting victims of the dominant consumer culture.

In earlier periods, Black communities within major American cities have provided the space in which counteridentities were forged and nurtured, but also places of resistance to hegemonic cultural forces and structures imposed as a result of institutional racism. This was especially evident in the 1960s and during the Civil Rights and Black Panther Movements. But the struggles of the 1960s, both cultural and legal, had ironic consequences. Along with open housing and other civil rights legislation which provided access to spaces that previously excluded Blacks, there were also special programs, like the earlier urban renewal, designed to transform "ghettos," precisely the places that had offered alternative meaning. By 1975 the places that had been home for many Black Americans began to disappear. Judged solely by standards that measure access, initially some of this change may have been seen as positive. Indeed, much of the redevelopment experienced in major cities like Los Angeles, Birmingham, Detroit, Washington, D.C., was completed during the terms of Black mayors.[3] The results of redevelopment have been disastrous for the poor Black community, however. Black Americans have lost a sense of place and with it, a sense of history. Much like the Black towns of the frontier that were lost without a marker for posterity, urban Black communities have been reduced to rubble or, more accurately, slated for redevelopment and thereby replacement without a trace.

The long-term processes associated with redevelopment and resulting in the loss of place for Blacks have had profound implications for residents and intellectuals alike. For residents the loss of space and place has created a rootlessness exacerbated by the separation of families. For intellectuals it has meant a separation of the discussion of identity, difference, and culture from material circumstances and a retreat to abstraction. It has contributed to the fragmentation of progressive politics and helped to obscure class alliances crossing race and ethnicity. Our loss of the battle for control of the street has been largely responsible for the absence or weakness of theoretical responses and frameworks aimed at aggrandizing political and economic power.

"Slum" Clearance for Profit

The restructuring of the American economy has reordered cities. As old neighborhoods disappear, new downtown financial districts are being built to house banks, insurance companies, and the headquarters of corporations on a scale representing the power of their occupants and clients. These changes have drastic consequences for industrial and social relations; they have forced us away from geographic communities and into what some call occupational groupings that reinforce inequality. More striking than any notion of a new basis for unity, therefore, is the new basis of disunity – inequality has been magnified by this restructuring of space to correspond to changes in the economy. The new cities of America have moved to eliminate their working-class constituents, in some instances replacing them with White and even Black professionals who are employed downtown; in other instances the working class is simply dispersed. A geographic inequality appears integral to the growth process.

There can be little doubt that race has been an important element of social policy in the urban landscape. Restrictive covenants, exclusive zoning, and other legal tools were used for the creation and maintenance of racially homogeneous communities. These kinds of policies were hindrances to government's role in generating and ensuring profits and economic health for the corporate sector. During the Depression corporations watched government become a major provider of jobs, housing, and services. There was little objection to this role as long as government did not *compete* with the private sector or disrupt corporate agendas for urban America. Corporations, developers, and financiers did identify limits for government. They wanted to continue to reap the benefits of government subsidies and insurance while eliminating government controls and guidelines. This became increasingly clear in the area of housing.

Responding to the needs of a population in economic crisis and attempting to preclude more violent disruption, the federal government made the dcision to build public housing in 1937. What the private sector demanded as a concession as government built inexpensive, quality houses and made them available to the working class was "slum clearance." To avoid oversupply or even adequate supply of affordable housing, private sector lobbyists forced the Congress to agree to the demolition of housing in areas designated as "slums." Similar policies with the same intended outcome of maintaining profits continued throughout the 1950s, 1960s, and 1970s. Slum clearance and urban renewal still remain as contemporary instruments for this purpose, but now "growth" and "redevelopment" are metaphors for the removal of poor people and people of color. The renovations, renewal, and reinvestment that have eliminated or moved inner city communities, however, have not solved the social and economic problems of cities.

Place and Resistance

Forms of resistance can be located in the shape and character of community. In *City and the Grassroots*, Manuel Castells asserts that "cultural identity is associated with and organized around a specific territory."[4] He concludes that the urban revolts of the 1960s emerged because "the ghetto territory became a significant space for the Black community as the material basis of social organization, cultural identity and political power."[5] It should not be surprising that the dismantling of community has been simultaneous with a decline in organized political action. The consequences of the new restructuring are dramatically demonstrated in the aftermath of the Los Angeles uprising of 1992. The mass unrest has been insufficient in providing new political leadership; existing political and physical structures threaten the fragile bonds of unity both within the Black community and between Blacks and Chicanos. In Los Angeles the social and economic conditions of the city stoked the flames of April and May 1992 as they did in 1965.

The conditions of unemployment, inadequate housing, and poverty in a city of glamour and fortune are the real causes of unrest, although police abuse and the miscarriage of justice are constants as well. Los Angeles has a poverty rate higher than the rest of the nation: 15.6 percent of residents live in poverty. Black unemployment for those between the ages of 25 and 54 is 19.5 percent; 14 percent of Los Angeles residents with full-time jobs live in poverty because of low-wage jobs. Los Angeles has more than its share of low-wage jobs: 17.5 percent of the jobs pay employees $11,000 or less per year; yet 75 percent of families living in poverty must pay half of their income for rent.[6] Los Angeles remains one of the most segregated cities in the country. As residents lose access to political organizations, they lose their voice. In the wake of the current urban redevelopment all inherent organizations are destroyed.

These economic conditions have been exacerbated by urban government debt and the call for austerity. As states and the nation move to balance the budget at the expense of the poor, we witness budget cuts in health, welfare, public housing, education, and other services. California's deficit stood at 25 percent of the state budget one month after the uprising and has been used to justify a wide range of cuts. Calls to eliminate deficits have become a political tool for the wealthy to maintain positions of power and influence. The exaggerated conditions of poverty that have resulted from such calls contribute to the deterioration in race relations. The popular response to these conditions has been protest and revolt. Los Angeles joined the ranks of these austerity protests on April 29, 1992.

The vast majority of Black residents in major American cities has been forced to succumb to new history carved by the bulldozers of redevelopment; they are the products of a new culture created by redevelopment. The old places in the community, the social clubs, churches, movie theaters, public spaces around which memories revolved have been displaced. In their place we find new structures and "restoration"/gentrification evoking nostalgia for a past that no one seems to know. Ironically, places that were so important to the Black community have been dismissed as meaningless by urban planners and designers, while new "places" are erected in the name of universal civic values.

There is a new private use of public space that not only destroys the territoriality of Blacks but is the essence of the new redevelopment. Under the guise of "urban renewal" emergent places and organizations are disrupted and destroyed. Because place is a historical as well as geographic reference, its elimination causes the disappearance of everything that makes life livable. Redevelopment manifests itself as a besieging of non-White cultures. Land-use decisions and planning have become tools of governmental violence. The displacement and removal of poor people are international issues. The elimination of the freedom to build a community, a place in one's own image, is a powerful way to break social forces as they emerge. Is there any wonder, then, that we have experienced a collapse of values, a surge of anarchy and anomie in modern society?

Re-Creating Social Justice

It is clear that growth and development can be sources of wealth, but also of death, destruction, and inequality simultaneously. As pointed out by Hazel Henderson, it is never a matter of growth versus no growth; rather, it is what is growing, what is declining, and what must be maintained.[7] If growth reproduces inequality, is it possible to limit growth and distribute goods more equitably? Henderson's statement helps us to see that the costs of growth may outweigh the advantages. It is most apparent in communities of color where we find the debris created on the road to perfection. The litany of problems should cause us to rethink economic development from the bottom up. Communities must develop solutions for themselves, solutions that are not only independent but may be antithetical to free-market approaches. We see, therefore, the possibility of developing economic institutions in the community that will parallel those in the larger society but that will also respond to local problems and needs – a type of economic "liberated zone."

These possibilities include alternative ownership arrangements, cooperatives, recycling, all sustainable production techniques, and nonmarket approaches to basic needs like housing. For example, we (the Twenty First Century Institute) believe that it may be necessary to ensure that some housing is removed from the commodity market and spared the pricing cycle produced by speculation. Pricing could be based on the income structure of communities. The objective must be to prevent displacement and maintain community stability. These alternatives are based on the establishment of new rules for economic enterprises that spring from some basic philosophical concerns and differences. These new rules flow from our efforts to establish a new and alternative philosophical base. Alternatives will develop as we reject the theory of markets as the basis for distribution, and by rejecting the philosophy of liberalism and its emphasis on individualism and property rights. As we embrace group rights and come to understand the threat that individualism poses to resources we hold in common (air, water, land), there may be a call for a new social contract.

The challenge feared most by the corporate sector is one that substitutes the collective good for the much-touted philosophy of individualism. When groups previously left out of formal parliamentary and electoral processes demand access or develop new methods of political action, capitalists feel threatened. For African Americans in this legally segregated, "separate but equal" society, the personal commitment to change was reflective of social concerns. Demanding broad social change was a prerequisite for expanded personal rights and freedoms. Unfortunately, industrial society has forced the separation of private and social concerns. As a result, individuals are locked into selfishly considering individual rights rather than cooperating to meet community needs.

The essence of a new social contract must be the reaffirmation of common good. Livable cities will only be possible when the collective good is understood to have meaning for each individual. A community agenda must replace the current corporate agenda for American cities so that we may consider issues of sustainability: full employment, livable space, resource management that avoids excessive waste, and pollution control as a health measure. But this community agenda would also revive a notion of the collective good; social concerns would become more central than private good. Individual and collective good can no longer remain separate. The false contradiction between social good and individual rights and needs has produced the current problems and crises. Individual property rights must no longer be permitted to infringe on the quality of life affecting everyone.

An alternative philosophical beginning can provide the basis for a progressive agenda. The new rules for economic enterprises must include, first, an equitable distribution of wealth, one based on a recognition of workers' real contributions, education, and experience as well as production; second, acceptance of workplace democracy as an alternative to current work processes; third, cooperative relations between enterprises and the surrounding community; and finally, environmentally sound production.

The Labor Community Strategy Center in Los Angeles produced a document in 1992, *Reconstructing Los Angeles from the Bottom Up*, calling for approaches to economic development different from corporate-approved ones proposed by the Ueberroth Commission in the wake of the urban insurrection following the first Rodney King trial.[8] The Strategy Center sees the need to set standards of social responsibility for corporations, particularly those that must locate in a particular area or market for resource considerations. As corporations abandon communities, citizens and residents must begin to look within for solutions and organize regionally to identify problems and solutions as well as a means of creating new economic alternatives. Inner-city communities, by identifying their basic needs, can begin the process of sustainable development. Embracing integrated regional approaches can make communities the center for the environmentally sound production technologies of the future.

The policies of redevelopment have caused urban residents to lose many of their rights as citizens. Minorities of varying income brackets lose political access and electoral strength as communities are dismantled and reassembled with new residents. Churches, schools, small businesses, neighborhood and civic groups, social clubs, and countless other associations are lost as communities disappear. While citizens are chided by political parties and media alike to participate, to be involved, government itself has facilitated the destruction of the very mechanism by which minorities, women, and poor people are able to organize and claim their own social justice – namely, through their communities and neighborhoods. Urban redevelopment has claimed millions of victims over the past decades. The process is not complete, however, and beyond the dismantling of communities and the complete transformation of cities into corporate entities we may all have been quietly socialized to believe that this process is both natural and necessary for human progress. But this is not always the case.

Notes

1. David Harvey, *Social Justice and the City* (Baltimore: Johns Hopkins University Press), p. 97.

2. Luis Aponte-Parés, "What's Yellow and White and Has Land All around It?: Appropriating Place in Puerto Rican Barrios," *Journal of the Center for Puerto Rican Studies*, vol. 7, no. 1 (1995), p. 10.

3. Cynthia Hamilton, *Apartheid in an American City: The Case of the Black Community in Los Angeles* (Los Angeles: Labor Community Strategy Center, 1988).

4. Manuel Castells, *City and the Grassroots* (Berkeley: University of California Press, 1983), p. xvii.

5. Ibid., p. 67.

6. Cynthia Hamilton, "The Belly of the Beast: Linking Militarization and Urban Plight in Los Angeles," *Positive Alternatives*, vol. 2, no. 4 (Summer 1992).

7. Hazel Henderson, *Politics of the Solar Age* (Indianapolis: Knowledge Systems, 1983).

8. *Reconstructing Los Angeles from the Bottom Up* (Los Angeles: Labor Community Strategy Center, 1992).

4

Black Voters and Urban Regime: The Case of Atlanta

Tony Affigne

In many important ways the three decades since the Civil Rights Movement of the 1960s have witnessed substantial progress for Black America. Most formal barriers to mass Black political participation have fallen, and overt legal protection for racially segregated political institutions has ended. These changes in the meaning of Black citizenship, combined with the political mobilization of African-, Latino-, Asian-, and Native-American communities, have indeed brought about new realities in the racial composition of the active electorate and the institutions of American government. As just one example, there were five times as many Black persons elected to local, state, and federal offices in 1992 compared to 1970, rising to more than 7,500. Most of these – nearly 5,500 – were in the South, where obstacles to Black empowerment were the strongest prior to 1965.[1] Many African-American entrepreneurs and professionals have seen substantial improvement in their economic status. The Black middle-income and college-educated classes have grown significantly; between 1970 and 1992 the number of Black households with annual incomes greater than $50,000 rose by 171 percent – twice the overall Black population's growth rate – from 537,000 to more than 1.4 million.[2]

Yet during the same period, economic prospects for the *majority* of Black Americans have deteriorated in absolute terms and when compared to White Americans. The gaps between Black and White family incomes, wealth, and poverty barely changed, while the unemployment rate for Black workers actively seeking employment more than doubled from 4.7 to 9.8 percent. The net result of labor market trends was that income rose for some Black households but fell for others, leaving their median income essentially unchanged. Between 1970 and 1992, median income for Black households fell by

$150 to less than $19,000, while the same figure rose by nearly $1,500 for White households – to more than $32,000. Likewise, relative per capita Black income hardly changed at all, rising slightly from 56 percent to 58 percent of the figure for the White population; annual income for each Black man, woman, and child in 1992 averaged just $9,296, compared to an average of nearly $16,000 for White Americans.[3] At nearly 43 percent, the proportion of Black households earning less than $15,000 in 1992 was double that of White households, a gap that *increased* since 1970. During the same two decades the proportion of all Black children living in poverty increased from 42 percent to 46 percent.[4] (See Table 4.1.)

Table 4.1 Political and Economic Trends for Black America, 1970–1992

	1970	*1992*	*Change*
Total Black Elected Officials, All Local, State and Federal Offices	1,469	7,517	+ 6,048
Unemployment Rate among Black Workers Actively Seeking Employment	4.7%	9.8%	+5.1%
Median Annual Black Household Real Income (measured in 1992 dollars)	$18,810	$18,660	−$150
Black Household Income per Person as a Percentage of White Income per Person	56%	58%	+2%
Percentage of Black Families with Household Real Incomes under $15,000 (measured in 1992 dollars)	41.3%	42.7%	+1.4%
Percentage of Black Children Living in Poverty	42%	46%	+4%

Sources: Joint Center for Political and Economic Studies, *Black Elected Officials: A National Roster* (Washington, D.C.: U.S. Bureau of the Census); *Current Population Reports*, P60–184; and *Statistical Abstract of the United States, 1994.*

Unremitting economic crisis has created severe social stress in many predominantly Black communities where the impacts of joblessness and poverty are concentrated. For residents of these communities the quality of life has worsened dramatically, with continuing high levels of unemployment – especially for young Black men – interacting explosively with readily available drugs and weapons. Police brutality, deterioration of public school systems, weak enforcement of minimum housing standards, disinvestment from public housing, low wages and job insecurity, and the inaccessibility of health, nutrition, and psychological services have all contributed to the pervasive sense of despair that afflicts much of Black America in the 1990s. Thus, we encounter the central political paradox that confronts Black America today. The most significant changes wrought by the Civil Rights Movement of the 1960s – the elimination of most formal barriers to Black political participation and increased access to previously segregated occupations and professions – appear to have had negligible impact on the nation's underlying racial hierarchy. The apparent stagnation in Black economic and social progress and the resurgence of racially divisive political rhetoric would both suggest that Black political empowerment has in fact been limited.

As the twenty-first century approaches, then, the primary political question troubling many Black Americans is understanding how their efforts expended on electoral politics can contribute concretely to the struggle for economic justice, social equality, and political power – a puzzle that poses important strategic dilemmas. Three decades after the Voting Rights Act, what hope is there that conventional participation, *along the lines practiced so far*, will yield tangible improvements for Black communities? Are there more effective ways to mobilize Black voters? Do internal politics and competitive calculations of the two major parties pose insurmountable obstacles to the attainment of Black political goals? Are the apparent limitations of Black empowerment the result of institutional racism, failures of leadership, or the nature of American federalism?

Contemporary conditions also raise new questions. What approaches, alliances, and conflicts are suggested by the ongoing emergence of Latino, Asian-American, Native-American, and immigrant political power? How should Black political leaders respond to fundamental changes in the global economy and the relative weakness of the labor movement? Finally, what new opportunities and dilemmas spring from a growing class, cultural, and generational diversity within the Black population itself? This chapter explores some of these questions with a close look at the racial dimensions of voter turnout and political conflict in Atlanta, Georgia, a major American city where race, democracy, and urban policy have been closely linked for more than ten years. Voter turnout analysis allows us to trace the emergence and extent of Black participation in urban democracy.

Atlanta provides a useful case study of broader issues because of its unique place in African-American political history and because social scientists have already produced a substantial body of research focused on Atlanta's politics, its race relations, and the interaction between the city's governmental and economic power structures.

Race and Power in Atlanta, Georgia

The city of Atlanta holds a prominent place in the history of Black America, the development of Black social thought, and the scholarly analysis of urban life in the United States. Crucial events of the nation's antebellum economic development, Civil War, Reconstruction, Civil Rights Movement, and post-civil-rights Black political emergence all occurred in Georgia's largest and most important city. From its founding as the nexus for Georgia's publicly financed railroad system in 1843 to its destruction by General William Tecumseh Sherman in 1864, Atlanta served as an important center of the Southern slave economy and White supremacist political power.[5]

Nearly a century later, pivotal moments of the post-World War II Civil Rights Movement took place in Atlanta. Here was held the 1954 strategy conference of the NAACP, called to coordinate the southern Black response to the Supreme Court's *Brown vs. Board of Education* ruling. Three years later, Atlanta was the site of the founding convention of Dr. Martin Luther King, Jr.'s Southern Christian Leadership Conference. Drawing on the city's several prominent, predominantly Black colleges, Atlanta was also the scene of increasingly assertive Black student action, culminating in lunch-counter sit-ins during 1960 and 1961. During the 1950s and 1960s, Black Atlantans witnessed all three of the early Civil Rights Movement's tactical thrusts – the legal strategy of the NAACP, Montgomery Improvement Association-style mass (boycott) actions, and the direct civil disobedience of the Black student movement.[6]

In the realm of electoral politics Atlanta was an early locus of emergent Black political power. Horace Tate's 1969 campaign for mayor represented one of the earliest Black electoral mobilizations in a major American city. Maynard Jackson's election as mayor in 1973 was – alongside similar victories in Detroit, Gary, Indiana, and Newark, New Jersey – among the first wave of successful Black electoral efforts in the country's growing number of majority-Black cities.[7] Andrew Young, a political ally of former governor and president Jimmy Carter, succeeded Jackson in 1981 after serving as the Carter administration's ambassador to the United Nations.[8] At the end of Young's eight years in office, Jackson returned for a third term from 1989 to 1993. In the 1993 elections, Jackson's protégé and former city councilman Bill Campbell was elected. Thus, an unbroken series of Black-led city administrations has governed the city for more than twenty years.[9]

Atlanta was also the birthplace of the scholarly study of the African-American experience in W. E. B. Du Bois's Atlanta University studies, the very foundations of contemporary Black social theory and social analysis. During the present century numerous other social scientists have studied the city of Atlanta in order to build and illustrate general theories of urban society, economy, and politics. Prominent examples include Floyd Hunter's *Community Power Structure*, M. Kent Jennings's *Community Influentials*, and Clarence Stone's *Regime Politics*.[10] In none of these scholarly studies, however, was much attention given to the potential impacts of racial differences in political participation. The reader is left wondering, in fact, just how much democratic institutions have to do with the governance of Atlanta at all. This is an important question given that if city government is only partially responsive to democratic influence – and cities are where most Black Americans live – then there may be good reasons why the mobilization of Black voters has had only limited impact.

Atlanta's Urban Regime: Elections Yes, Democracy No

Neither Hunter nor Jennings provided any empirical evidence regarding the level of mass Black participation in Atlanta's electoral politics. Their elite power studies barely mention mass participation, emphasizing instead the political activities of social and business elites. Hunter's study identified Black political power with the integration of Black leaders into the White power structure, while Jennings attributed the Black community's political power to its malleability and willingness to follow the directives of the city's Black elite.

Stone used an analysis of public policymaking in Atlanta to show the existence of an enduring *urban regime*, a more-or-less stable alliance linking the city's downtown business leaders with a political class made up of elected and appointed public officials. But Stone gave slight attention to changing voter turnout, observing only that during the 1960s and 1970s the participation of African-American electors increased substantially, while pointing out that recent gains

in the *apparent* political empowerment of Atlanta's Black population
have not generated across-the-board improvements:

> Increased political power has produced significant gains for the Black
> middle-class, but little for the Black poor and working-class. Scarce
> attention is paid to the employment and housing needs of those who have
> limited education and income. Class differences in policy gains rule out
> any simple connection between electoral power and group benefit.[11]

There is ample reason to suspect that class tensions are still
important features of Atlanta's civic culture, affecting the nature of
relations within the Black political elite as well as that elite's linkages
to the broader public. Between the 1960 and 1970 censuses, Atlanta's
population became majority-Black, and the establishment of the city's
Black political regime in the 1970s followed shortly afterward. During
the same time period, suburbanization and the outmigration of
affluent White families produced the current demographic patterns in
Fulton County, a somewhat exaggerated variant of a classic American
pattern: an affluent, overwhelmingly White tier of suburbs sprawls
north of the city; located midcounty, the city itself is two-thirds Black;
the southern end of the county is predominantly Black and rural.[12]
By 1990, 67.1 percent of Atlanta's 394,000 residents were African
American, the third highest proportion among large U.S. cities, after
Gary, Indiana, and Detroit, Michigan. While about 61 percent of
Fulton County's total population and voting-age citizens lived within
the city limits in 1990, Atlanta was home to more than 82 percent of
the county's Black residents, and nearly 90 percent of its poor
families.[13] Within the boundaries of the city itself, Atlanta is a
bifurcated community whose population is largely segregated into
predominantly White and predominantly Black neighborhoods. It is
also polarized in terms of economic status. In 1989, the median Black
family income was $18,451 – *less than 30 percent* of the median
White family income of $59,133. Black families in poverty made up
32.3 percent of the Black community, compared to a poverty rate of
just 4.6 percent among Atlanta's White families – and Black poverty
rates were increasing, while poverty among White Atlantans had
declined.[14]
In short, Fulton County's large Black community is concentrated
within the city limits of Atlanta, is predominantly low income, and
lives apart from an affluent suburban White population – but adjoins
an equally affluent White population within the city. Yet this Black populace is governed by a middle-class political stratum also composed of

Black people, but which is closely allied with the White leadership of the local economy. Moreover, if the socioeconomic data are any indication, the Black political elite's two decades of governance have not significantly altered the broader community's typical conditions of increasing poverty and residential segregation.

With these characteristic features – a nationally significant history of Black mobilization, strong and visible alliances between political and corporate elites, a classic American urban–suburban cleavage defined by race and class, an enduring Black-led political regime, and the all-too-common constellation of contemporary urban problems including high crime, rising poverty, and economic restructuring – it should be apparent that understanding the racial and class dimensions of electoral participation in Atlanta may provide valuable insights into political conditions facing Black voters in other American cities.

In light of Atlanta's long history of Black political mobilization, it is possible that the majority of Black citizens gives tacit or active support to the city's Black leadership; after 130 years of White-dominated politics, the Black community may very well be willing to tolerate limited progress toward social and economic equity in exchange for the symbolic achievement represented by the accession and endurance of Black-led city government. Alternatively, however, the broader Black populace may feel no more invested in a weak, White-allied, corporate-oriented Black elite than in its predecessor White regimes. One way to determine which of these alternatives is accurate is to analyze electoral participation patterns. Consistently high levels of voter turnout across the city's diverse neighborhoods, reflecting high levels of grassroots mobilization in Black neighborhoods and White among the rich and the poor, would suggest that the regime enjoyed widespread public support or, at least, that the general public felt sufficiently invested in the formal mechanisms of local democracy to participate, whatever its feelings may have been toward the particular incumbents or their challengers. The 1993 mayoral election provides a good opportunity to test this possibility.

Atlanta's 1993 Mayoral Election

Following Maynard Jackson's decision to retire after serving as mayor for twelve years, Councilman Bill Campbell emerged as an early front-runner in the jockeying to replace Jackson. Fellow city councilor Myrtle Davis also declared quickly, hoping to capitalize on the 1992 election season's so-called year of the woman, and expecting to attract widespread support from the city's female voters. Women made up more than 56 percent of the city's registrants, and Black women alone represented a bloc of nearly sixty thousand voters, more than a third of the total. Longtime Atlanta power Michael Lomax, at the time chairman of the Fulton County Commission, resigned his post to enter the mayoral race, with the eventual backing of former mayor Andrew Young; Campbell had been endorsed by Jackson. Nancy Smith Schaefer, a conservative White activist, also emerged during the campaign as a surprisingly energetic candidate, attracting a small but significant following of predominantly White voters.

With twelve mayoral candidates on the ballot, including three prominent African Americans (Campbell, Davis, and Lomax), high levels of campaign spending and television advertising, and a flurry of high-profile endorsements and counterendorsements, Atlanta voters in 1993 were treated to a spirited and busy municipal campaign. Unfamiliar at first to most voters, Campbell was able to build visibility and maintain momentum by conducting a largely symbolic campaign, pledging to prepare the way for the city's hosting of the 1996 Olympics. Davis was even less well known than Campbell and was unable to assemble an effective campaign organization, changing campaign managers and press spokespersons at a dizzying pace. Lomax suffered with high negative poll ratings, due primarily to his administration of an unpopular property tax reevaluation. Schaefer was not taken seriously by the media or political commentators until late in the campaign and never attracted much support beyond the city's coterie of White conservatives.

The campaign ended on November 2, 1993, much as expected, with Campbell in the lead – but shy of the outright majority needed to avoid a runoff – followed by Lomax, Davis, Schaefer, and the eight minor candidates. In the November 23 runoff, Campbell over-whelmed Lomax with nearly 75 percent of the vote, the biggest landslide in decades. Campbell thus inherited, with a convincing show of electoral support, the legacy of Atlanta's Black-led governing regime and spent subsequent months preparing his administration for the demands of hosting an international gathering in 1996. He also faced the daunting task of reducing the nation's highest crime rate, while maintaining control over a fractious and independent-minded police department. The magnitude of Campbell's election victory might have represented a high point in the political empowerment of Atlanta's Black electorate and should have given him a strong hand in addressing the city's social and political problems. Analysis of voter registration and turnout records, however, shows that Campbell won office with a significant majority of a *very small fraction* of the city's eligible electorate. Despite the campaigns of twelve candidates, including three strong African-American contenders, on election day barely one-fourth of the city's voting-age population cast ballots (see Table 4.2).

Table 4.2   Atlanta's Voter Turnout by Race, 1993

Race/Ethnicity and Gender	Turnout among Registered Voters	Turnout among Voting-Age Residents
White	45.2%	35.1%
Male	45.1%	
Female	45.2%	
Black	45.8%	22.1%
Male	43.1%	
Female	47.5%	
Latino	21.4%	1.8%
Asian	19.7%	4.5%
Native American	33.3%	6.6%
Total	45.4%	25.8%

Sources: Fulton County, Georgia Count of Voters by Precinct and District (VRE1438) (Atlanta: Fulton County Department of Elections, 1993); voting-age population estimates derived from data reported in the *County and City Data Book 1994* (Washington, D.C.: U.S. Department of Commerce, U.S. Bureau of the Census, Data User Services Divisions, 1995).

Moreover, despite the Atlanta Black community's long history of political mobilization, the active electorate in 1993 was disproportionately White; Atlanta's 200,000 eligible Black voters only cast 44,000 votes, while the White population – less than half as numerous (93,000) – cast nearly 33,000. The gap between the majority-Black population's potential and actual voting strength resulted from a lower rate of voter registration among eligible African Americans; less than half of Atlanta's Black residents of voting age – 48.2 percent – were registered to vote, compared to nearly four-fifths – 77.8 percent – of the city's White voting-age residents. Comprising 67 percent of the city's population, African Americans made up only 57 percent of its registered voters (see Table 4.3).

Among those Black residents who *were* registered, turnout in the 1993 election was actually slightly higher than among White registered voters – due entirely to higher participation levels among Black women. Thus, while significant changes have occurred in the racial composition of the city's active electorate, and compared to the 1969 elections African-American voters now exercise much greater control

Table 4.3   Atlanta Voter Registration by Race, 1993

Race/Ethnicity	Voting-Age Population	Registered Voters	Registration Rate
White	92,846	72,197	77.8%
Black	200,575	96,664	48.2%
Latino	5,711	490	8.6%
Asian	2,655	603	22.7%
Native American	427	84	19.7%
Total	299,690	170,038	56.7%

Sources: *Fulton County, Georgia Count of Voters by Precinct and District*; voting-age population estimates derived from data reported in the *County and City Data Book 1994.*

over the outcome of local elections, the 43.1 percent turnout among Black male registrants continues to lag behind that of both White men and White women. Were African-American women not voting at *higher* than average levels, Black turnout averages would *still* be lower than for Whites, despite the past two decades' gains in voter access and the election of Black officials to the entire range of positions in Atlanta, from U.S. Congress, to the school board, the county commission, the city council, and the mayor's office.

Atlanta's pool of registered voters also included less than 9 percent of voting-age Latinos, and only about one-fifth of voting-age Asian or Native Americans. For Latinos and Asian Americans, lower levels of citizenship would suppress levels of voter registration in any case, but this does not explain the low levels of registration and voting by Native Americans or the extremely low levels of voting among those Latino and Asian Americans who *are* citizens and were *already* registered to vote. Overall turnout among registered Whites in 1993 was 45.2 percent compared to 45.8 percent among Blacks, and 21.4 percent among Latinos. One-third of the city's registered Native Americans cast ballots, as did less than 20 percent of its Asian Americans.

When measured as a share of voting-age residents, electoral participation by Atlanta's growing Latino and Asian American populations as well as its Native Americans was virtually nonexistent. For these groups, *fewer than one in ten* voting-age residents cast ballots in 1993. Atlanta's Black empowerment, to the extent that such empowerment has occurred, has barely touched the city's other minority populations. The 1993 elections were also characterized by extremely low levels of voting by Atlanta's youngest citizens, exactly those people on whom the city government's hopes for a more peaceful, egalitarian, and legitimate future must rest (see Table 4.4).

Table 4.4 Turnout by Age Group

Age Cohort	Turnout Among Registered Voters
18–21	12.0%
22–35	28.2%
36–50	51.4%
51–65	65.3%
65+	61.8%

Source: Fulton County, Georgia Count of Voters by Precinct and District.

In other words, the Atlanta urban regime's electoral base is skewed even more strongly by age than by race, ethnicity, or gender. In fact, eighteen-to-twenty-one-year-olds were the only demographic grouping that voted at a lower rate than did the city's Latino, Asian- and Native-American registrants. These young citizens, and the slightly more participatory twenty-two-to-thirty-five-year-olds, are overwhelmingly African Americans.

Finally, turnout rate differences reflecting class divisions have actually *widened* over the past two decades among both Black and White voters. Recent years' improvements in African-American registration and turnout levels have not been evenly distributed across the city; large and important areas continue to show extremely low levels of participation. Precinct-level data show that it is in the lower-income, economically and socially stressed neighborhoods – both Black and White – where democratic participation in Atlanta city government continues to lag.

Political Incorporation and the Future of Black Empowerment

Thirty years after the Voting Rights Act and two decades after Maynard Jackson's election, an active electorate so clearly skewed by age, race, and socioeconomic class does not bode well for the city's governability in the future or its capacity to correct existing local inequalities over which it might otherwise have some control. If our definition of empowerment includes the broad participation of Black publics in the selection of political leaders and the determination of public policies, the case of Atlanta shows that the process of Black empowerment is dramatically incomplete, with wide variations in levels of voter turnout linked to generational, racial, and class differences within the electorate.

The gains made by Atlanta's Black political elites in electability and control over city government are important, but they have not yet involved the majority of the city's African-American population. Less than half of Atlanta's voting-age Black residents were registered to vote in 1993, and *barely one-fifth* of the potential Black electorate cast ballots in the mayoral election. The city's most participatory citizens were thirty-five-to-fifty-one-year-old African-America females; its *least* participatory were young African Americans between the ages of eighteen and thirty-five. As with Latino, Asian, and Native American citizens, low turnout among African-American youth reflects a detached population with slight investment in conventional politics. Sharply limited participation by young citizens should be especially troubling to the city's elected and appointed governors; these youths are, after all, the victims of educational and social disinvestment, of the urban world's unpredictable violence, and of the adult world's seeming indifference. They are also very much the city's future. An aging population of political and social elites, drawn from traditional leadership families and the ranks of civil rights veterans, cannot hope to manage a diverse twenty-first-century city without the cooperation and participation of the city's younger generations, its Latino, Asian, and Native-American peoples, and its populous inner-city communities. If nothing else, Atlanta's distorted voter turnout patterns show that the city's widely cited urban regime rests on very weak democratic foundations.

With its Black-led city government, vibrant African-American cultural life, large Black middle class, and national prominence, Atlanta can appear to be the "promised land" to Black Americans in other, less empowered communities. It is discouraging to learn that even here the urban political culture is characterized by low and extremely uneven levels of mass participation, increasing social inequality, and limited involvement of the poor in local democratic politics. If the situation in Atlanta – where Black empowerment is well advanced – reflects conditions elsewhere, then the future contribution of electoral politics will depend on how Black America *changes* its approach to conventional political participation. Despite years of electoral effort, the nation has not yet achieved a profound transformation in its racially stratified political, economic, and social institutions. Yet with all its limitations, abandoning electoral action altogether is not an option for Black America, which can either fight for control of local government or see local power used to obstruct, divert, and repress the broader struggle for Black freedom, racial justice, and an equal share of the American promise.

A more complete mobilization of Atlanta's poor and working-class

Black majority will not occur, however, until the aspirations and needs of that majority become central features of the city's political culture. While some legal and logistical obstacles to full registration and voting still exist, these are surmountable and are not the most important barriers to greater local democracy. Full participation by Atlanta's Black community is now blocked more effectively by the limited attention that candidates, political parties, and independent organizations devote to the community's most pressing needs. As long as the city's political discourse revolves primarily around the interests of an elite, corporate-oriented urban regime, emphasizing capital development and profitability over human needs; until candidates for citywide office routinely articulate people-oriented solutions to long-standing problems of affordable housing, quality education, and equitable public services; until the shared class interests of Black, Latino, Asian, Native American, and White workers – stable employment, higher wages, and universal health care – become decisive electoral issues; and until the most important problems confronting urban youth, including police harassment, unemployment, boredom, poverty, and fear, are added to the city's public agenda, there will be little progress toward either democracy or equality in Atlanta, or in any other American city where similar conditions prevail for Black people and communities of color.

Full electoral mobilization would spark heightened conflict between the established Black leadership and an increasingly restive Black population, shaking business confidence in the existing leadership and destabilizing the developmental consensus that has for three-quarters of a century dominated the city's political agenda. Once before, such intra-Black tensions culminated in bitter divisions between student activists and "Atlanta establishment" Black leaders during the Civil Rights Movement, when the Black community supported more assertive political action than much of the middle-class Black leadership was willing to endorse.[15] Widespread frustration with the uncertain benefits of Black cooperation with the existing regime could also lead to the emergence of new coalitions, especially those advancing progressive agendas in which social and economic as well as political equality was more central. In this regard, Atlanta is no different from other U.S. cities in which decades of neglect and disinvestment are sparking explicitly class-conscious, community-level mobilizations.[16]

The preconditions for a more democratic Atlanta can be seen in the very places where today democracy is most absent. They include effective alliance-building among the city's diverse populations of poor and working-class African Americans, Whites, Latinos, Asian

Americans, and Native Americans. They are visible in the disdain that young Atlantans feel toward politics in general, and electoral politics in particular. And they are clear in the current political system's subservience to an aloof suburban corporate culture whose leaders for three decades have commuted past Atlanta's social crisis, holding city government hostage to the demands of regional development. The next stage in the liberation of Black Atlanta – and Black America – will arrive when Black voters declare their independence from the politics of the high-rise urban regime, find equality and human needs among their electoral choices, and forge alliances with *all* the city's – and the nation's – other disenfranchised communities.

Notes

1. *Black Elected Officials: A National Roster 1993*, 21st ed. (Washington, D.C.: Joint Center for Political and Economic Studies, 1994).
2. *Statistical Abstract of the United States: The National Data Book* (Washington, D.C.: U.S. Government Publications Office, 1995), table 706.
3. Ibid., tables 650, 706, 728, 726, 742.
4. Income data are from the U.S. Bureau of the Census, *Current Population Reports, P60–184*. Unemployment and childhood poverty also have increased among the nation's White population: between 1970 and 1992 for White children, poverty rates rose from 10 percent to 16 percent, while for White workers unemployment increased from 3.1 percent to 5.0 percent.
5. See the documentary and narrative accounts in Mary L. French and William F. Swindler, *Chronology and Documentation Handbook of the State of Georgia* (New York: Ocean Publications, 1973) and Pete Wallenstein, *From Slave South to New South: Public Policy in Nineteenth Century Georgia* (Chapel Hill: University of North Carolina Press, 1987).
6. Atlanta's place in the Civil Rights Movement is chronicled in Doug McAdams, *Political Process and the Development of Black Insurgency 1930–1970* (Chicago: University of Chicago Press, 1982) and David Garrow, *Atlanta, Georgia 1960–1961: Sit-ins and Student Activism* (New York: Carlson Publishers, 1989).
7. For the story of Atlanta's transition to Black-led city government, see Charles S. Rooks, *The Atlanta Elections of 1969* (Atlanta: Voter Education Project, 1970); Glenn F. Abney and John D. Hutchinson, "Race, Representation and Trust: Changes in Attitudes after the Election of a Black Mayor," *Public Opinion Quarterly*, vol. 45 (Spring 1981), pp. 91–101; and Clarence Stone, *Regime Politics: Governing Atlanta 1946–1988* (Lawrence: University Press of Kansas, 1989).
8. See Charles S. Bullock, III and Bruce A. Campbell, "Racist or Racial Voting in the 1981 Atlanta Municipal Elections," *Urban Affairs Quarterly* (December 1984), pp. 149–64.
9. Mack Jones offers a critical assessment in "Black Empowerment in Atlanta: Myth and Reality," *Annals of the American Academy of Political and Social Science*, vol. 439 (September 1979), pp. 90–117.
10. Floyd Hunter, *Community Power Structure: A Study of Decision Makers* (Chapel Hill: University of North Carolina Press, 1953); M. Kent Jennings, *Community Influentials: The Elites of Atlanta* (London: Collier MacMillan, 1964); Stone, *Regime Politics*.
11. Stone, *Regime Politics*, p. 177.

12. For a detailed view of this era in Atlanta's political history, see Ivan Allen, Jr., and Paul Hemphill, *Mayor: Notes on the Sixties* (New York: Simon & Schuster, 1971).

13. Population and income data are from the *County and City Data Book 1994* (Washington, D.C.: U.S. Department of Commerce, U.S. Bureau of the Census, Data User Services Division, 1995), Geocode 0520; voting and registration data are from *Fulton County, Georgia Count of Voters by Precinct and District (VRE1438)* (Atlanta: Fulton County Department of Elections, 1993).

14. Residential segregation by race can be seen in Fulton County's voter registration data in which the race of registrants is reported. Comparative Black–White income data were reported in Obie Clayton and Anna Grant, "Atlanta's Black Families," in Bob Holmes, ed., *The Status of Black Atlanta 1994* (Atlanta: Southern Center for Studies in Public Policy, 1994).

15. For the story of Atlanta's early Black student movement, see Garrow, *Atlanta, Georgia 1960–1961*.

16. For a discussion of Black community organizing and its role in advancing a distinctively Black political agenda, see James Jennings, *The Politics of Black Empowerment* (Detroit: Wayne State University Press, 1992); for critical assessments of Atlanta's uneven economic development, see Anthony Downs, "Urban Realities: Some Controversial Aspects of the Atlanta Region's Future," *Brookings Review*, vol. 12, no. 3 (1994), p. 26; and John Heylar, "The Big Hustle: Atlanta's Two Worlds: Wealth and Poverty, Magnet and Mirage: The Metropolitan Area Grows as the Core City Shrinks: Will a Shooting Star Fall?" *Wall Street Journal* (February, 1988), p. 1.

Black and Latino Political
Conflict in Chicago

John J. Betancur and Douglas C. Gills

This chapter assesses the Black and Latino coalition that was initiated
under Mayor Harold Washington in Chicago in the early and mid-
1980s. How was it put together? Who was involved? How did it
unfold? What was its agenda? How were internal conflicts and
contradictions approached? What were the accomplishments and
shortfalls? And, most importantly, what were the lessons gained for
application to future work in urban and big-city politics, and in terms
of minority strategizing for social change? This topic is important in
light of the continuing urban crisis – the local manifestation of the
deepening political–economic crisis of capitalism, the ensuing efforts
to resolve it through globalized restructuring, and the resultant social
and political dislocations that these changes are causing. It is also
about how activists have responded and might respond to this overall
crisis through multinational collective action and advanced organization. One possible route leads to intensive conflict and political
polarization among national minorities increasingly concentrated in
central cities. The other alternative is to engage in dialogue and joint
efforts among members of minority communities aimed at fostering
greater cooperation, collaboration, and collective social action.
Analysis of experiences of cooperation can help promote other
joint actions while avoiding the mistakes and resolving the shortcomings of past efforts at political collaboration and public policy
intervention.

One such collective experience was the movement and organization
underpinning the Washington mayoral experience in Chicago during
the 1980s. An aspect of it was the specific coalitional experience of
African-American and Latino political activists during the period of
the Harold Washington–David Sawyer regime. This experience has

serious implications for the present situation in Chicago and elsewhere in cities where Blacks and Latinos are politically significant.

We argue that in the development of the Black–Latino coalition process in Chicago internal contradictions were not successfully resolved because of the absence of conscientious thought and action. Contending agendas were often pushed – or, in some cases, divergent agendas withheld for fear of weakening further a fragile, tenuous coalition formation. There were also the ever-present efforts of the old-guard political machine to destroy it, and the less visible efforts of the urban growth consortium to co-opt or to control the progressive movement within the emergent political process in Chicago, while advancing its own narrowly interested economic development agenda.[1] As has been the case in many Black-mayor-led cities (and we suspect in Latino-led cities, as well) over the past three decades, the political–economic power of white elites has remained intact.[2] In Chicago, moreover, there was an underlying tension between the various forces active in the emergent coalition and the more encompassing popular forces within the African-American and the multifaceted Latino communities driving the new popular regime.[3]

Some key goals were pushed and achieved to some degree. Yet there were challenges that were not addressed in the short period between the Washington election campaign of 1981 and the time of his death in 1987. The mismanagement of political dynamics and the traumas of moving from opposition politics to leadership in City Hall may have severely hurt the capacities of grassroots groups to sustain the engagement in progressive politics, to exercise independence and initiative at the citywide level and may also have set back the development of solidarity among Black and Latino community groups. A consequence of these developments may have been the weakening of an independent political movement rooted in grassroots community groups and organizations of Chicago. Efforts to attract the White-voter constituency by broadening the regime's political support base may have detracted from the advance of a progressive agenda or prevented such an agenda from emerging.[4] The mobilization of nationalism within the political process of empowerment by the leadership of these movements within the Black and Latino communities may have been more significant as an internal factor determining the demise of the progressive coalitional effort than the racist reaction of the White political elites had been an external factor in sustaining the solidarity effort among Blacks and Latinos.

Laying the Groundwork

The movement underpinning Harold Washington's successful election originated outside the political mainstream and within Black and Latino communities allied temporarily with some Whites interested in government reform. It was inspired by the common feeling of alienation caused by years of corruption, monopoly of power, exclusion, racism, and neglect by the Democratic machine. It was a movement of hope; could the election of a reform-minded Black mayor open up City Hall to minorities and redirect equitable public resources to their communities? Washington was a viable and attractive candidate for this challenge. His record was unique although a product of "the Machine." He had broken with it and now opposed it, and its patronage system that bred corruption, exclusion, and social inequities. Its practices were outright racist. Not only was his legislative intervention highly impressive in its support of fairness, equal opportunity, and reform, but his links to progressive groups and politics also made him particularly attractive as a reform candidate.

Meanwhile, discussions were held in the early 1980s in the Puerto Rican and Mexican communities about this emerging reform movement. Progressive forces tied to Puerto Rico's independence led the way in the near northwest Puerto Rican community. CASA (Centro para Acción Social Autónoma), a group advocating the rights of documented and undocumented Mexican workers, organized the near southwest Mexican community. Members of other Latino groups, linked by joint struggles in the 1970s, met to discuss an overall strategy for their community. From the beginning, discussions included the possibilities that could be brought about by a Black mayor or a Black–Latino coalition. There was no independent White progressive in 1982–83 who had the capacity to mobilize the Black and Latino vote outside the Democratic Party machine in light of the disappointment of Jane Byrne's administration's policies and practices.

Earlier contacts between Black and Latino organizations and leaders facilitated dialogue between the two communities. Particularly crucial were the independent political organizations of Blacks and Latinos that had been formed in the early 1980s following efforts to support independent candidates and to look for access to power for these communities. Equally important were relationships among Black and Latino leaders developed as part of the common struggles of both communities. The coalition was, in fact, made possible by preexisting

Black–Latino networks. Such networks had been forged through years of common struggle and search for social change, particularly among progressive elements of these communities. When the opportunity of the candidacy of Washington presented itself, these groups joined forces on the basis of such relationships and networks. They in fact provided the foundations and linkages of the Black–Latino coalition under Harold Washington. Among these coalitions were the Housing Agenda, a network of housing and tenant advocacy groups; the Chicago Rehab Network, the first multiracial coalition of community-based housing rehabilitation and development groups; and the Community Renewal Society, which made great strides in bringing community groups together.

In 1981 the Illinois Coalition Against Reagan Economics (I-CARE) was formed as an urban policy advocacy and protest coalition linking welfare rights groups, community organizations, social workers, and labor unions, and drawing heavily upon Blacks and Latinos as well as liberal Whites. On the eve of the Illinois gubernatorial election in the summer of 1982, the People Organized for Welfare Economic Reform (POWER) was formed as a direct action coalition of grassroots activists and disabled and unemployed workers sponsored by community-based groups from within Black, Latino, and poor White communities. More than any other group, POWER expressed the radical populist spirit of social change underpinning the Washington mayoral campaign. POWER was a principal force in the expansion of the popular electorate through massive voter registration campaigns that put 160,000 newly registered voters on the books prior to the 1983 municipal elections. There was also the emergence of the Community Workshop on Economic Development, a coalition of community development corporations and support assistance intermediaries targeting low-income residents in communities of color. These organizations carved out the urban policy framework that subsequently drove the Washington administration's development policies. Without this earlier groundwork, interviewees suggested, these two communities could not have possibly come together and coalesced in the way in which they did.

Latinos did not have the numbers that Blacks did. Together, however, these two communities could have a major impact on Chicago politics. Challenging the machine, however, was a formidable task requiring not only many people, but well-organized people as well. Election of a Black mayor with Latino support was a possibility. Within this context, the Black–Latino coalition came together and elected a mayor. They also joined forces to challenge redistricting in court and were able not only to gain executive control of city government and its powers of appointment and resource allocation, but to become a force to be reckoned with in local politics.

Within the African-American community there was a massive upsurge of community-based political and civic activism. Teachers and preachers were organized by Operation PUSH and led by Jesse Jackson. Nationalist organizations participated in this upsurge; they included Chicago Black United Communities, under the leadership of Lu Palmer, the prominent broadcast journalist; Chicago Black Ministerial Alliance, led by Rev. Al Sampson; and Citizens for Self Determination. There was the civic alliance called Vote Community led by longtime activist Tim Black and business magnate Ed Gardner. The Black community–labor coalition was led by labor activist Charles Hayes. But perhaps the single most important umbrella coalition formed within the African-American political community, uniting all segments of political activism, was the Task Force for Black Political Empowerment. The Task Force, first under reform leadership and then subsequently nationalist leadership, was the principal mobilization and coordinative force of cohesion representing some degree of unity in the African-American political community. This body was the main source of nationalist influence on the Washington–Sawyer regime.[5]

The main sources of Black–Latino coalition-related work within the African-American community, however, came from political progressives in the Left and community-based activists such as Nancy Jefferson and Bob Lucas, and from the Black labor and workers movement led by the Coalition of Black Trade Unionists, chaired by Harold Rogers. All these groups saw in the motion behind Washington's campaign for mayor an opportunity to empower various sectors and strata within the African-American community and to share power under a realignment of political relations between members of communities of color and the White minority. Thus, there was a submerged tension around the core forces giving leadership to the movement underpinning the electoral coalition. Traditional middle-class leadership in both the Black and Latino communities, by the way, came on board late in the mobilization and were slow in providing support for Harold Washington's candidacy.

Finally, the candidacy of Harold Washington attracted some progressive sectors of the White community, including liberal government reformers. Traditionally excluded from the political process or deeply opposed to the corrupt and monopolistic ways of the Democratic machine, they had a particular interest in government reform and saw Harold Washington as a once-in-a-lifetime opportunity for political reform and for altering relations between ordinary citizens and a corrupt antidemocratic municipal bureaucracy.[6]

The Black–Latino Electoral Coalition Under Mayor Harold Washington

Two aspects of the Black–Latino coalition under Harold Washington need to be distinguished: the electoral and the governance coalition. Though integral parts of the same effort, these two dynamics bear important differences and help to highlight the strengths and weaknesses of the coalition and, finally, its early dissolution. The Black and Latino electoral coalition was facilitated by the coincidence of feelings of alienation and exclusion among vast sectors of the Black community and more limited, largely progressive White and Latino sectors. It was a coalition of outsiders looking for a way into government. While the sharing of this feeling, coupled with conditions of exclusion and marginalization, facilitated collaboration, the actual coalition was a combination of forces from outside and inside of the political mainstream as well as from within and outside the Washington campaign that conducted broad outreach and education and secured votes.

Within the coalition, there was the perceived need to attract voters beyond the Black community as Blacks alone could not elect Washington. Outside, there was the excitement that his candidacy produced among progressives, community activists, and others (well-educated, upwardly mobile Black and Latino professionals) seeking opportunities in the public sector. While outside support had come with his candidacy, inside recruitment of other groups went rather slowly. The case of Latinos and Whites participating in the election is illustrative.

Latinos had difficulty getting the campaign to accept their input and direct participation. Similarly, it took some effort for the Washington camp to accept that Latinos would manage the campaigns in their communities. The reluctance to allow forces outside the "established" campaign office to run the ward and precinct organization was experienced within the predominantly Black wards as well. Washington was caught in a situation where he had learned to trust very few political leaders within and outside the party. These factors prevented trust building and positive working relationships from developing earlier. They also produced unnecessary tensions and, in the long run, alienated potential supporters. Interviewees mentioned as a problem the strong presence of people in the inner circle of political advisers who saw Harold's election as "the turn of the Black community" and were insensitive to the priorities of other groups in the electoral front.

Initially, the main support for Washington came from African Americans (most sectors) and from progressive groups in the White and Latino communities. Once he won the primary, other sectors previously supportive of other candidates joined in. Latino voting for Washington, for instance, changed dramatically, from less than 15 percent in the primary to nearly 75 percent in the general election. This increase was attributed to various factors, including strong commitment of and campaigning by Latino leaders; Latino loyalty to the Democratic Party; Washington's commitment to a Latino agenda, including support of Latinos for office, contracts, and jobs; the "bandwagon" effect; and the defeat of the candidates who had previously captured the Latino vote – Richard Daley and Jane Byrne.

While the split in the White vote facilitated Washington's primary victory, its reunification in the general election under an unknown White Republican candidate – in one of the most racist campaigns in the country's history – made the support of Latinos and White progressives crucial for winning the mayoralty. It also suggested early that a Washington victory might encounter serious difficulties with governance. While Washington did move to create a governance organization through his transition team reflecting the social and demographic characteristics of the city, the financial management team more closely mirrored traditional mayoral transition to governance organizations. It represented the conscious effort to send a message to corporate Chicago and the banking and finance community that there was nothing to fear from a Black-led, reform government, and that corporate business would go on pretty much as usual. In this sense, there was nothing revolutionary about the emergent regime under Washington's leadership.[7]

The coalition developed by Washington was largely tied to the electoral process. It included people and groups with multiple interests and agendas. While the initial core of supporters knew each other somewhat or had collaborated before, most had not. They either lacked the experience of cooperation or had not developed a high degree of mutual trust. Many political activists in the campaign process were not necessarily committed to the idea of a Black–Latino coalition or to the ideals of a progressive movement. While the coalition of *outsiders* looking for a way into political power was strong enough to bring Latinos and Blacks together, their experience of electoral collaboration was limited to the local efforts mentioned. As such, it was largely dependent on the ability of a small core of people and the mediation of Washington to keep it together. Each group's members were separately looking for the opportunity to get government contracts and jobs, to elect their representatives to office, and to get a fair share of government services and development in their communities. Given the task at hand, not enough attention was placed during the campaign on what happens after gaining power.

The Governance Coalition

Once elected, the Washington administration confronted the formidable task of governing under political siege. A city council controlled by the Democratic machine obstructed almost every effort of the new administration. City employees, most of them carryovers of previous administrations, boycotted initiatives for reform and change. The business establishment resisted any new policies, and the media used every opportunity to criticize Washington. As a result, the city remained deeply polarized between the emerging reform forces and supporters of the old machine – the latter looking for any opportunity to regain power. Furthermore, the administration was being called upon to provide sound crisis management, maintain the electoral support, and deliver to a constituency with very high expectations at a time of federal retrenchment and urban crisis. Could the coalition provide the foundations required for this work?[8]

While the electoral coalition had reached its goal, its members were anxious about the opportunities and resources of government. Turning this electoral force into a governance and support coalition was a major challenge. Once Washington was in power, the issue was no longer one of exclusion, but of distribution. Only an experienced and strong coalition could successfully meet these challenges. The forces of the election collaboration did not make the transition well. Adding to this difficulty, Washington had started to bring into the emergent governance coalition new people who had not been active in the campaign or in the movement underpinning it. Many of these new agents had no appreciation for the sensitive nature of coalition building and the fragility of its relations, primarily because they did not play a role in building Washington's electoral coalition.

Unfortunately, the governance coalition under Harold Washington was too new and fragile. The Black–Latino coalition as the organized force behind the broader African-American and Latino communities had dissipated into a small circle of activists that followed Washington into city government. Thus, the electoral coalition that made the election possible was separated from the broader movement in the community. Moreover, there was no coordinative organization or forum that served to bring diverse elements together and to facilitate unity of action. There was no movement-driven coalition of Blacks and Latinos that was independent from City Hall and community associations and agency staffs that organized around specific agendas in housing, economic development, health, and human services. There was no center of the coalition, and, therefore, there could be no joint efforts to bring about a coherent, comprehensive public policy, social, or political agenda. The Black–Latino coalition was unable to fully make the transition from an electoral to a governance administration with an independent agenda.

POWER, the center of the electoral coalition, was quickly dissolved. The Task Force for Black Political Empowerment had succumbed to a narrow Black power agenda, disowning any talk of progressive coalitions. The left organizations in Chicago were preparing to move on to the Jesse Jackson presidential bid. The labor movement was engaged in divisive struggles, disjointed from those of communities of *place* and of *condition*. Broad-based African-American and Latino community coalition building had no priority outside the context of City Hall electoral politics. It would be four more years before the issue of Black and Latino community coalition would resurface as a factor in the mass politics of Chicago.

Another problem with the transition was that the electoral coalition was highly uneven, with African Americans at the core, a strong group of White supporters close to them, and Latinos as a supporting cast. Some people in the Black community insisted on the importance of Latinos as the swing vote and the need to integrate them into the coalition's leadership and, ultimately, governance structures. This call led to the highest ever participation of Latinos in government jobs and contracts. Their share, however, was never close to their percentage in the city, the workforce, or the electorate. Similarly, their appointment to executive and central decision-making positions was dismal. In contrast, African Americans gained control of key executive and policymaking positions and were able to push their own agenda – an agenda of middle-class empowerment and embourgeoisement. This was consistent with the results of the election: not only had African Americans provided the majority of the votes, but the mayor himself was Black. The election, however, did provide limited incentives for other groups, Latinos in particular, to stay within the coalition. The agenda of both the administration and the coalition suffered tremendously from the resulting tensions.

Sources of Black and Latino Contention

Within the context of electoral and governance coalitions, five main factors contributed to the tenuous character of a Black–Latino collaboration during the administration of Harold Washington: (1) outside forces; (2) a limited tradition of coalition politics; (3) ethno-centrism; (4) limited efforts to create an agenda inclusive of all groups; and (5) the inability to resolve objective differences and contending interests between the two groups.

Outside Forces

Though removed from formal power, the Democratic machine still controlled the bureaucracy of City Hall, the media, political resources, the economic elites, and the electoral process throughout Washington's terms. It used every opportunity, then, to undermine the coalition and to prevent its consolidation. Holding a majority in the Chicago City Council until 1986, the Democrats were able to obstruct appointments and policy reforms, rendering the administration ineffective. They submitted Washington to a continued political siege, slowing down his work and blocking every initiative to implement new social, political, and economic reforms.

To its credit, the Washington administration was able to make some significant accomplishments. In addition to establishing enforcement of affirmative action in employment, government contracting for services, and set-aside contracts for construction and capital repairs (as well as working to certify women and minority business enterprises to qualify for municipal contracts), Washington's administration was able to establish a Chicago first-source hiring and contracting policy that favored Black and Latino business interests. Under Washington's leadership the number of certified community-based, nonprofit service providers was expanded from less than one hundred under the Byrne administration to more than five hundred by the end of the Sawyer administration.

One of Washington's main accomplishments was to transfer more than $13 million in federal Community Development Block Grants (CDBG) funds directly to support community development capacity

building in minority neighborhoods. In terms of community improvements, Washington expended more than $100 million annually over
the first four years of his administrations on repairing streets, sidewalks, alleys, sewers, viaducts, street lighting, gutters, and vaulted
sidewalks; on removing rubbish and refuse; and on bringing fly
dumping under control. More money was spent on repairing units of
privately owned rental housing, targeting low-income families, than
at any time in the city's history, prior to or after this administration.
More important, Washington also increased the flow and the forms
of communication between citizens at the community level and the
offices of the government, while systematically increasing community
activist input into public policy reform. In fact, perhaps the greatest
accomplishment of the Washington administration was its commitment to opening up citizen participation in government policy formation processes – for example, community planning, implementation
through building partnership of communities with city and private
actors in urban development, and other arenas of the regime's policies
and problem-solving strategies.

The progressive character of the regime was demonstrated, ultimately, by the establishment of a neighborhood-based approach
driving public policy at all levels, with community-based agencies
being treated as full partners in the development of local policies and
development projects. Moreover, the administration under Washington's leadership was open to encouraging innovation and experimen-
tation while maintaining high standards of performance and
accountability. The defining distinction between the Washington
regime and all other administrations prior to or ever since was
Washington's effort to work collaboratively with previously underrepresented constituencies to raise their capacities to participate in the
"mainstream" of governance.

In short, the approach of the Washington administration was to
have its agents work jointly with community groups and agencies in
the policy development and implementation process rather than to
disqualify them ipso facto for their organizational development and
management shortcomings. Perhaps it was this attribute, in a period
of urban crisis and declining economic and fiscal resources, that was
also the Achilles' heel of the regime. The expectations of the many
sectors involved were too high to be realized, given the structural and
ideological limitations on the regime and the support base underpinning it. Harold Washington was not a revolutionary, and the organization of his supporting cast struggled to retain a progressive
character.

Limited Tradition of Coalition Politics

Historically, Blacks and Latinos had been engaged in separate political
action efforts in Chicago, often at the neighborhood level. Latinos
had been scattered in small clusters throughout the city and had only
recently consolidated in areas such as Pilsen-Little Village (Mexicans)
and West Town-Humboldt Park (Puerto Ricans). Many of them were
recent immigrants, highly uneducated, politically disenfranchised in
their home countries, and ignorant about the U.S. political system.
While Black–White dynamics had always been in the forefront,
Latinos had only recently achieved a significant size and presence in
the city. They were still largely viewed as a negligible force. Segregation in the inner city had limited the struggles of Blacks and Latinos
to the local level, with each community carrying its own fights locally
within a highly fragmented and isolated context.

While Blacks were highly concentrated, not fragmented by different
national origins, and had a longer tradition of struggle in Chicago,
they had been divided by the actions of the Democratic machine into
a limited, ineffectual stratum of co-opted insiders and a large mass of
outsiders. City Hall had often acted to co-opt the local Black and
Latino leadership by keeping a selected number of them on the city's
payroll. While Blacks and Latinos had come together before around
key issues and struggles, often on a short-term basis, they lacked a
consistent tradition of collaboration around political interests. This
effort to elect Washington and then to support his reform regime was
in fact their first major conscious undertaking in the city that extended
beyond community-based struggles.

While progressive elements within the administration were highly
committed to the coalition, many had joined in the search of
opportunity, power, and position for themselves. Although the core
of the coalition consisted of people who believed deeply in it or those
who had practiced Black–Latino coalition-building efforts before
around specific policy issues, there was never a clear-cut, overall
commitment to the coalition and its needs. The mayor was perhaps
the main force keeping the group together. With his death and the
absence of a strong figure to take over, people broke apart and looked
for the best option available within the emerging political forces.

Ethnocentrism

In response to the frustration of many years of struggle and limited results, the Black and Latino communities had developed a strong sense of self-help. Many Black leaders and individuals looked at the mayoralty of Washington as "their turn." This attitude was resented by Latinos, who themselves felt left out of power, opportunity, and influential positions. Latinos, in fact, expressed these feelings openly throughout the administration of Washington. Individuals who did not receive what they expected were among the first to leave the coalition following the death of the mayor.

Meanwhile, nationalism among different Latino groups also led to internal and external tensions about the allocation of jobs and opportunities among the different nationalities. This strategy was particularly manipulated by individuals in both communities for their personal gain and the formation of enclaves of patronage within the administration. As a result, there was a continuous tension over the distribution of power and opportunities between Blacks and Latinos and among the various Latino groups. Nationalism expressed itself in a series of actions from competition for positions and power through mutual accusations and recriminations and often diverted focus from issues of collective fairness, justice, and reform.

Limited Efforts to Create an Agenda Inclusive of All Groups

As discussed earlier, the emergent coalition had come together as a result of common frustrations, opportunities, and circumstances. It had been facilitated by limited preexisting networks both within the Latino community and between Latinos and African Americans. Many of the individuals and organizations involved lacked much experience in building coalitions and had not developed the discipline and commitment required for a long-term effort of this nature. The immediate task of organizing government and staying in power had left little time and energy for strengthening the coalition through forging an agreed-upon agenda and a system of mutual accountability. Issues were addressed on an ad hoc basis. Conflicts often went unresolved. While this issue was not particularly important in the campaign to get Washington elected, it became a continuous source of tension during governance when the struggle for positions, resources and influence unfolded. In the absence of an open dialogue and agreement, opportunism often prevailed over coalition and collective solutions to problems presented by reform and policy change.

Inability to Resolve Differences and Contending Interests

Following the death of Mayor Washington, the leadership, even among progressives, bowed to nationalism and opportunism. Once in government, Latinos and Blacks ended up disagreeing on priorities and other matters related to objective differences between the two communities. Not only had they been unable to recognize and sort out these differences ahead of time, but they were also unable to address them in any significant way during the administration. As a result, elements within these communities, as well as outside forces, often manipulated such conflicts to their own advantage. The movement that brought Washington to power moved into City Hall, lost its independence, and failed to keep a close watch on the administration and the struggle for reform.

In our view, the electoral coalition was built from the outside in, while specific aspects of the governance coalition, as a political expression of the movement, were built from the inside out. Founded from the beginning on a narrow electoral base and having accomplished its initial objective – the election of a Black mayor – the coalition's demise signaled the fragmentation of the movement that fueled it. That it disintegrated is not surprising. That it happened so suddenly is a cause for inquiry and assessment that may teach some invaluable lessons to social action researchers and political activists alike. We further argue that once the electoral coalition that spearheaded the movement to elect Harold Washington as mayor of Chicago had accomplished its initial goal, it was not able to reconsolidate on some new bases to meet the challenges of *coalition management* and to refuel the movement driving the broader Washington coalition. This occurred because the leadership of the coalition was transferred from grassroots activists, who came into the electoral arena, to a leadership that was institutionalized as a group of government functionaries, bureaucrats, and politicians. Thus, the coalition lost its progressive cutting edge. It became self-interested; its members became less concerned about a social change agenda and more concerned about self-preservation and individualized opportunities for power and privilege. It finally disintegrated and became polarized with Washington's death in 1987, less than five years after its crystallization.

The story of the systematic demobilization of the political base that energized the Washington coalition is a significant one, still yet to be appreciated. Not only has the Black and Latino coalition dissipated, but the community-based forces and the disadvantaged sectors of the city have also been rendered politically ineffective in developing and promoting an agenda capable of winning sufficiently broad support within or outside the electorate. Despite the existence of significant networks and coalitions organized around empowerment and community development agendas, the constituents of these associations, networks, and community-based coalitions have not been able to launch a counteroffensive to the new coalition or consortium that shaped City Hall's policy under the Daley administration. With no clarity about common objectives beyond the death of Washington, the movement and the coalition fragmented because during the Washington–Sawyer regime its agenda (and that of its constituents) was subsumed under other agendas in such a way that its aims and payoffs were not immediately and concretely identifiable for a significant sector of the coalition's base.

From the beginning, Washington had combined progressive views with pragmatism. His progressivism, in this case, seemed to consist of a process that allowed for all interests to be represented, for all voices to be heard. In practice, it was an effort to achieve a balance between community and business interests and between downtown and the neighborhoods. His governance coalition also included progressives and nonprogressives. Under the Sawyer administration and its consolidation around Black nationalist influences, any hope for an inside-out progressive Black–Latino coalition had been lost. The community and progressive movement outside of City Hall had been demoralized and exhausted. In sum, the African American–Latino coalition of Harold Washington had two clearly discernible aspects: an electoral and a governing one. Spurred by the movement to elect a Black, reformist mayor, the coalition was brought together by a common sense of political exclusion and the opportunity to overcome the governing Democratic machine. While the main support came initially from African Americans, progressive elements in the Latino and White communities attracted some support from these groups. Along with Blacks, they represented Washington's electoral base for the primary elections. The surprising victory of Washington in the primary election and the defeat of Byrne and Daley, who had captured the Latino vote earlier, dramatically increased Latino support for Washington. Within a highly racially polarized general election, Latinos provided the swing vote that got Washington elected.

Once in power, however, the coalition was largely dominated by African Americans in close association with a core of members of the White community – liberals and progressives, in particular. Latinos became relatively marginal in the governance phase of the new regime. This contradiction made the governing coalition highly fragile. In spite of the best performance of any administration in providing minority jobs and contracts in the history of the city of Chicago, its record was still below minimum Latino expectations. While Latinos continued supporting Washington, they were clearly disappointed by their marginal role and participation. Internal and external forces continued to undermine the coalition and to bring forth its contradictions. Internal factors included issues of nationalism between and within the Latino and Black communities, the uneven nature of the coalition, the lack of a clear commitment to a minimum coalition agenda, a limited coalition experience, and the inability to work out objective differences and expectations among its constituent groups. External factors included the accelerated urban crisis brought about by globalization and neoconservative federal politics and the siege of the old guard, which engaged in a virulent attack on the Washington administration.

In short, although the coalition was formed to *gain power*, it did not materialize into a coalition to *share power*. Polarization prevented formation of a more inclusive, expanded front. Once the main element that kept things together was gone, many individuals and forces who had gained power, privilege, and access panicked and opportunistically looked for a place for themselves in the midst of an unsettled scramble for power. The existence of the *urban crisis* and its various aspects meant that Washington inherited an administration in a city with a declining manufacturing industry, employment, and tax base. All are crucial for addressing problems among families and individuals in the neighborhoods who are becoming increasingly reliant upon local government at a time when revenues to address social welfare expenditures are declining.

Conclusion

Despite this pessimistic analysis, it is important to note that many activists we have talked to feel that the major thrust of Latino–Black coalition building has yet to be experienced. There were factors cited that led to this optimism, such as economic exploitation among the vast majority of Black and Latino people, and the persistence of racial exclusion in political and social life, coupled with the continuation of national oppression that provides a structural context for potential unity building. Moreover, there are continuing networks that have facilitated dialogue and activities enabling African Americans and Latinos to work collaboratively on common issues, ranging from struggles against housing displacement and residential gentrification to education improvement and school reform, to efforts to resist the dismantling of the social welfare system of health care, human capacity enhancement, and social service support systems. Finally, the overall rise in right-wing political dominance has resulted in the promotion of the most reactionary policy agendas at the local, regional, and national levels. On the perceptual level, the brunt of these attacks is aimed at the masses among, and the most vulnerable sectors within, the African-American and Latino communities.

A set of implications can be extracted from this chapter. First, we have a clearer understanding about the nature of the Black–Latino coalition under Harold Washington. Any new coalitional efforts appear to require building on a broader social basis than on narrow electoral politics. This is true since the returns on the political investment are too limited to realize substantial benefits for the vast majority of Blacks and Latinos, especially if the direct benefits to the middle class are discounted. Second, the coalition must be built upon a broader basis than nationalism, for the failure to do so will only result in the eventual polarization of their nationalist leadership elements and in the misguidance of the masses of people to further compete for presumably scarce resources in the public economy.

From our vantage point, it would appear that the progress of new political struggles to come lies in the realization that the main sources of oppression of urban Blacks and Latinos are within the prevailing political–economic relations that bound members of both groups to oppression, domination, and exclusion. Moreover, effective political coalitions are built on the basis of traditions of interaction and joint activity, where people learn trust through testing each other in practical struggles and under conditions of risk and sacrifice. The framework of electoral politics alone is too narrow to yield anything but short-term outcomes. Electoral activity is subject to crass opportunism and is not necessarily a source for building lasting, principled relationships. The frame for building effective coalitions must be broadened beyond election mobilizations to embrace much broader, more substantial reforms that weaken a system requiring the reproduction of racism, national oppression, and political polarization in order to sustain the status quo.

Notes

1. Gregory D. Squires, Kathleen McCourt, Larry Bennett, and Philip Nyden, *Chicago: Race, Class, and the Response to Urban Decline* (Philadelphia: Temple University Press, 1987).

2. See Peter Eisenger, "Black Mayors and Politics of Racial Economic Advancement," in William C. McCready, ed., *Culture, Ethnicity and Identity: Current Issues in Research* (New York: Academic Press, 1983). Also see James Jennings, *The Politics of Black Empowerment: The Transformation of Black Activism in Urban America* (Detroit: Wayne State University Press, 1992); and Pierre Clavel and Wim Wiewel, eds., *Harold Washington and the Neighborhoods: Progressive City Government in Chicago, 1983–1987* (New Brunswick, NJ: Rutgers University Press, 1991).

3. G. Rivlin, "Everybody's Mayor," *Reader: Chicago's Free Weekly*, vol. 21, no. 24 (March 20, 1992), pp. 16–29.

4. William J. Grimshaw, *Bitter Fruit: Black Politics and the Chicago Machine, 1931–1991* (Chicago: University of Chicago Press, 1992), chapters 8–9.

5. Douglas Gills, "Chicago Politics and Community Development: A Social Movement Perspective," in Clavel and Wiewel, eds., *Harold Washington and the Neighborhoods*, pp. 34–63. Also see Abdul Alkalimat and Douglas Gills, "Black Political Protest and the Mayoral Victory of Harold Washington: Chicago Politics 1983," *Radical America*, vols. 17–18, Special Issue (November 1983–February 1984), pp. 111–27.

6. See Grimshaw, *Bitter Fruit*, chapters 8–9; also Richard Simpson, ed., *Chicago's Future in a Time of Change* (Champaign, IL: Stipes Publishing, 1992), p. 187.

7. For a full discussion of this theme, see Abdul Alkalimat and Douglas Gills, *Harold Washington and the Crisis of Black Power in Chicago* (Chicago: Twenty-First Century Books and Publications, 1989), pp. 123–26.

8. Ibid. See also Gills, "Chicago Politics," pp. 58–61; and John J. Betancur and Douglas Gills, "Race and Class in Local Economic Development," in Richard D. Bingham and Robert Mier, eds., *Theories of Local Economic Development: Perspectives from across the Disciplines* (Newbury Park, CA: Sage Publications, 1993), pp. 191–212.

6

The Political Economy of
White Racism in Great Britain

Louis Kushnick

The plight of the white working class throughout the world today is directly traceable to Negro slavery in America, on which modern commerce and industry was founded, and which persisted to threaten free labor until it was partially overthrown in 1863. The resulting color caste founded and retained by capitalism was adopted, forwarded and approved by white labor, and resulted in the subordination of colored labor to white profits the world over. Thus the majority of the world's laborers, by the insistence of white labor, became the basis of a system of industry which ruined democracy and showed its perfect fruit in World War and Depression.

W. E. B. Du Bois, *Black Reconstruction in America* (1935)

Racism has blighted the lives of millions of people of color all over the world and has functioned worldwide to maintain class-stratified societies. Racism has been contested for its entire history. Whites and people of color, as both individuals and groups, have resisted the imposition of racist ideology and the racialized organization of society. Given the continued influence of racism, it is important to understand the conditions within which some Whites have opted for a more inclusive definition of "us."

The acceptance by most of the working class of the inevitability of hierarchy, and the racist determinants of their place in the hierarchy, has weakened the working class's ability to resist the ideological and cultural hegemony of the ruling class. Control over the culture-producing institutions gave the capitalist the capacity to define the public good. The inability of the British working class and its allies to create alternatives was a major factor in the continued domination of the working class. Racism is "artificially kept alive," as indicated by Karl Marx in a letter to Friedrich Engels, "by the press, the pulpit, the comic papers – in short, by all the means at the disposal of the ruling classes." Racism explains the impotence of the British working class despite its organization.[1]

Britain's first immigration controls were established to keep Jews out in 1905. The arguments used in favor of control were remarkably similar to those used later in the 1950s and 1960s against Black immigrants and later still in the 1980s and 1990s against refugees and asylum seekers. Virtually all of the English trade union movement campaigned for immigration control, and after 1892 it was official Trades Union Congress policy. In the Parliamentary debates of 1904, not a single Labour member spoke, and only three voted against the bill. Although they opposed it in the 1905 session, there is little evidence that they acted to oppose the scapegoating and division that characterized trade union policy. Thus, the trade union movement supported racism toward the periphery, the Irish, and immigrants.

Racism, Welfare Capitalism, and the Authoritarian State

In the aftermath of the Great Depression and World War II welfare capitalism emerged in mature form. The state, it was commonly argued, was now the protector of the weak and defenseless, the provider of a safety net and services on the basis of need rather than the ability to pay. Power was dispersed because of widespread stock ownership, and the new managers in the postindustrial society were responsive to more than the hitherto exclusive concern for profit maximization. There were no longer to be struggles over the distribution of scarce resources in an age of plenty and affluence. Class had become an irrelevant concept and, consequently, there was an end to ideology.

The actions of corporations and the state in capitalist societies in the past decade have revealed these claims to be ideological fairy tales. The soulful corporation has turned out to be a transnational entity moving production and jobs around the globe in a search for ever greater profits. These corporations use their mobility to force their workforce to accept an escalating series of "take-backs" as a condition of employment. The state has turned out to be more committed to capitalism than to welfare. The social safety net is being eroded as a strategy to keep and attract jobs. These challenges to the hegemonic ideology did not, however, lead to a reconsideration of their ideological assumptions by mainstream ideologues. Rather, it was either the genetic or the cultural inferiority of the victims that accounted for continuing and increasing inequality. Indeed, it was the very welfare components themselves that created a dependency culture and, thus, these outcomes.[2] Racism continues to be a central characteristic of British societies. Indeed, racism has played a crucial role in the current attack on the modern capitalist welfare state.

Racism in Modern Britain

Britain acquired a Black population because of the need for cheap labor, not out of a spirit of high-mindedness or in a fit of absence of mind, as some liberals have argued.[3] Black workers were first brought to Britain during World War I. In 1919 there were race riots in centers of Black population such as Liverpool and Cardiff. White seamen were faced with demobilization and job insecurity and, consequently, responded with a struggle against non-Whites.[4] In South Shields, attacks on Arab workers were encouraged by the leadership of the National Union of Seamen.[5] Attacks on the Jewish community rose as well. There was a rise of support for fascism and racism in general. For example, Member of Parliament David Logan (Labour, Liverpool) asked in the House of Commons, before the end of World War II:

> Is it a nice sight, as I walked through the south end of the city of Liverpool to find a black settlement, a black body of men – I am not saying a word about their colour – all doing well, and a white body of men who face the horrors of war walking the streets unemployed? . . . To see Chinamen . . . in the affluence that men of sea are able to get by constant employment while Britishers are going to public assistance committee?[6]

The turning point for Britain's becoming a multiracial society occurred in the 1950s. British capitalists demanded cheap labor to rebuild the economy, to staff the public services, and to cheapen indigenous labor. The British state responded in a variety of ways to these demands. Between the end of World War II and 1957, more than 350,000 Europeans were allowed into Britain under a variety of programs. But this number was insufficient to meet labor requirements, and thus Britain turned to the dependent economies of the periphery. These colonies had a surplus of labor, and, therefore, Blacks were recruited into British industries as cheap labor.

Immigrants typically did the jobs that indigenous workers were unwilling to take. For example, the textile industry in Lancashire introduced new technology that required the continuous operation of a night shift. Even the weak unions in this industry would not accept capital's demand that there be no night-shift differential for White male workers. Women were "protected" by law from working the night shift. The union leaders and rank and file, however, were ready to agree to a solution that satisfied almost everyone. Asian male workers were hired to work a permanent night shift at single rates of pay.

In this period Afro-Caribbean and Asian immigrants entered a racist political culture where the White working class had largely accepted the dominant racist ideology. However, this acceptance was not irrevocable. Some British political leaders during World War II found the British public to be insufficiently vitriolic towards people of colour, perceived as outsiders to British society, similar to the reactions of white landowners in the South United States after emancipation of poor whites in this region.[7] Labor leaders acted on the basis of their own racist attitudes or on the belief that their rank and file were racist.[8] For example, Black labor was put into an antagonistic racial relationship with White labor over housing. Similarly, many politicians used immigrants as scapegoats for the social problems facing the country.

Racial scapegoating was legitimized by a series of racist immigration laws in the 1960s and 1970s. The 1962 Conservative Party's Commonwealth Immigration Act and the Labour Party's 1965 Immigration White Paper established a quota of 7,500 for the New Commonwealth and one thousand for Malta and abolished the "C" entry voucher for unskilled workers without a specific job. Labour's 1968 Kenya Asians Act abolished the right of entry for non-White holders of a type of British passport. The Conservative government's 1971 Immigration Act ended the right of entry for non-White Commonwealth citizens as primary immigrants. Family members were kept apart, attempts to reunite families were portrayed as attempts by those illegal immigrants to flood into the country, and women and children were subjected to indignities, humiliations, and doses of radiation. These are but a few examples of how institutional racism underpins and legitimates popular racism in Britain. These laws only served to strengthen the racist belief that Black people cause existing social problems.

Racist scapegoating reinforced the operation of a system based on the reproduction of class inequality. Thus, although the system of welfare capitalism constructed after World War II was a major reform of capitalism, it did not mark the shift of all power to the working class. Despite overall improvements in the health and education of the working class, class inequality remained.[9] Capital continued to control the framework for debate about economic policy. While the business community demanded a fundamental restructuring of the postwar political economy in the late 1970s and 1980s, the working class had not yet been able to create a coherent alternative culture to counter the ruling-class-based culture and, therefore, has continued to be divided. Despite the creation of rights to benefits and income transfer programs, the image of welfare recipients as "scroungers," "spongers," or "lead-swingers" was assiduously fostered by employers, the media, and the state.[10]

Racism has always provided the means for business and conservative politicians to bring about the restructuring of the relationship between capital, labor, and the state. Margaret Thatcher played the race card in January 1978 with her infamous "swamping" speech, in which she declared that the British people had a legitimate fear of being swamped by people of an "alien culture." This was the first of four successful uses of the race card to ensure sufficient support for destroying the old social contract from sections of society whose interests would be harmed by the restructuring. This political manipulation was further facilitated by the vigorous and vicious racism of the British press.[11]

The triumph of Thatcherism in Britain resulted in a fall in real wages, massive cuts in the social wage, and increasing insecurity for workers. Needless to say, these depressed social conditions generated greater tendencies toward racial violence.[12] In their study of racial harassment in the London borough of Waltham Forest, researchers found a pattern of "White territorialism" operating during this period. A recent study has shown that local authorities were failing to protect tenants from racial harassment.[13] These findings reinforce a large body of work that has identified the crisis of racial violence affecting Britain's Black communities. For example, the Home Office in 1981 calculated that West Indians were thirty-six times more likely to be the victims of a racial attack than were Whites. The figure for Asians was fifty times as likely. The Policy Studies Institute found that of those who had experienced racial harassment, 60 percent had not reported these cases to the police. This study calculated that the incidence of racial harassment was probably ten times that estimated in the 1981 Home Office survey.[14]

The Greater London Council in 1984 concluded that "racial harassment in London is an increasingly serious problem."[15] A poll commissioned by London Weekend Television's London Programme in 1985 found that one in four Asians in the boroughs of Redbridge,

Waltham Forest, Tower Hamlets, and Newham had been racially attacked.[16] A report commissioned jointly by Sheffield City Council and the Commission for Racial Equality concluded that "no Black person, male or female, young or old, from any ethnic group, is safe from harassment and violence."[17]

A survey by the Leeds Community Relations Council found 305 cases of harassment over an eighteen-month period in a population of about four thousand, which suggested a level ten times that estimated by the 1981 Home Office survey.[18] The Scottish Ethnic Minorities Research Unit of Glasgow found in 1987 that 44 percent of racial incidents were not reported to the police.[19] Moreover, a 1986 survey found that one in four of Newham's Black and ethnic minority residents were victims of racial harassment in the twelve months prior to the survey, and that two out of every three victims had been victimized on more than one occasion. Only one in twenty of the 1,550 incidents recorded by the survey had been reported to the police, and 80 percent of the Black and ethnic minority victims were dissatisfied with the police handling of the cases.

The Waltham Forest study also found dissatisfaction with the police which reinforced the findings of the Institute of Race Relations in both its 1979 report on *Police Against Black People* and its 1987 report on *Policing Against Black People*.[20] The European Parliament's Committee of Inquiry into Racism and Xenophobia indicted Britain for its "intolerably high level of racial harassment and violence" and estimated that there was a racist attack every twenty-six minutes in Britain.[21] A special report in the newspaper *The Guardian* (13 February 1995) documented the massive rise in racial attacks in Britain that were seen as more widespread than in Germany. In 1992, eight people were killed as a result of racist attacks, and Home Office figures for 1993, the last year for which they are available, indicated that there were nearly nine thousand racial attacks in that year.[22] The Anti-Racist Alliance indicated that only one in ten such attacks are reported and that a more accurate estimate of the number of racial attacks that occurred in 1991 alone would be close to seventy thousand.[23] The government has been forced to recognize that the situation is even worse than this estimate. Peter Lloyd, a former Minister of State at the Home Office, reported to the Home Affairs Select Committee of the House of Commons that racial attacks could be as much as twenty times the reported level. Although the British Crime Survey reported 7,793 attacks a year, nearly double the 1988 figure, the true figure could be as high as 140,000 – with the 1993 figure of around 9,000 leading to a probably more accurate figure of 180,000. The level of racial violence in Britain during the last decade has been the worst in the European Community.

The deaths of at least seventeen people in racist attacks in 1993 and 1994 and the high rates of racial violence and harassment in Britain may be indications of the consequences of popular racism fostered by the activities of the state and the media. The ending of primary Black immigration did not, as its proponents asserted, lead to the ending of the issue of immigration in British politics and the production of good race relations. Instead, immigrants continue to be portrayed as outsiders who do not belong; right-wing politicians continue to raise the specter of "swamping" and the replacement of church bells with calls to worship at the mosque. For example, as an indication of this thinking, Member of Parliament Winston Churchill asserted that:

> We must call a halt to the relentless flow of immigrants to this country, especially from the Indian subcontinent. . . . The population of many of our northern cities is now well over 50 percent immigrant, and Moslems claim there are now more than two million of their co-religionists in Britain. . . . With this government continuing to bring in immigrants each year at a scale, in Mrs. Thatcher's immortal phrase of 15 years ago "equivalent to a town the size of Grantham", a halt must be called – and urgently – if the British way of life is to be preserved.[24]

Two years later Member of Parliament Charles Wardle resigned as a junior minister at the Department of Trade and Industry on the grounds that membership of the European Union will lead to floods of immigrants coming into Britain. Wardle stated that "if the back door at Dover, at Folkstone, at all the Channel ports, was left open as the European Commission envisages, uncontrolled numbers of people could come in here."[25] Right-wing newspapers, columnists, and politicians have played the race card to its fullest. For example, right-wing columnist Paul Johnson, writing in the newspaper of Little England, *The Daily Mail*, asked whether Britain should have become multiracial:

> The smouldering anger among the British people reflects the fact that they believe they have been lied to twice. The first time was when a flood of Commonwealth immigrants arrived without anyone asking the British electorate if they were welcome. Within a generation, fundamental changes had taken place in the composition of the nation and we had become a multi-cultural, multi-racial society without any of us being given the smallest choice in the matter.[26]

The Conservative government, suffering the worst public opinion standing of a government since polling began, has begun looking yet again at playing the race card. The Home Secretary, Michael Howard, announced in mid-March 1995 that the government was considering legislation to "crack down on illegal immigrants." The proposed measures would further restrict the rights of asylum seekers following the passage and implementation of restrictive legislation in 1993.[27]

A report in *The Guardian* reported the Home Secretary's decision in the following terms:

> Mr Howard's decision to prepare legislation to be published this summer and introduced this autumn indicates that the government sees a need to placate the demands from the Tory right for further tough action. Immigration welfare groups have voiced concern that ministers were prepared to play the "race card" in an attempt to reverse the spiralling decline in party fortunes.[28]

Financial Times reported yet another government measure playing the race card:

> A vision of a UK swamped by immigrants was revived by a Department of the Environment report on Monday. It forecasts a net inflow of 50,000 people a year for the next two decades, whereas a 1991 report had predicted no net immigration. Indeed, for the year to June 1993, the last period for which figures were available, there was an outflow of 11,000 people and tougher checks and the unreliability of figures may mean that the projected flood of migrants – few of them the "benefit tourists" or low-skilled workers of Mr Wardle's vision – could never materialize. If they do not, the forecast of 4.4m new households in England over the next 20 years – an increase of nearly a quarter – begins to sound dubious too.[29]

The combination of racist state policies legitimating popular racism and the destruction of working-class jobs created a collapse of hope and sense of community in Britain's cities. This process has been exacerbated by the failure of the Labour Party and trade unions to defend these communities. The racism of the White working class has left them susceptible to the appeals of the far right racist and fascist movements.[30]

One recent indication of the disastrous potential for the rights of Black people of these developments was in a September 1993 council by-election in Millwall, in east London, where the British National Party (BNP) candidate, Derek Beacon, was elected in a predominantly White working-class ward. Although he was defeated in 1994 when he stood for reelection and other BNP candidates have lost elections, there has been an increase in racial violence and attacks in areas where the BNP has been active. The playing of the race card by politicians and the press continues to encourage popular racist attitudes. But interestingly, a poll conducted for *The Guardian* in mid-March 1995 found that 79 percent of White Britons polled think there is prejudice toward Black people – defined as those whose families originally came from the West Indies or Africa.[31]

The reality of the choices facing British society is brought home by these results and the danger of collusion of the mainstream parties in state racism and in the attacks on the living standards of large parts of the British population – Black and White. The consequences of free-market economic strategies combined with attacks on organized working-class resistance have included a massive increase in insecurity in people's lives. Secure jobs have been replaced by joblessness, temporary and part-time jobs, or insecurity of tenure for those still in full-time employment. Greater inequality of income and wealth has been accompanied by cuts in the welfare support systems leading to greater insecurity for the majority of society dependent upon collective provision for health, education, and support for the elderly or for periods of unemployment. Unfettered greed in the boardrooms and scandals in the Conservative government and among its backbenchers have led to increasing cynicism toward government and public institutions. The Labour Party under its new leader, Tony Blair, has been striving to achieve respectability and electability by appealing to what is called "middle England" at the expense of its traditional supporters in the inner cities and in the former industrial heartlands. The questions facing Labour in forthcoming elections are what to do about a decade and a half of decline in collective provision, increasing inequality and dislocation, and their structural causes, without appearing to favor those outside of middle England.

Notes

1. Karl Marx and Friedrich Engels, *On Britain*, 2nd ed. (Moscow: Foreign Languages Publishing House, 1962).
2. For a critique of these ideas, see Thomas D. Boston, *Race, Class and Conservatism* (London: Unwin Hyman, 1988); Joseph Graves, Jr. and Terri Place, "Race and IQ Revisited: Figures Never Lie, But Often Liars Figure," *Sage Race Relations Abstracts*, vol. 20, no. 2 (1995), pp. 4–49; James Jennings, *Understanding the Nature of Poverty in Urban America* (New York: Praeger, 1994); K. Mann, *The Making of an English 'Underclass'?: The Social Divisions of Welfare and Labour* (Philadelphia: Open University Press, 1992); Valerie Polakow, "Savage Distributions: Welfare Myths and

Daily Lives," *Sage Race Relations Abstracts*, vol. 19, no. 4 (1994), pp. 3–29; and Adolph Reed, "The Underclass as Myth and Symbol: The Poverty of Discourse about Poverty," *Radical America*, vol. 24, no. 1 (1992), pp. 21–40.

3. D. Nandy, "Foreword," in J. McNeal and M. Rogers, eds., *The Multi-Racial School* (New York: Viking, 1971).

4. Roy May and Robin Cohen, "The Interaction between Race and Colonialism: A Case Study of the Liverpool Race Riots of 1919," *Race and Class*, vol. 16, no. 2 (1974), pp. 111–26; and Peter Fryer, *Staying Power* (London: Pluto Press, 1984).

5. David Byrne, "The 1930 Arab Riot in South Shields," *Race and Class*, vol. 18, no. 3 (1977), pp. 261–77.

6. This quote is cited in "Black Workers and Trade Unions," *Liberator*, no. 1 (1980).

7. Graham Smith, *When Jim Crow Met John Bull* (London: I. B. Tauris, 1987).

8. Shirley Joshi and Bob Carter, "The Role of Labour in the Creation of a Racist Britain," *Race and Class*, vol. 25, no. 3 (1984), pp. 53–70. Also see Clive Harris, "Configurations of Racism: The Civil Service, 1945–60," *Race and Class*, vol. 33, no. 1 (1991), pp. 1–30.

9. John H. Westegaard and Henrietta Resler, *Class in a Capitalist Society: A Study of Contemporary Britain* (London: Heinemann Educational Books, 1975). Also see Peter Townsend and Nick Davidson, eds., *Inequalities in Health: The Black Report* (Harmondsworth: Penguin Books, 1982); and Carey Oppenheim, *Poverty: The Facts,* revised ed. (London: Child Poverty Action Group, 1993).

10. See Fiona Williams, *Social Policy: A Critical Introduction* (New York: Blackwell Publishers, 1989) for an overview of how these sectors use such images to describe poor people receiving welfare from the state in both England and the United States.

11. Nancy Murray, "Anti-Racists and Other Demons: The Press and Ideology in Thatcher's Britain," *Race and Class*, vol. 27, no. 3 (1986), pp. 1–20. Also see Chris Searle, "Your Daily Dose: Racism and the *Sun*," *Race and Class*, vol. 29, no. 1 (1987), pp. 55–72.

12. See, for example, Liz Fekete, "Racist Violence: Meeting the New Challenges," *Race and Class*, vol. 30, no. 2 (1988), pp. 71–76; N. Ginsburg, "Racial Harassment Policy and Practice: The Denial of Citienship," *Critical Social Policy*, vol. 26 (1989), pp. 66–68; *Policing Against Black People* (London: Institute of Race Relations, 1987); and Keith Tompson, *Under Siege: Racism and Violence in Britain Today* (Harmondsworth: Penguin Books, 1988).

13. *Beneath the Surface: An Inquiry into Racial Harassment in the London Borough of Waltham Forest* (London: London Borough of Waltham Forest, 1990).

14. Colin Brown, *Black and White Britain: The Third PSI Survey* (London: Heinemann, 1984).

15. *Racial Harassment in London* (London: Greater London Council, 1984).

16. *Racial Attacks – Survey of Eight Areas of Britain* (London: Commission for Racial Equality, 1987).

17. Sheffield Racial Harassment Project, *Because Their Skin Is Black* (Sheffield: Sheffield City Council, 1988).

18. Independent Committee of Inquiry into Racial Harassment, *Racial Harassment in Leeds, 1985–86* (Leeds: Leeds Community Relations Council, 1987).

19. *Racial Harassment in Glasgow* (Glasgow: Scottish Ethnic Minorities Research Unit, 1987).

20. *Police against Black People* (London: Institute of Race Relations, 1979); and London Borough of Waltham Forest, *Beneath the Surface*.

21. Glyn Ford, *Fascist Europe: The Rise of Racism and Xenophobia* (London: Pluto Press, 1992).

22. R. Klein, "Where Prejudice Still Flares into Violence," *The Times Educational Supplement*, no. 4097 (1995), p. 9.

23. *The Guardian*, 20 February 1993.

24. Quoted in *The Daily Express*, 29 May 1993.

25. Quoted in *The Guardian*, 13 February 1995; for Churchill, see *Manchester Evening News*, 7 February 1995. The paper in one of its regular readership polls asked its readers whether he was right and received more responses than on any issue other than whether Moors murderer Myra Hydley should be released from prison, with 96 percent responding yes and 4 percent no. *Manchester Evening News*, 9 February 1995.

26. Paul Johnson, *The Daily Mail*, February 1995.

27. See Louis Kushnick, "Immigration and Asylum in the European Union," *Outsider*, vol. 42 (April 1995), p. 3.

28. *The Guardian*, 14 March 1995.

29. *Financial Times*, 8 March 1995.

30. A similar process is in operation throughout Europe; see Louis Kushnick, "Immigration and Asylum," p. 3.

31. *The Guardian*, 20 March 1995.

7

Hands across the Atlantic: Comparison of Black American and Black British Electoral Politics

Clarence Lusane

Although written more than thirty years ago, Ira Katznelson's insight that "the systematic study of comparative race politics is in its infancy" maintains salience.[1] Few studies have been produced that examine relationships between Blacks in the United States and Blacks in Britain.[2] Yet a comparison of race relations and the Black response to racism in the United States and Britain is relevant and compelling for several reasons. A number of writers, most notably Paul Gilroy, are developing a body of literature focusing on the cultural links among Blacks in the two nations. Gilroy refers to this area of the diaspora as the "Black Atlantic."[3]

Ronald Walters notes that political linkages between these two communities can be summarized in five themes: (a) structural similarity of social, political, and economic systems between Britain and the United States in promoting similar policy approaches to race relations; (b) cultural similarity with regard to racial attitudes of Whites in Britain and the United States; (c) similar political and social reactions by Whites to the presence of Blacks – given the maturing state of the British Black community; (d) similar political reaction by the respective Black communities to the reception by the White host societies; and (e) similar violent racial conflict patterns in each society.[4] As minority communities functioning in racially unequal societies, Blacks in the United States and in Britain have had to employ similar strategies to pressure the larger society to address their concerns. In similar ways Blacks in both circumstances have moved from "protest to politics" as they have become more incorporated into the mainstream of society, while class differences have crystallized within those communities. In addition, there continues to be an evolving bond between political activists in each country across the ideological spectrum and different time periods.

Blacks in the United States

One feature that makes the comparison between the political participation of Blacks in the United States and Britain important is the socioeconomic status of Blacks in comparison with the majority group in their respective countries. There are several similar factors driving the poverty rate in the Black communities in both countries. Fundamental changes in the global economy have had devastating consequences for the working classes in the United States and Britain, particularly for poor people. Capital flight and receding domestic investments have had an especially harsh impact on these Black communities. The downturn in manufacturing – for Britain in the late 1960s and for the United States in the 1970s and 1980s – has meant a sharp drop in economic opportunities for hundreds of thousands of Blacks.

Blacks in the United States and Afro-Caribbeans in Britain are minorities who account for about 12 percent and 1.6 percent, respectively, of their populations. In both instances, Blacks on average are not only suffering more than the majority White population, but generally more than other groups of color with the sole exception of the Native-American population in the United States and the Bangladeshis in Britain. In the areas of poverty, employment, education, housing, and police relations, Blacks fare the worst. The latest figures on poverty in the United States show that the number of Americans living in poverty in 1993 grew to 39.3 million. This is an increase of 1.3 million over 1992. The official Black poverty rate is 33.1 percent, or more than ten million people, which is higher than for Hispanics (30.6 percent), Asians/Pacific Islanders (15.3 percent), or Whites (12.2 percent).[5] Close to half of all Black children live in poverty.[6] The crisis threatening African Americans is not simply that there exists extensive Black poverty; rather, it centers around the chronic nature of that poverty. Under the Reagan and Bush administrations, more than 1.6 million additional African Americans fell below the poverty line during the period from 1989 to 1991.[7]

The current median income for Whites is $32,960, for African Americans $19,532, for Hispanics $22,886, and for Asians/Pacific Islanders $38,347. Black median income is still only 59 percent that of Whites, or essentially what it was thirty years ago. Black median income is only 50 percent that of Asians/Pacific Islanders and 85 percent that of Hispanics.[8] According to the Urban League, Blacks have fewer savings accounts than Whites (44.5 percent vs. 76.6 percent), fewer checking accounts (30.1 percent vs. 50.9 percent), fewer stocks (7 percent vs. 23.9 percent), less equity in their homes (43.5 percent vs. 66.7 percent), and fewer IRAs (6.9 percent vs. 26.4 percent).[9] Black household net worth is $26,130 compared to $111,950 for Whites. While Whites were earning $6,162 at financial institutions, Blacks were earning only $735; while Whites had $3,846 worth of equity in their businesses, Blacks had only $351.[10] The Black civilian labor force comprises about 14.4 million, which constitutes 11.1 percent of the nation's total labor force.[11] In the past two decades, the Black unemployment rate has been roughly three times that of Whites. In 1993, the Black unemployment rate was 13.4 percent while the White rate stood at 5.2 percent; Blacks made up 21.7 percent of the nation's unemployed.[12] For those young Black males with criminal records, the rate of which in some cities is higher than 50 percent, employment opportunities have virtually disappeared. A study by the National Bureau of Economic Research found that while 50 percent of those incarcerated had a job before they entered prison, only 19 percent had jobs after they left prison.[13]

Downturns in the economy in recent years have also been felt unevenly across racial lines. According to the *Wall Street Journal*, "Blacks were the only racial group to suffer a net job loss during the 1990–91 economic downturn."[14] African Americans lost close to sixty thousand jobs at companies surveyed by the Equal Employment Opportunity Commission. At companies such as W.R. Grace, BankAmerica, ITT, Sears, Roebuck, Coca-Cola, Safeway, Campbell Soup, Walt Disney, and General Electric – all of which have been globalized – Blacks lost jobs at a rate twice that of Whites. The jobs that were lost by Blacks at these companies ranged the entire job spectrum from entry-level positions to management. These economic retreats alone go a long way in explaining – though by no means justifying – the move by so many young and unemployed African Americans into the underground economy, particularly the illegal drug trade.[15] In the last fifteen to twenty years the degree of economic deterioration among the Black poor has grown sharper and its existence appears permanent. In the 1980s, a fairly conscious assault on labor and the Black community by the Reagan administration, in collaboration with Congress, destroyed all hope of extensive economic opportunities for Black youth.[16]

Under the theme of anticommunism Reagan ballooned the military budget by going after "programs targeted to low-income families and individuals – one tenth of the federal budget."[17] Cuts in these programs constituted nearly one-third of the 1981–83 budget cuts.[18] In the years 1981–86 job training funds had been "reduced from $7.6 billion to $3.6 billion or 52 percent in real terms and it is argued, had the President's budget proposals been accepted each time, funding for job training programs would have fallen 62 percent below the funding level for the 1981 fiscal year," according to Keith Jennings.[19] As a result of these policies and the normal operations of the labor marketplace, by 1986 Black youth unemployment was officially 39.3 percent.[20] According to the National Urban League, Black teenagers suffered the sharpest increase in unemployment since 1960 of all groups.[21]

Nearly a decade later little has changed. In 1994, in the midst of an economic recovery, Black teen unemployment rose. In January 1994 official Black teen unemployment was 32 percent; in May, it had risen to 40 percent (males, 44 percent; females, 37 percent).[22] In contrast, the May unemployment rate for White teens was 15 percent. While 60 percent of White youth who are out of high school (either graduated or dropped out) have full- or part-time jobs, only 33 percent of Black youth in the same situation have such employment.

Blacks in Britain

Much of this crisis mirrors the situation facing Blacks in Britain. The Afro-Caribbean population constitutes about 1.6 percent (880,000) of the total Great Britain population of about 52 million.[23] And, like many Blacks in the United States, they are concentrated in inner cities. About 70 percent of Blacks in Britain live in metropolitan areas, with 41 percent of all Blacks living in London.[24] Economically, Blacks are significantly disadvantaged compared to White Britons. As David Owen states, "ethnic minorities experience higher rates of unemployment, hold less-skilled jobs and are employed in older industries than White people."[25] Blacks are disproportionately concentrated in the service sector, which has grown substantially since the decline of manufacturing in Great Britain in the mid-1960s. Caribbean Black males, with the exception of their work in the transportation industry, tend to somewhat mirror White males in terms of occupational categories – construction, engineering, and distribution; most Black males are concentrated in the service sector.

More than 25 percent of Africans, however, work in unskilled service occupations.[26]

Police harassment and deaths in police custody have also been a critical issue in the British Black community. Discussion of strains between the Black community and the police echoes many of the same sentiments found in the Black community in the United States, particularly as these relations impact Black youth. A. Sivanandan writes, for example, that "young Blacks are frequently stopped and questioned on the basis of no more than a generalized suspicion that if they are Black and young and on the streets they can be up to no good. And the way that Blacks are subjected to violent arrest stems from another presumption: that Blacks are violent and aggressive by nature and must, from the outset, be dealt with violently and aggressively."[27] This tension, however, is not limited to just the youth. As Sivanandan notes further, "Black people experience racism in the criminal justice system not just as a set of statistics or as generalized discrimination, but with a deep sense of fear at any point at which they, or members of their communities, come into contact with the custodians of the law."[28]

Sivanandan's analysis echoes the crisis that African Americans confront in terms of the criminal justice system. In 1995, it was reported that 32.2 percent of all young Black males (compared to about 6 percent of White males) between the ages of eighteen and thirty are incarcerated, on parole, or on probation; in Washington, D.C., 42 percent of all young Black males are in those circumstances.[29] One study estimates that at the current incarceration rate, by the year 2000, 40 percent of all African-American men between the ages of eighteen and thirty-five will be in prison or jail.[30] The Rodney King beating, which received massive publicity throughout British society, underscores the unresolved problem of police brutality that still plagues many inner-city Black neighborhoods in both countries.[31]

Finally, it appears that there is a significant hard-core sector of the White British population that holds intolerant views toward Blacks. In 1986 a national survey found that "over 90 percent of adults believe Britain is a racially prejudiced society, about 40 percent believe racial prejudice is getting worse, and the same proportion believe it will go on getting worse, as opposed to under 20 percent who believe it will get better. Moreover, over 30 percent are prepared to admit that they themselves are prejudiced against people of other races."[32]

Black Political Participation in the United States

Prior to the Civil War of 1860–65, formal Black political participation was reduced to limited voting in a few states as more than 90
percent of the Black population was held in bondage. Although three
Blacks were elected to public office prior to the Civil War, the years
following the war would see an unprecedented growth in Black
elected officials.[33] During the Reconstruction era, about two thousand
Blacks held political office, but this political renaissance came to an
end after the fall of Reconstruction in 1877, and by the turn of the
century virtually no Black elected officials existed anywhere in the
nation at the federal or state level.[34] Although a trickle of Black
elected officials began to appear again by the late 1920s, it was not
until the passage of the 1965 Voting Rights Act that the vast majority
of Blacks were able to vote relatively freely and the number of Black
elected officials grew rapidly.

Between the Civil War and the 1930s, Black party participation
was fairly restricted to that of the Republican Party, which had fought
to end slavery. The Democratic Party, the home of southern racists,
was unattractive to Blacks until the New Deal era of Franklin
Roosevelt, whose programs benefited Blacks more than any initiated
by the Republican Party. Since that time Black voters have overwhelmingly supported the Democratic Party, and the majority of all
Black elected officials are Democrats.

What is notable about African-American political participation in
the electoral arena is not its support for one party or the other, but its
collective response. Except for the transitional period of the 1930s,
Black political behavior has operated with a somewhat clear consensus at least in regards to electoral behavior. This would indicate that
race and perceptions of racial interest are salient and have not
significantly deteriorated in spite of growing class divisions in the
Black community. Political scientist Michael Dawson calls this
phenomenon of collective group interest the "Black utility heuristic."
Dawson's thesis is "that as long as African Americans' life chances
are powerfully shaped by race, it is efficient for individual African
Americans to use their perceptions of the interest of African Americans as a group as a proxy for their own interests."[35] Dawson
contends that this theory should be applicable to other socially
subordinate groups whose race, ethnic, or religious identity makes
them vulnerable to oppression and perhaps even annihilation.[36] It is
argued below that the Black utility heuristic is operationalized in
Britain as Blacks consistently demonstrate a political cohesion that,

within limits, transcends class divisions. This has meant that Blacks have backed the Labour Party with similar patterns of support in the way that the African Americans have supported the Democratic Party.

Black Political Participation in Britain

Researcher Terri Sewell argues that the major political parties sought to ignore race as a relevant factor in British politics prior to 1962 and the subsequent debates about immigration. She calls this approach the "peripheralisation of race" and believes that it operated in the context of a bipartisan consensus.[37] While race has become more a focus of public debate in terms of Black participation in mainstream politics, most observers still believe that class remains the dominant variable shaping Black political behavior. It is argued here, however, that class is perhaps viewed through the prism of race given the predominant working-class nature of England's Black community. From this perspective, Dawson's Black utility heuristic appears relevant and provides an appropriate starting point for assessing Black British political behavior and views.

Surveys provide some evidence of how class and race interrelate in the British context. In a 1983 Harris poll it was found that only 31 percent of Asians and 7 percent of Afro-Caribbeans said that their support for the Labour Party was because "they support Blacks and Asians."[38] Instead, Whites, Asians, and Afro-Caribbeans all stated that they made their party choices because of the "general image" of what the party stood for. For those Afro-Caribbeans who supported Labour, 66 percent said they did so for this reason.[39] One could infer, therefore, that rather than disaggregate race and class as separate identities or interests, Blacks see these as intertwined and not functionally separable.

Black Britons also appeared to be remarkably close in how useful they view particular strategies in advancing their agenda. In a 1985 survey Blacks, more than any other group, saw pressure group politics as more effective than voting or lobbying. Only about 15 percent of Blacks surveyed found voting an efficacious political approach.[40] As political analysts Zig Layton-Henry and Donley T. Studlar have observed, "we are faced with the paradox that the group least likely to vote [West Indians] participate more than Whites and Asians in these other respects [political activities other than voting]. . . . In each instance, it is the Blacks who are more likely to participate."[41] Given these views, it is not surprising that Asians have a higher registration and voter turnout than Blacks and even higher than some Whites in particular areas.[42] Thus, a paradox exists of a high voting rate by a relatively apolitical Asian community compared to a low voting rate, by a politically active Afro-Caribbean population.[43]

Afro-Britons have been active in all major party groups: the Conservative Party and the Labour Party. Political researcher Marian Fitz-Gerald divides the Conservatives into two categories: populists who pander to racism and dominate the party, and progressives who "believe in equal opportunity before the law."[44] Right-wing populists tend to be ideologically close to the ultraconservatives in the U.S. Republican Party. For example, in a survey given to Young Conservatives in 1983, it was found that a quarter thought that "the best kind of society for Britain would be exclusively White, 14 percent advocated compulsory repatriation of Black immigrants, and 56 percent thought immigrant controls should be tougher."[45] This view echoes the sentiments of many in the Republican Party and most of its leaders who are calling for tighter controls on (non-White) immigration to the United States as expressed in the campaign for California's Proposition 187, which seeks to deny public education, health services, and other opportunities to the children of undocumented immigrants.[46]

The Conservative Party has made some outreach efforts toward Blacks over the years. In 1976, it set up the Community Affairs Department to conduct outreach to various groups including Blacks. That venture closed down in 1980. The party then established the separate Anglo-Asian and the Anglo-West Indian Conservative Societies. Each of these lasted about ten years, enduring the criticism that they were more vehicles for individual advancement than efforts to reform the party on questions of race.[47] After those efforts failed, the party created the One Nation Forum, which functions in an advisory capacity and little else.

Black rejection of the Conservatives is rooted in the policies that have been exercised by the party. Margaret Thatcher, an ideological twin of Ronald Reagan, launched harsh attacks on the British working class and Blacks including the privatization of some public utilities, tax cuts for the rich, the ending of price controls, tougher policing in the wake of the 1981 and 1985 riots, a more rigid immigration policy, and little enforcement of the Race Relations Act. As she stated, "the philosophy of this government is a non-interventionist one."[48] This would account for why, in a 1987 Harris poll, 76 percent of all Blacks disapproved of the Conservative record, particularly regarding racial concerns.[49] While there is little indication of increased Black voter support, the Conservatives have continued to increase the number of

Black candidates that run for office each election. This is believed to be a result of the growing Black middle class and some Black frustration with the disappointing performance of the Labour Party.

In the 1983 and 1987 elections, the Liberal Party and the Social Democratic Party (SDP) formed an electoral alliance. They sought to pool their small resources and bases as well as break off a sizable chunk of the Afro-Caribbean and Asian vote. Both parties had fairly good records of supporting Black causes and challenging racism both within and outside of their parties. Both had expelled members in the past for espousing racist views.[50] Indeed, the constitution of the Social Democrats states: "The Social Democratic Party exists to create an open, classless and more equal society, which rejects prejudices based upon sex, race, or religion."[51] The SDP also had at least two people of color on their national executive committee. In both the elections cited, the Alliance ran Black and Asian candidates.

The Alliance promised in 1983 to work to achieve racial equality, to fight for progressive antidiscriminatory immigration reform, and to struggle to ease the road to citizenship for immigrants.[52] However, despite these progressive views, neither the Alliance nor each party separately has been able to win a healthy vote from the Black community. In 1983, the Alliance won only 11 percent of the Black vote, though that was higher than the 7 percent received by the Conservatives. The Alliance did worse in 1987, then getting only 7 percent of the Black vote and 10 percent of the Asian vote.[53] The Alliance likely suffered from the same political phenomenon as in the United States, where third parties have a difficult time winning the vote of what should be their natural constituencies because voters are hesitant to vote for candidates or parties that cannot win.

The principal battleground for Blacks in the formal political system has been within the Labour Party (LP). Marian FitzGerald has argued that a chief reason why Blacks have been so loyal to Labour is that Blacks settled initially in labor areas and, therefore, developed close ties with Labour officials.[54] While this is undoubtedly a factor, FitzGerald acknowledges but underestimates the degree to which policy initiatives by the Labour Party and individual Labour activists and officials were attractive and distinct from the Conservatives. For example, Labour has a long history of support for colonial freedom and took an antiapartheid position early on.[55]

The downturns in the economy in the mid-1960s began to erode Labour's White and labor base. As its traditional base began to waver, the party increasingly saw the importance of the Black vote. After losing the government in 1979, the party's national executive issued a self-critical report titled *Labour and the Black Electorate* that stated: "In spite of the party's long-standing commitment to anti-racism we have, so far, failed to convince Black people that we deserve their active support. Instead, they have increasingly been organizing politically into self-help and pressure groups, largely spurning mainstream party politics. Indeed, many Black people – especially the youngest members of the community – are openly suspicious of the party."[56] Recommendations were made as to how to improve outreach and to make the party more welcoming for Blacks and Asians. The now-defunct Greater London Council (GLC), controlled by Labour and a conduit for funds for community-based Black organizations, had been active and even declared 1984 the GLC Anti-Racist year.[57]

Inside the party, beginning in 1975, Blacks, Asians, and even White leftists began to organize race-related caucuses and groups. Whites created the Labour Party Race Action Group, for example. This effort was viewed as being paternalistic and did not last long. Blacks and Asians also began to create their own groups including the Asian Labour Party Alliance, the Afro-Asian and Caribbean Alliance for Labour, and the Standing Conference of Afro-Caribbean and Asian Councillors.[58] However, it was the battle over the creation of a constitutionally recognized Black Section that became the defining struggle for Blacks inside the Labour Party. The fight began in 1983 and lasted seven years. The party had already established a Women's Section and a Youth Section, so Afro-Caribbeans and Asians felt justified in pressing for their own official recognition within the party. Yet they found resistance at every turn.

Ben Bousquet, Billy Poh, and Ray Philbert had initiated the idea in May 1982 and brought it to the LP national party conference in 1983. They sought the same privileges, rights, and authority as the other recognized sections, as well as a seat on the National Executive Committee of the party. Their resolution stated in part:

> In this unequal society there is no real equality of opportunity in that working-class people, women and ethnic minority groups suffer severe discrimination. . . . Our party itself is unfortunately not free from this and therefore accepts the principle of positive discrimination in favour of disadvantaged groups . . . in particular the right of Black members of the party to organise together in the same way as Women's Sections and Young Socialist branches.[59]

The resolution was opposed by all party leaders and not even allowed to be brought to a vote. But the movement for Black Sections would not go away. In July 1984, the first National Black Sections Conference was held. More than three hundred delegates, mainly Afro-Caribbean, attended and vowed to continue the fight within the Labour Party. It is interesting to note that the conference took place around the same time as the Democratic National Convention in San Francisco, where Rev. Jesse Jackson was leading a fight for more democracy within the Democratic Party. Although no explicit links were made between the two efforts, it would appear that in that period, when the Soviet Union was in the midst of a major and ultimately revolutionary reform and when the socialist nations were liberalizing, the major parties in the industrialized countries were not immune to the global call for democratic change.

At every national party conference between 1984 and 1989, resolutions advocating a Black Section were proposed and defeated. Meanwhile, in numerous local party situations, unofficial Black Sections were established. Black Sections conferences also continued, although the movement began to suffer from internal divisions that eventually took their toll and turned early supporters against the movement. Two of the four Black Parliament members, Paul Boateng and Keith Vaz, became openly critical of the movement. At the October 1990 party conference, a compromise was finally reached. Composite 8, as it was called, stated that the National Executive Committee would (a) recognize formally and support Black members' right to organize together for effective participation and representation; b) make provisions for the representation of Black members at all levels of the party; and c) adopt the working party's proposal on Black members' organization within the party that were presented to the National Executive Committee on 26 July 1989, namely, the setting up of a single affiliated organization for members of African, Caribbean, and Asian descent, with local and regional groups and direct representation on the National Executive Committee.[60]

The outcome of this resolution was the creation of the Black Socialist Society. Although this entity had constitutional recognition, it fell far short of the Black Sections goal that the activists had sought. The value of the Black Sections fight was mostly symbolic, but still very important. For seven years, Black activists had pushed the party to confront the issue of race. The affiliated status of the Black Socialist Society provided an in-road to the party leadership in a formal and consistent way. The movement had also galvanized and mobilized the Black community around systemic politics in a manner that had not previously occurred. In this way, as did the 1964 losing fight by Blacks and White liberals from Mississippi to unseat the traditional, all-White Mississippi delegation at the Democratic National Convention, the battle that was lost helped the overall war because it broke the opposition's wall of confidence and complacency and forced concessions that otherwise would not have been made.

It was logical that the Labour Party would be the battleground for Black electoral politics because it was there that Black elected officials initially emerged and remain. The first Black elected official in Britain was Richard Archer. He was the first Black municipal council member and also England's first Black mayor. In November 1906 Archer was elected as one of the six councilors in the London borough of Battersea, which was dominated by a radical faction of the Labour Party. In November 1913 Archer was elected mayor of Battersea by a vote of 40:39. In his acceptance speech, Archer stated: "You have made history tonight. . . . Battersea has done many things in the past, but the greatest thing it has done is to show that it has no racial prejudice, and that it recognises a man for the work he has done."[61] This important historic moment was noted by African Americans including W. E. B. Du Bois, who wrote enthusiastically about the elevation of Archer to mayor in *The Crisis*, the official publication of the NAACP, recognizing it as a victory for colored people around the world. *The Crisis* noted that Archer "fears no man, and brooks no insult because of the race to which he is proud to belong."[62] Following Archer, there were very few Black elected officials, and those were at the local level. The electoral consequences of Black immigration and settlement began to take effect by the late 1960s and 1970s. This was starkly revealed in 1974. A Commission for Racial Equality study found that there were fifty-nine seats in the Parliamentary elections where the Black population was larger than the majority of the winning candidate's vote total, and that it could be assumed that the Black vote was the balance of power in thirteen of the seventeen seats that Labour won from the Conservatives. The number of Black elected officials during this time was relatively small. Reportedly, there were only about 150 Black city councilors out of twenty-five thousand seats available.[63] Yet Blacks continued to run for office both at the local and national levels. In 1979, five Blacks ran for Parliament; by 1983, that number had grown to eighteen and in 1987, twenty-seven persons ran.[64]

The 1987 elections saw Black politics come of age. There were sixty Parliamentary seats that had Black populations of 15 percent or more, the highest being Vauxhall in London with a population of 30.3 percent non-White. The average in those sixty areas is about 30 percent.[65] Prior to the 1987 elections, no one of African descent had been elected to the 650-seat Parliament. But in that historic year, three Afro-Caribbeans – Paul Boateng (Brent South), Bernie Grant (Tottenham), and Diane Abbott (Hackney North and Stoke Newington) – and one Asian, Keith Vaz (Leicester East), won seats in Parliament.[66] John Taylor, the first Afro-Caribbean to run as a Conservative Parliamentary candidate, lost. They joined Lord Pitt, who had been appointed to the House of Lords in 1975. Pitt had first run for Parliament in 1959. He ran again in 1970, and, in what has become an infamous incident in Black political history, he lost in what was considered a safe Labour seat when 10.2 percent of the vote shifted to the Conservatives, twice the national average.[67] While Pitt was reluctant to totally blame race, most interpretations of the vote held that Whites simply refused to support a Black man.

The election of the four colored candidates was significant in a number of ways. First, it meant that the Afro-Caribbean community now possessed a potential national platform within the system to raise issues and concerns. Just as African Americans have used Congress as a vehicle to spotlight national concerns of the Black community, Black Britons now had such an opportunity. Second, the election demonstrated that Whites, whether out of party loyalty or liberalized racial views, were willing to vote for Black candidates, given that none of the areas represented by the candidates was inhabited overwhelmingly by people of color. According to 1987 estimates, Boateng's Brent South was the only area of the four, at 55.6 percent, that had a majority of people of color. Grant's Tottenham was 45.3 percent, Abbott's Hackney North and Stoke Newington was 37 percent, and Vaz's Leicester East was only 31.7 percent.[68] As Abbott stated, "there is no District you can win in Britain without holding your White vote. You can't just appeal to the Black vote."[69]

A third lesson from the 1987 contest was that it demonstrated that those Blacks who had the best chance of getting elected were those who had previous government experience. All four candidates had come up through the process. Grant, for example, had been chairman of Haringey Council. Abbott was a city council member for four years. A similar situation has developed in the United States. In 1992, when an additional sixteen new Black members were elected to Congress, all except one, Mel Reynolds (D, IL), had extensive government and office-holding experience. In Britain, this path of electoral success is problematic, however, given the small number of Black elected officials in Britain.

Fourth, a number of incidents between 1983 and 1987 had raised the racial consciousness of the nation. This included the struggle over

Black Sections within the Labour Party, the riots of 1985, and, though acknowledged by few observers, Jesse Jackson's campaign for the Democratic nomination in 1984. The Jackson campaign had captured the imagination of millions of people around the world and undoubtedly served as a vehicle for legitimizing the electoral arena as a site of progressive and Black struggle. Jackson's efforts were certainly not lost on Blacks in Britain, who have always kept an eye turned toward the Black struggle in the United States.

In 1992, twenty-three Blacks ran for Parliament. This included ten Labour candidates, which was actually down from the fourteen who ran in 1987. The Conservatives had eight Black candidates in 1992, while the Liberals had five. Although all the Black Conservative candidates lost, they received high-profile and controversial endorsements from a number of Black celebrities and athletes including singer Shirley Bassey, soccer star John Barnes, Olympic swimmer Sharron Davies, and former Olympic champion Tessa Sanderson. Black Tory candidates also had to face racist attacks from their own base, where leaflets were circulated that urged voters not to vote for the "Conservative" Black candidates.[70]

Finally, it should be mentioned that just as Britain's past Black community activists and liberal political reformers had been influenced by developments in United States Black politics, so had those in Parliament. The Black and Asian members of Parliament, with the exception of Boateng, formed the Parliamentary Black Caucus (PBC), an organization analogous to the Congressional Black Caucus (CBC) in the United States. Indeed, the CBC played a strong role, in a comradely fashion, of helping the PBC form and sharing its experience in taking on similar tasks in the U.S. Congress. At the PBC inaugural in April 1989, a number of CBC members and some of their staff went to Britain and participated in a series of workshops, celebrations, and meetings with their British counterparts. The CBC members present were Ronald Dellums (D, CA), Charles Rangel (D, NY), John Conyers (D, MI), and George Crockett (D, MI).[71] PBC chair Bernie Grant enthusiastically welcomed the CBC members and others in the U.S. delegation, whom he referred to as "our kith and kin from across the water."[72]

The Black Members of Parliament had been meeting informally for about a year amid rampant rumors that they would form a caucus. After several months, they contacted the CBC for guidance and help. Lord Pitt, who was the sole Black representative in Parliament for a dozen years, declared at the inaugural: "This is a moment for which I've prayed. The election of four Black MPs in 1987 opened the door of opportunity for our people."[73] By 1995, however, both the Black members of Congress and Parliament had serious political setbacks. The 1994 congressional elections resulted in the control of Congress going to Republican conservatives, and one of their first tasks was to eliminate funding and staffing for the CBC. In Britain, the energy around the PBC fizzled, and by 1995 it no longer existed. Both groups of Black elected officials confront challenging times ahead as the major parties abandon any pretense of addressing Black interests and progressive concerns are marginalized.

Conclusion

As minority populations in their respective settings, African Americans and Afro-Britons have had to withstand majority attacks on their group interests and well-being. This has meant, in effect, that collective responses and political behavior have not only been desirable but necessary. In this sense, the group responses of the two communities have been remarkably similar. It would be a mistake, however, to overestimate the similarities. First, the U.S. Black community constitutes a much larger percentage of the population than the British Black community – 12 percent versus 1.6 percent. Also, the British Black community is even more fragmented by nationality groups both within the Caribbean sector and the African sector. While these differences may erode to a secondary or peripheral nature over time, particularly given the lack of distinction made by Whites and the political system, at present they are a factor to consider in grasping some of the obstacles to unity that exist.

Second, the British political system is much more rigid than that of the United States. Traditions are strong and the political culture is resistant to change. A cautionary note, however: that rigidity may be weakening, given the reality of global political and economic changes. Already, the Labour Party has been shaken from its traditional base as described above.

Third, how the balance between class and racial interests is viewed and acted out on the political stage is different in each country. In Britain, class consciousness is relatively high, even among Blacks who appear to have fashioned a political synthesis of sorts that links race and class as a political whole. For many, a Black identity is synonymous with a working-class identity. While the growth of a Black middle class may be producing some cracks in that framework, identity with working-class concerns is still strong. On the other hand, in the United States, the large and still growing class differences within the Black community are showing powerful signs of a major fracture between the Black middle class and the Black poor and underclass. A small, but not insignificant sector of Blacks has joined the conservative movement, mainly through the Republican Party, and is challenging social programs and agenda of liberal Blacks. These conservatives clearly separate their class interests as they perceive them from any racial interest. Indeed, most deny that there is any group racial interest at all.[74]

Despite these differences there are a number of factors driving the two Black communities along the same path. The rise of racism and anti-Black policies in Europe, in general, and in Britain and the United States, in particular, has the potential to unify the Black communities within their countries.[75] Internationally, the rise of racism also has the potential of bringing together a global coalition of people of color searching for common ground in the struggle for security and development.

Additionally, both communities appear to increasingly recognize the limits of electoral redress. While Black leaders on both sides of the ocean are not calling for an abandonment of involvement in electoral work, emphasis on base building at the community level and con-structing (or reconstructing) what some call the "civil society" is becoming a priority. It is acknowledged that as even the traditional liberal parties (i.e., the Democratic Party and Labour Party) cast off their liberal and progressive social agenda, it will be harder to win policy victories for the Black community unless that community is mobilized and working in coalition with those who have similar interests. Thus, party labels and affiliations will likely lose their relevance for Black communities in the period ahead as they have already for Whites.

In 1992, the election of Bill Clinton signaled the rise of the so-called new Democrats, which in practice has meant a distancing of the Democratic Party from its most loyal constituents, including Blacks, Latinos, and labor. As Clinton and Al Gore wrote, "Our policies are neither liberal nor conservative, nether Democratic nor Republican. They are new. They are different."[76] The Republican control of Congress has likely moved Clinton to the political Right, deepening the Black community's frustration with the Democratic Party. In 1994, the election of Tony Blair to head Labour reflects the same process of change happening in England to the Labour Party. Blair, who has frequently been compared to Clinton, was elected on the pledge that he would bring the party closer to the political middle and away from its traditional base in the trade unions. Abandoning what he views as the negative leftist image of the party, Blair declared: "We are the mainstream voice in politics today."[77] Blair – whom his opponents derisively call "Tony Blur" in reference to his hesitation to be nonspecific about his proposals and his attempt to walk the middle ground – says that the party must "break out of the past."[78] In Britain, to break with the Left is a direct hit on the Black community, which has had to locate itself on the left side of the political spectrum in its fight for Black and working-class interests.

In addition, for progressive Black politicians at the national level there may be little choice but to go back to the community because the possibility of further electoral expansion seems remote. In both the United States and Britain, those seats that could possibly be won by Black candidates, given the racial voting patterns of Whites, may be exhausted. In fact, the paradox may be that it will be Black Republicans and Conservatives who will gain in the near future. For both Black communities, it will be a case of going from protest to politics to community mobilization – what Bernie Grant has termed "extra-parliamentary activity"[79] – as the next stage of political empowerment. Yet it is this need for greater community mobilization within a context of increasing globalization that will require greater racial unity, domestic and international, than ever before. Thus, both communities will continue to find that as common interests remain, the reach of political solidarity across the ocean is not as far as one thinks.

Notes

1. Ira Katznelson, *Black Men, White Cities: Race, Politics, and Migration in the United States, 1900–30, and Britain, 1948–68* (Chicago: University of Chicago Press, 1973), p. 17.
2. In Britain, the term "Black" is sometimes used to describe only those of African descent, and at other times it refers to all people of color in the country. In this essay the first usage is applied unless specifically noted otherwise.
3. See Paul Gilroy, "The Black Atlantic as a Counterculture of Modernity," in Paul Gilroy, ed., *The Black Atlantic: Modernity and Double Consciousness* (New York: Verso, 1993), pp. 1–40.
4. Ronald Walters, *Pan Africanism in the African Diaspora: An Analysis of Modern Afrocentric Political Movements* (Detroit: Wayne State University Press, 1993), pp. 193–4.
5. Press release, *Census Bureau Announces Number of Americans in Poverty up for Fourth Year although Poverty Rate Unchanged; Household Income and Health Care Coverage Drop* (Washington, D.C.: U.S. Department of Commerce, October 6, 1994).
6. For an overview of poverty in the United States, see James Jennings, *Understanding the Nature of Poverty in Urban America* (Westport, CT: Praeger, 1994).

7. *The State of Black America, 1993* (New York: National Urban League, 1993), p. 168.

8. Press release, *Census Bureau Announces Number of Americans in Poverty up for Fourth Year.*

9. *The State of Black America, 1993*, p. 102.

10. Scott Minerbrook, "Home Ownership Anchors the Middle Class," *Emerge* (October 1993), p. 46.

11. Frank McCoy, "No Real Recovery for Black Jobs or Income," *Black Enterprise* (June 1994), p. 188.

12. Frank McCoy, "Can Clinton's Urban Policies Really Work?" *Black Enterprise* (June 1994), p. 182.

13. Figures quoted in Jonathan Marshall, "How Our War on Drugs Shattered the Cities," *Washington Post* (May 17, 1992), p. C1.

14. Rochelle Sharpe, "In Latest Recession, Only Blacks Suffered Net Employment Loss," *Wall Street Journal* (September 14, 1993).

15. For a more detailed analysis of the impact of the drug crisis on the Black community, see Clarence Lusane, *Pipe Dream Blues: Racism and the War on Drugs* (Boston: South End Press, 1991).

16. Keith Jennings, "Understanding the Persisting Crisis of Black Youth Unemployment," in James Jennings, ed., *Race, Politics, and Economic Development: Community Perspectives* (New York: Verso, 1992), p. 154.

17. Ibid.

18. Ibid.

19. *The Quality of Life Alternative Budget* (Washington, D.C.: Congressional Black Caucus, U.S. House of Representatives, 1987), p. 57.

20. *The State of Black America, 1993*, p. 183.

21. *The State of Black America, 1986* (New York: National Urban League, 1987), p. 214.

22. Steven Pearlstein and DeNeed L. Brown, "Black Teens Facing Worse Job Prospects," *Washington Post* (June 4, 1994).

23. David Owen, *Black People in Great Britain* (Coventry: Centre for Research in Ethnic Relations of the Economic and Social Research Council, 1994), p. 1.

24. Terri Sewell, *Black Tribunes: Black Political Participation in Britain* (London: Lawrence & Wishart, 1993), p. 17.

25. David Owen, *Ethnic Minorities in Great Britain: Economic Characteristics* (Coventry: Centre for Research in Ethnic Relations of the Economic and Social Research Council, March 1993), p. 8.

26. Owen, *Black People in Great Britain*, pp. 14–16.

27. A. Sivanandan, *Deadly Silence: Black Deaths in Custody* (London: Institute of Race Relations, 1991), p. 1.

28. Ibid., p. 3.

29. See Marc Mauer, *Young Black Americans and the Criminal Justice System: Five Years Later* (Washington, D.C.: Sentencing Project, October 1995), p. 3; and Jason DeParle, "Young Black Men in Capital Study Finds 42 Percent in Courts," *New York Times* (April 18, 1992).

30. "Violence in America," *JaxFax*, National Rainbow Coalition newsletter, (December 2, 1993).

31. For an analysis of the King rebellions and the ongoing confrontation between Black youth and the police, see Robert Gooding-Williams, ed., *Reading Rodney King/ Reading Urban Uprising* (New York: Routledge, 1993).

32. Marian FitzGerald, *Black People and Party Politics in Britain* (London: Runnymede Trust, 1987), p. 41.

33. Lerone Bennett, Jr., *Before the Mayflower: A History of Black America* (New York: Penguin Books, 1993), pp. 458–61; and Bruce A. Ragsdale and Joel D. Treese, *Black Americans in Congress, 1870–1989* (Washington, D.C.: U.S. Government Printing Office, 1990), p. 74.

34. See Eric Foner, "African Americans in Public Office during the Era of Reconstruction: A Profile," *Reconstruction*, vol. 2., no. 2 (1993), pp. 20–32.

35. Michael Dawson, *Behind the Mule: Race and Class in African-American Politics* (Princeton, NJ: Princeton University Press, 1994), p. 61.

36. Ibid., p. 10.

37. Sewell, *Black Tribunes*, pp. 22–3.

38. FitzGerald, *Black People and Party Politics*, p. 12.

39. Ibid., p. 13.

40. *Survey of Political Activity and Attitudes to Race Relations* (London: Greater London Council, 1985).

41. Zig Layton-Henry and Donley T. Studlar, "The Electoral Participation of Blacks and Asians: Integration or Alienation?", *Parliamentary Affairs* (Summer 1985), pp. 312–13; cited in Sewell, *Black Tribunes*, p. 32.

42. Sewell, *Black Tribunes*, p. 31.

43. FitzGerald, *Black People and Party Politics*, pp. 16–17.

44. Ibid, p. 27.

45. Ibid, p. 28.

46. John Roemer and Marta Sanchez-Beswick, "Can SOS Be Stopped?", *San Francisco Weekly* (August 24, 1994), pp. 13–15.

47. FitzGerald, *Black People and Party Politics*, p. 28.

48. Sewell, *Black Tribunes*, p. 61.

49. Ibid., p. 86.

50. FitzGerald, *Black People and Party Politics*, p. 37.

51. Ibid., p. 34.

52. Ibid., p. 35.

53. Sewell, *Black Tribunes*, pp. 78–9.

54. FitzGerald, *Black People and Party Politics*, pp. 20–1.

55. Ibid., p. 30.

56. Ibid., p. 31.

57. Ibid., p. 32.

58. Ibid.

59. Sewell, *Black Tribunes*, p. 102.

60. Ibid., p. 117.

61. Peter Fryer, *Staying Power: The History of Black People in Britain* (London: Pluto Press, 1984), pp. 290–1.

62. See *The Crisis* (January 1914), pp. 120–21 and *The Crisis* (March 1914), pp. 224–26; cited in ibid., p. 291.

63. Sewell, *Black Tribunes*, p. 14.

64. Ibid., p. 14.

65. Ibid, pp. 18–19.

66. Ibid., p. 13.

67. Ibid., p. 133.

68. Muhammad Anwar, *Race and Politics* (London: Tavistock Publications, 1986), pp. 165–66.

69. "The Politics of Race and Class in England: An Interview with Diane Abbott," *Point of View* (Winter 1988), p. 31.

70. Clarence Lusane, "England's Black Vote," *Black Political Agenda* (April 1992), p. 5.

71. Walters, *Pan Africanism in the African Diaspora*, p. 190.

72. Ibid., p. 191.

73. Sheila Rule, "British MP's Form Caucus to Advance Rights of Minorities," *New York Times* (April 3, 1989).

74. See Thomas Sowell, *Civil Rights: Rhetoric or Reality?* (New York: Morrow, 1984), as representative of this argument.

75. For an analysis of racism in Europe, see Liz Fekete and Frances Webber, *Inside*

Racist Europe (London: Institute of Race Relations, 1994), and the Institute of Race Relations's quarterly bulletin, *European Race Audit* (London).

76. Bill Clinton and Al Gore, *Putting People First: How We Can All Change America* (New York: Times Books, 1992), p. viii.

77. John Darnton, "British Labor Party Sheds Marx for Middle Class," *New York Times* (October 5, 1994).

78. Ibid.

79. Darcus Howe, "Darcus Howe Interviews Bernie Grant at the House of Commons," *Race Today* (January/February 1988), p. 10.

PART II

Empowering Black Communities in the United States

8

Black and Latino Coalitions: Prospects for New Social Movements in New York City

William W. Sales, Jr. and Roderick Bush

The potential for empowerment of Blacks and Latinos has increased as New York became a "minority" city. James Regalado and Gloria Martinez view political empowerment (including political coalition building, participation, representation, access, and influence) as a condition in which "a minority group becomes politically organized to such an extent that its concerns, agendas, and demands can no longer be ignored by current power groups."[1] The concept also includes the sense that such empowerment can be institutionalized and reproduced from one election to the next. This notion of empowerment is tied to the idea that Blacks and Latinos can effectively confront the mounting problems of their existence in urban America through electoral politics. This has proven to be no easy task. Nevertheless, there have been some strikingly positive developments in New York City. Since the early 1960s Latino and Black political strength has made it almost impossible for any Democratic politician to gain a citywide office without supporting civil rights.[2]

In the 1980s redistricting increased the number of Blacks and Latinos in the city council and the state assembly, and most important, this augmented electoral strength led to the election of David Dinkins as the first non-White mayor of New York City. Demographic changes reflected in increased electoral power have given the Latino community its first real presence in the corridors of power. Latinos now make up 25 percent of New York City's population, but only 15 percent of its registered voters (500,000 votes).[3] This emerging potential is all the more notable in the face of the national and local explosion of a White backlash, fueled by the eras of Ronald Reagan and Edward Koch. Latinos, who in the early 1980s showed a propensity for conservative voting, having turned out significantly for both Reagan and Koch, later began to shift their voting pattern toward Jesse Jackson and the Rainbow Coalition agenda in 1984, and even more forcefully in 1988. Dinkins won the mayoralty in 1989 with two-thirds of the Latino vote.[4] Nydia Velasquez won election in a newly created district in Brooklyn when Blacks and Latinos, neither alone constituting a majority, coalesced to elect her to Congress. In fact, it was the Black vote in the district that created her winning majority.[5] Another example of Black and Latino cooperation in the electoral arena is found in Brooklyn's 51st council district where Felix Ortiz was elected with support from heavily populated Latino Sunset Park and Black Red Hook.[6]

Yet despite these important electoral achievements serious problems are frequently reported, for instance, that Latinos feel they are treated as second-class citizens, even by Black elected officials. These officials sometimes forget the importance of building trust and bridges with Latinos in dispensing patronage and benefits, and thus play into divide-and-conquer schemes of more powerful interests. There may also be ideological divisions. Angelo Falcon, President of the Institute for Puerto Rican Policy, recognized that many Puerto Ricans belong to an emerging conservative bloc that opposed the Rainbow Coalition and supported Rudolph Giuliani. No previous Republican mayoral candidate had gotten more than one-third of the Latino vote, although some observers claim Giuliani's total was close to 40 percent.[7]

The mobilization of majority coalitions composed of Blacks and Latinos to gain elective office has not been easy. There are three immediate problems associated with structuring such coalitions: (1) intraethnic difficulties, (2) interethnic difficulties, and (3) problems associated with the restructuring of the capitalist political economy. In the literature, the traditional problems associated with building unity between Black and Latino communities are associated with cultural differences, lack of a strong tradition of cooperation, and the opportunistic behavior of traditional political entrepreneurs who have provided leadership to these communities in the electoral arena.[8] Milga Morales-Nadal gives an example of one of the issues of greatest divergence between Blacks and Latinos. She describes School District 17 in a neighborhood in Brooklyn, Crown Heights, where there is some contention between Blacks and Latinos over the issue of bilingual education. Blacks think that Latinos are receiving special treatment. Bilingual classes are smaller, and thus they are seen as a privilege. Some Latino teachers, according to Morales-Nadal, complain about the mistreatment of Latino students by Black teachers. So far this tension pales in terms of the Black and Jewish conflict, the most visible example of social conflict in Crown Heights. Morales-Nadal reports that there was no significant Latino participation in the Black and Jewish confrontation over the accidental killing of seven-year-old Gavin Cato.[9]

At the national level barriers to Black and Latino coalition are considerable. The Black and Latino populations of New York City have experienced increasing ethnic differentiation since immigration from the Caribbean and Latin America has greatly increased due, in part, to the 1965 immigration reforms and the impact of "structural adjustment" on the economies of their homelands. Different components of these populations have varying perceptions of nationality, communal allegiances, citizenship, and perceived capacity to participate in electoral politics. This point has been demonstrated in the work of Charles Green and Basil Wilson, and Rodolfo de la Garza et al.[10] For both communities the notion of an undifferentiated, culturally and ethnically homogeneous community is erroneous.

In discussing future possibilities for Black and Latino coalition, it is important to desegregate the Latino population in terms of ethnicity, class, race, nationality, culture, specific histories associated with their homelands, and reasons for immigration. There is a large number of groups who are included in the designation Latino: Puerto Ricans, Dominicans, Cubans, Salvadoreans, Mexican Americans (or Chicanos), Mexicanos, Nicaraguans, Panamanians, Colombians, and Venezuelans. The barriers to coalition seem less salient with Puerto Rican–Black relationships, as may be the case with the Dominican–Black and Dominican–Puerto Rican bonds.[11]

The greatest potential for coalition has traditionally resided in the Black and Puerto Rican communities, for they are closest in most of the variables cited above. For the immediate future what is significant is that the fastest-growing Latino grouping, the Dominicans, also share with African Americans significant affinities, which in a racist society will probably strengthen rather than weaken over time. Certainly, among Latinos the Dominican community has the strongest of cultural, class, and linguistic affinities with Puerto Ricans. To the extent that there is a growing involvement in electoral and protest politics in the Dominican community, the factors fueling this involvement will push Blacks and Puerto Ricans and Dominicans closer together, not farther apart. For those Puerto Ricans and Dominicans who cannot physically "pass" for white, they may find themselves much more "naturalized" into the African-American community than assimilated into white middle-class America. This reality may encourage them to hold onto their ethnic identity far longer than previous generations of immigrants from Europe.

The electoral potential of a Black and Latino coalition in New York City remains as a possible rather than actual power bloc since Blacks and Latinos are still underrepresented among registered voters, elected officials, and in the decision-making bureaucracy of the city. It is important to recognize that while both Blacks and Latinos are underrepresented, African Americans are notably better off in all of these areas than Latinos. In addition, the needs of Latinos have often been submerged under those of the Black community, and when some of these needs are met for Blacks it is unjustifiably assumed that the condition of Latinos has also been ameliorated. This phenomenon has given rise to a demand from Latinos that they become visible as a distinct entity in the political process whose agenda must also be explicitly addressed. Some of this unrealized potential is rooted in the inability of a stable and extensive Black and Latino coalition to emerge. Moreover, we must question the extent to which the latent power of these two communities can be galvanized if electoral politics remains the primary arena of focus and contention of the established community leadership.

To be sure, racism has had an important impact on the capacity of Blacks and Latinos to coalesce around political issues. There has been a tendency in the Black experience to think of political coalition in terms of powerful groups in the White community such as the Jewish community or organized labor. Blacks have not traditionally viewed Latinos as power brokers and thus have more often sought coalition possibilities with other groups. Latinos have been subjected to a direct or indirect process of colonization by powers committed to White superiority and Black subordination. To the extent that Latinos have internalized racist assumptions of their colonial past, it is difficult to accept a Black person as a decision maker, an elected official, or a prominent businessperson. With the exception of Cuba, the Dominican Republic and Puerto Rico, almost no Blacks have achieved prominence in any Latin-American country in government, politics or business. In Latin America, politicians are traditionally visualized only as those whose skin is white.[12]

As a result of the lack of power Black and Latino communities have become increasingly impoverished and marginalized. Due to restructuring of the capitalist world economy, New York City lost about 350,000 jobs under Dinkins's administration. At the same time, approximately one million New Yorkers were on welfare, while the city was characterized by inferior schools and rampant crime. Michael Tomasky's assessment of Dinkins's "mosaic" suggests that while he could not be faulted for these kinds of problems, his administration's response to it was totally inept.[13] In the arena of electoral politics, the impact of capitalism's restructuring has produced distressing tendencies on the part of leaders. In conceding that capitalism cannot be fundamentally altered to meet the material needs of all the members of their communities, they approach politics as a zero-sum game. They exploit ethnic allegiances at every turn and engage in traditional clubhouse politics. This behavior, in turn, reinforces divisiveness and cynicism at the grassroots level and contributes to the political weakening of both Black and Latino political leadership.

In New York City there are notable examples of the kind of behavior mentioned above. In the 1985 mayoral primary the Black and Puerto Rican leadership split over the endorsement of a primary challenger to the incumbent Democratic mayor, Ed Koch. Rather than support Herman Badillo, a candidate who had a real chance of unseating Koch, the Harlem leadership working within the Coalition for a Just New York eschewed coalition with Latinos to settle old scores with Badillo. It backed one of its own who had no chance of victory, the clubhouse hack Herman "Denny" Farrell. While the political leadership in Harlem could have been expected to behave this way, the insurgent African-American politicians in Brooklyn like Al Vann and Major Owens ultimately abandoned principle and supported Farrell, reinforcing the suspicion and distrust of the Latino community. Badillo consequently ran with Giuliani on a "fusion" ticket during the 1993 mayoral election but he lost and Latinos stuck with Dinkins.

In the 1989 mayoral election the Black and Latino coalition was crucial in making David Dinkins the first Black mayor of America's largest city. Latinos expected their contribution to the Dinkins victory would be proportionately acknowledged with patronage and attention from the mayor. Threats to the Dinkins coalition included the feeling of Latinos that their community got too few appointments under Dinkins and, in this respect, they were no better off than under Koch. There were notable disappointments with the Dinkins administration's lack of concern for the needs of their communities and the dearth of his appointment of Latinos to crucial decision-making positions. Falcon identifies additional problems that Latinos had with the Dinkins administration, including shutting out his liaison with the Latino community from the real decision-making process, cutting off funds for high-profile projects in the Bronx, and generally poor attention given to the needs of Latino neighborhoods. On August 5,

1993, Bronx Borough President Fernando Ferrer sued the Dinkins administration for the conditions of the highways and streets in the Bronx.[14]

In the 1993 mayoral election, despite serious reservations and some premature press reports that Latinos would abandon Dinkins, the Latino vote remained loyal to Dinkins. Despite reports to the contrary, their support was not down 5 percent from the 67 percent of 1989; if anything the most accurate reports indicate that Dinkins received about 74 percent of the Latino vote.[15] Both the Black and Latino turnouts were slightly down from 1989. On the other hand, the White vote for Giuliani increased by 7 percent. The slightly smaller Black and Latino turnouts in crucial election districts were enough to allow the Republican challenger, Rudolph Giuliani, to reverse his defeat of 1989 and make Dinkins a one-term mayor.[16]

Mostly recently, the political leadership of both communities parted company around the project to construct a major supermarket in East Harlem. The established political and religious leadership of Central Harlem broke ranks with Puerto Rican leadership in East Harlem to push through approval for the construction of a Pathmark supermarket, which many local Latino businessmen and politicians felt would have a devastating impact on the smaller Latino-owned supermarkets in East Harlem. Ironically, the deciding vote was cast by the first-elected Dominican member of the city council, who broke ranks with Puerto Rican political leaders at the eleventh hour.[17] The redefined empowerment zone in New York City that now excludes previously included sections of the Bronx has also soured relationships between Black Harlem politicos and their Latino Bronx counterparts.[18]

It must be noted that the difficulties and the behavior outlined above are merely the end product of selfish individuals or narrow-minded leadership. Both the political and economic structure of New York and the larger society tend to produce and reproduce this kind of counterproductive behavior in the arena of electoral politics. The electoral sphere, however, cannot at one and the same time respond to the demands of Blacks and Latinos and retrench the public sector as required by the restructuring process of capitalism. Some degree of electoral influence has failed to force municipal government to meet pressing material needs of our communities; consequently, it cannot be the main arena of our struggle for liberation. While political entrepreneurs providing electoral leadership may at times support and even encourage coalition, they do so opportunistically in order to get elected or reelected without lasting commitment to foster and institutionalize the coalition. It is to the arena of activism and protest that one must turn to find the best examples of Black and Latino cooperation, and it is upon these building blocks that effective coalitions might be constructed for the future.

While the tradition of Black and Latino coalition has not yet firmly institutionalized itself at the level of electoral leadership, there are some radical and activist organizations that uphold such a tradition. This tradition is at least a quarter of a century old in New York City and is one of the most important legacies of the 1960s. The stimulus for Black and Latino coalition emerged out of commonly shared objectives associated with both the operation of the metropolitan economy and the functioning of public institutions in relation to both communities. This is especially true in that while living in separate neighborhoods, Blacks and Latinos have had to use the same schools, hospitals, and city bureaucracies and thus have come to share the same enemies.

One of the earliest examples of Black and Latino cooperation in New York City was associated with the student and community mobilization around the Open Enrollment Struggle (OES) in the City University of New York. Initiated in the period between 1968 and 1970, the OES saw its birth at campus-based institutions that brought together Black and Puerto Rican students, faculty, and other staff to pressure for unrestricted entrance of people of color and others to the CUNY system. One example of such cooperation was the Black and Puerto Rican Student Faculty and Counselor Coalition at Queens College (CUNY). There was a similar organization at City College in 1969, and the model rapidly spread to other CUNY campuses. In addition, the Open Enrollment movement of 1969 in CUNY led to fundamental curriculum reforms in the area of racial and ethnic studies, while vastly expanding the presence of Black and Latino faculty on CUNY campuses.[19]

This tradition of cooperation has continued up to the present and is much stronger today than ever. One of the most important developments in the CUNY student mobilization is the role played by student leadership from the immigrant Caribbean and Latino communities. In the struggle to preserve CUNY, there is the recognition that public higher education in New York City has been one of the most important vehicles for immigrant upward mobility. That avenue of advancement is being fundamentally threatened and with it the dreams and aspirations of the most recent generation of immigrants. There have been two major budgetary crises in the CUNY system within the past decade. Each crisis has seen the mobilization of student coalitions grounded in the unity between Black and Latino students. Joining with progressive White and Asian students, this coalition has exhibited a militancy and a capability to engage in civil disobedience on campuses and in the streets not seen since the 1960s. The present Black and Latino students in CUNY are even more capable protesters than those of the 1960s, although somewhat behind that generation in their political sophistication.

The principal instance of Black and Latino cooperation in Brooklyn occurred with the 1968 Ocean Hill-Brownsville struggle for community control of the schools. As in most cases of Black and Latino cooperation, the cooperating parties were African Americans and Puerto Ricans (two groups that occupy similar positions in the social structure of New York City). According to Luis Fuentes, the first Puerto Rican superintendent of schools on the Lower East Side, the community control movement was a community response to forced integration. The school system wanted to move Black and Latino students from their schools and place them in all-White schools to achieve "what they call integration." Fuentes argues that parents wanted their schools to be as effective as they had been in Puerto Rico or in the South. They wanted schools that were responsive and teachers and administrators who would be accountable to the community and to the public. The parents wanted quality education, "not integration" (at least not in the sense that it was being proposed). The strongest opposition to the community control movement, Fuentes states, came from the United Federation of Teachers (UFT). The parents did not want to run the schools as the UFT claimed; they simply wanted to develop a system of working together that did not exist until that time.[20] Fuentes maintains that it is no small matter that the parents involved in the community control movement were influenced by the Black Panther Party, the Young Lords Party, and all of the movements that were part of a general mood to move away from poverty. Fuentes gives major credit to the Black movement for social justice and civil rights. "The rest of us," Fuentes adds, "simply followed."[21]

The fight for community control in Ocean Hill-Brownsville represented a major ideological and power struggle. The activists and teachers who came together in the African-American Teachers Association (ATA) challenged the liberal integrationist orthodoxy of the United Federation of Teachers. They refused the de facto dismantling of neighborhood schools and challenged the belief of White teachers that Black students could not be expected to be high achievers because they were afflicted with a "culture of poverty." The ATA, under the leadership of Leslie Campbell (now Jitu Weusi), argued that White teachers could not teach Black children, not because of a culture of poverty but because of "an unwillingness to respect a Black lower class that was economically deprived but culturally rich."[22] The ATA argued that it was the White, middle-class values of the teachers that reflected a profound cultural impoverishment in their emphasis on "making it" in society as it is, pursuit of material gain, and individualism and competitiveness.

Similar efforts continue today. Most recently, the Caribbean Cultural Center has organized Azebache,[23] a Black and Latino youth group. Azebache is composed of young people representing youth organizations in largely Latino Washington Heights and African-American and Caribbean Central Brooklyn. It organized and held a conference on "Steps of Resistance" in June 1995 at Medgar Evers College (CUNY). This was a training conference bringing together young community organizers with veterans from traditional resistance organizations like the Black Panther Party, the Young Lords, the Student Non-violent Coordinating Committee, The East, and the trade unions.

A host of ad hoc coalitions in Bushwick, Washington Heights, the Bronx, and East Harlem has continued the trend first seen in the mobilizations around the racist murders of Michael Griffith in Howard Beach and Yusuf Hawkins in Bensonhurst. The City-Wide Coalition Against Police Violence and the activities of the Puerto Rican Congress also demonstrate that Latinos are prepared to give leadership in these struggles and to demand parity in the activist leadership on these shared issues of Black and Latino concerns.[24]

Support work around the issue of political prisoners has been another important area of Black and Latino cooperation that goes back almost two decades. Four busloads of supporters from the largely Dominican neighborhood of Washington Heights attended the massive rally in Philadelphia for Black political prisoner Mumia Abu Jamal. Congresswoman Nydia Velasquez also broke ground in this area in the electoral arena when she issued a statement of support for Mumia's right to a new trial. This coalition effort around political prisoners grows out of earlier work that dates back to the uprising of a largely Black and Latino prison population at Attica State Prison in New York. It also reflects the commitment that brought a contingent of a couple of thousand Latinos to the rally in Central Park Against Apartheid and to the Free Nelson Mandela rally.[25] The December 12th Movement has joined with Puerto Rican and Native American activists to achieve a breakthrough in getting some measure of recognition internationally on issues pertaining to America's Black, Latino, and Native-American political prisoners. In the area of

political prisoners, grassroots activism has forced some elected politi-
cians to take a position on an issue most would rather avoid. Bronx
Congressman Jose Serrano has lent his support to the cause of Puerto
Rican political prisoners, as has the Black and Latino membership of
the New York City council, which has also indicated its support for
Black political prisoners.

Environmental racism has also been the basis for cooperative efforts
in New York City between Blacks and Latinos. Grassroots coalitions
in the Bronx, Manhattan, and Brooklyn have won important victories
in the struggle against urban pollution and toxic dumping in inner-
city neighborhoods. The South Bronx Clean Air Coalition has led the
fight against a medical waste incinerator in the South Bronx. On
Manhattan's West Side, Blacks, Puerto Ricans, and Dominicans have
coalesced in the successful struggle for neighborhood compensation
for the sewage plant constructed in Riverside Park. In Williamsburg
and Fort Greene, Latinos have led a similar struggle against the
projected incinerator scheduled for construction at the old Brooklyn
Navy Yard site.

The public service unions in New York City have a large number
of African Americans and growing numbers of Latinos in their
memberships. Paralleling the racial and ethnic transformation of their
memberships over the past three decades has been an increasing
willingness of these unions to champion and become a part of
interracial and ethnic coalitions that lobby for government social
welfare and employment programs of direct benefits to these communities. Demographic changes have been reflected in the emergence
of Black leadership in unions, like Stanley Hill's presidency of District
Council 37 of AFSCME (American Federation of State, County, and
Municipal Employees), District 65 of the United Auto Workers, and
Local 1199 and Local 420, both locals of Black and Puerto Rican
Hospital workers. As Puerto Rican membership has increased in the
public service sector, their presence and role in these unions has also
increased.[26] Dennis Rivera's rise to the presidency of Local 1199
reflects not only the numerical growth of the Latino presence but the
maturity of Puerto Rican leadership to the point of extending leadership and support to the Black and Latino coalition.[27] Rivera was a
major player in the 1988 Jesse Jackson primary victory and in the
significant shift of Latino voters to Jackson between 1984 and 1988.[28]
The Rainbow Coalition's initial efforts in 1984 with Jackson were
helped in New York City by an insurgent group of Puerto Ricans for
Jackson, with Puerto Rican leaders like Jose Serrano, who was then a
state assemblyman, and city councilman Jose Rivera.[29]

Some activists see the necessity for a bridge between activism, protest, and the electoral arena. Their argument is that protest tends to be immediate, parochial, and ad hoc. Its weakness is in its lack of permanence in terms of issues and organizations. This weakness lends itself to co-optation, piecemeal solutions, and a tendency for the status quo to dominate. These activists feel that a third party solution might open up electoral politics in such a way that lasting institutional change is possible. The Campaign for a New Tomorrow under the leadership of Jesse Jackson's former campaign manager, Ron Daniels, has attempted to build the preconditions for a third party upon the notion of a coalition of people of color. While two member of its coordinating committee are Latino, this preparty effort thus far is still attempting to pull together a solid core of African-American support. Daniels's efforts parallel earlier attempts associated with the Majority Party with which Dennis Rivera was associated as an organizer, and those of Jitu Weusi to get a third party on the ballot in New York State. All of these efforts at least paid lip service to the notion of Black and Latino coalition as a prerequisite for effective electoral action to transcend the limitations of two-party politics.[30]

Conclusion

Without suggesting a rigid dichotomy, it has been our position that the arena of protest and civil disobedience is a more fruitful source of Black and Latino empowerment. Our reading of the post-World War II history of New York suggests that more progress at coalition building and empowerment has transpired at the grassroots than in the electoral arena. Why has this been the case? We concur with political scientist Marcus Pohlmann who argues that

> in the United States, both the election process and political party process are inherently biased against fundamental redistributive change. . . . A number of . . . [practices in the electoral arena] continue to institutionalize race and class inequalities. Registration and campaign finance procedures are prejudiced against working and lower-class people, and a two-party system guarantees that the major parties will be virtually incapable of educating and leading the public in any direction that would fundamentally challenge the socioeconomic status quo.[31]

We also recognize, along with Pohlmann, that electoral mobilization has led to control over some institutional levers of political power enabling some Blacks and Latinos to improve their life situations. It has provided an organizational structure for sustaining the vigilance and pressure needed to perpetuate those gains. It is certainly true that the right to vote is a fundamental democratic right worthy of pursuit in its own right and essential in developing the consciousness of the people in their struggle for a lasting empowerment. But Pohlmann is also correct when he concludes that in the American context the electoral process alone would not appear to be a sufficient mechanism for achieving self-determination and liberation.

Political scientist Hanes Walton, Jr., has echoed Ralph Bunche in warning of the limitations of making the vote a fetish.[32] Walton argues that traditionally electoral institutions have functioned to neutralize the Black vote politically. Wherever one sees low registration rates or low turnout rates in elections for African Americans, Walton cautions that this might be better explained not as apathy or ignorance but as the end product of a process of political neutralization that proceeds through legal as well as extralegal means.[33] American political institutions are biased against any but incremental, evolutionary change. They tend to be unresponsive to groups whose established electoral institutions are so structured that in their normal operation they neutralize the potential power of insurgents and facilitate the re-creation of the status quo. James Regalado posits a two-tiered theory of pluralism and notes that it provides for only marginal inclusion of minorities in the political process. The subordinate status of minorities in political life, in fact, is emphasized where pluralism "exists in form but not fully in fact for some groups."[34] Two-tiered pluralism reflects, for Latinos and African Americans, an institutionally subordinate status in political and economic life; thus the theory represents an important theoretical and political dilemma for American liberal democracy.[35] In the postindustrial period, the city and its political institutions have almost no latitude to make concessions to the pressing needs of increasingly impoverished urban dwellers through the normal operation of local electoral institutions. In this context directing the bulk of political activity into the electoral arena diverts pressure away from the real centers of power and demobilizes communities as cynicism appears in response to electoral victories that produce no programmatic payoffs.

Limiting political activity to the electoral arena facilitates the co-optation of grassroots leadership or the emergence of an elite rooted in officeholding or the public service bureaucracy. In fact, this is a major way in which class differentiation is advanced in poor, exploited communities of color. The electoral arena allows for the identification of insurgent leaders who are targeted for co-optation by the real centers of power. Once their class standing and standard of living are rooted in officeholding, they develop a stake in the status quo and can no longer give leadership to their constituencies without jeopardizing their class privilege.

True threats to institutionalized power tend to be mounted outside of the normal channels of political discourse. Under these circumstances, groups that do not have routine access to institutionalized power have as a major weapon only their ability to disrupt the normal operation of the system.[36] It is our opinion that the essence of Black and Latino coalition building is to enhance the ability of both groups through a combination of protest, civil disobedience, and tactics in the electoral arena to institutionalize the capabilities of these communities to disrupt the normal operation of society's political and economic institutions whenever their vital interests are threatened. There is in New York City a long tradition of Black and Latino grassroots activism out of which such a disruptive potential can mature and grow.

Notes

1. James A. Regalado and Gloria Martinez, "Reapportionment and Coalition Building: A Case Study of Informal Barriers to Latino Empowerment in Los Angeles County," in Roberto E. Villarreal and Norma G. Hernandez, eds., *Latinos and Political Coalitions: Political Empowerment for the 1990s* (New York: Praeger, 1991), p. 131.

2. Editorial, "Rainbow's End," *The Nation*, vol. 1257, no. 17 (November 22, 1993), p. 609.

3. Eric Pooley, "Dave's Latin Test," *New York*, vol. 26, no. 44 (August 23, 1993), p. 14.

4. Andy Logan, "Two Percent Solution," *The New Yorker*, vol. 69, no. 32 (November 15, 1993), p. 53.

5. Interview with Utrice Leid, *The City Sun* (August 27, 1995).

6. Interview with David Winyard, Office of Councilman Felix Ortiz (August 31, 1995).

7. Pooley, "Dave's Latin Test," p. 14. See note 15.

8. James Jennings, "The Puerto Rican Community: Its Political Background," in Chris Garcia, ed., *Latinos and the Political System* (Notre Dame, IN: Notre Dame University Press, 1988), pp. 75–8.

9. Interview with Dr. Milga Morales-Nadal, Office of the President, Brooklyn College of the City University of New York (August 29, 1995).

10. See Charles Green and Basil Wilson, *The Struggle for Black Empowerment in New York City* (New York: Praeger, 1989); and Rodolfo de la Garza et al., *Latino Voices: Mexican, Puerto Rican, and Cuban Perspectives on American Politics* (Boulder, CO: Westview Press, 1992).

11. Pooley, "Dave's Latin Test," p. 14.

12. Interview with Esperanza Martel, Washington Heights, New York City (September 4, 1995).

13. Michael Tomasky, "Identity Politics in New York City: The Tawdry Mosaic," *The Nation,* vol. 256, no. 24 (June 21, 1993), p. 864.

14. "Rainbow's End", p. 608; also Pooley, "Dave's Latin Test," p. 15.

15. Angelo Falcon has nevertheless raised doubts about polls that report that Giuliani received 40 percent of the Latino vote. These assertions are based, he says, on exit polls that are limited methodologically by language problems. In addition, Falcon was able to ascertain that these exit polls have a margin of error of +/− 10 percentage points. After an exhaustive analysis of returns from Latino election districts, the Institute for Puerto Rican Policy gave Giuliani no more than 26 percent of the Latino vote. Interview with Angelo Falcon (September 6, 1995).

16. Pooley, "Dave's Latin Test," p. 14.

17. *The New York Times* (April 24, 1995), p. B3.

18. The case of Nelson Antonio Denis should be mentioned here. Denis, who opposed the East Harlem Democratic machine, ran for the seat of recently deceased boss Angelo Del Toro. The Democratic county machine joined with the established Latino party leadership to topple his candidacy. He was seen as too much of an insurgent, especially given his commitment to a Black and Latino coalition. Interview with Utrice Leid (August 27, 1995).

19. Andres Torres, *Between Melting Pot and Mosaic: African Americans and Puerto Ricans in the New York Political Economy* (Philadelphia: Temple University Press, 1995), p. 135.

20. See James Jennings and Francisco Chapman, "The Community Control Movement," excerpts from an interview with Luis Fuentes in *Critica* (August 1995).

21. Ibid., p. 8.

22. See Jerald Podiar, " 'White' Values, 'Black' Values: The Ocean Hill-Brownsville Controversy and New York City Culture, 1965–1975," *Radical History Review*, vol. 59 (1994), pp. 36–59.

23. The name Azebache refers to an amulet used by Africans and their descendants to protect small children from harm. It is an African ritual whose practice is also found in Puerto Rico. Interview with Lumumba Bandele (September 5, 1995).

24. Interview with S. E. Anderson, Network of Black Organizers (August 26, 1995).

25. Interview with Esperanza Martel (September 4, 1995).

26. Torres, *Between Melting Pot and Mosaic*, pp. 77, 116.

27. Interview with Utrice Leid (August 27, 1995).

28. *The Nation*, vol. 256, no. 24 (June 21, 1993), p. 862.

29. Torres, *Between Melting Pot and Mosaic*, p. 204.

30. Interview with Mary France, Campaign for a New Tomorrow (September 4, 1995).

31. Marcus Pohlmann, *Black Politics in Conservative America* (New York: Longman, 1992), p. 132.

32. Hanes Walton, Jr., *Invisible Politics: Black Political Behavior* (Albany, NY: State University of New York Press, 1985) p. 73.

33. Ibid., p. 77.

34. See the review of Rodney Hero's work *Latinos and the United States Political System: Two-Tiered Pluralism* (Philadelphia: Temple University Press, 1992) by James A. Regalado in *American Political Science Review*, vol. 88, no. 3 (September 1994), p. 766.

35. Ibid.

36. Charles Tilly, *From Mobilization to Revolution* (Reading, MA: Addison-Wesley, 1978), pp. 115–16.

9

Black Neoconservatives in the United States: Responding with Progressive Coalitions

Lewis A. Randolph

Black neoconservatives of today are not actually "new" in terms of their message of self-reliance, supporting Black businesses and extolling the virtues of personal responsibility. However, the strategy of trying to organize the African-American community from the "outside" is a new twist that is different from that practiced by Booker T. Washington and his Tuskegee machine more than a hundred years ago. The other new twist that the current Black neoconservatives have employed and that is detrimental to the well-being of the African-American community is the reckless willingness to imply that the so-called Black underclass is the cause of social and economic problems of Black America.

The Black neoconservative agenda for the African-American community generally consists of the following positions: first, do away with affirmative action; second, follow the "Booker T. Washington approach" to uplift the Black poor; third, do not rely on government to address race problems in America; fourth, focus exclusively on self-help programs and activities for resolving problems in the African-American community; and finally, demand that the African-American middle class take responsibility for instructing the Black poor about morals and family values as a way to fundamentally assist them in escaping poverty.

Black neoconservatism has a long history in American politics. A strand of conservatism was evident during the New Deal and in earlier periods. The leading Black conservative during the New Deal was the journalist George Schuyler. A cynical social critic, Schuyler not only opposed the New Deal but also would later run for Congress in New York as a candidate for the Conservative Party on a platform opposing civil rights. Although Schuyler was a former supporter of Black nationalist causes and a former member of the Socialist Party, he eventually became disenchanted with socialism and became a "committed conservative."[1] Schuyler, as columnist for the *Pittsburgh Courier*, a major Black newspaper during this era, used his column to espouse a strident conservative philosophy.[2]

Schuyler and other less notable Black neoconservatives were eclipsed during the New Deal period because the African-American political leadership was aligned with the emerging Democratic sector of the American voting electorate. African-American Democratic politicians along with Black intellectuals who emerged during this period were more liberally inclined than Black neoconservatives and pursued policies that sought to eradicate segregation. This sector also demanded increased governmental intervention into the political and social arenas on behalf of those Blacks who were repeatedly being victimized by racist violence because of the state's failure to protect the lives and rights of its Black citizens.[3] Thus, an implicit alliance between liberal and left Black intellectuals in resonance with a liberal Black electorate, and an emerging White moderate electorate as a dominant political force, considerably weakened Black neo-conservatism.

The Civil Rights Era

Black conservative politics was relatively inert during the Civil Rights period in the 1950s and 1960s. One factor that might explain this situation, especially in the South, was that both parties excluded the participation of Blacks at the state and local level of their respective organizations in many parts of the country, even though a few Blacks had attempted to join the Dixicrat party in 1948.[4] Given the blatant hostility directed toward Blacks in general, there were no incentives in the 1950s for Black neoconservatives to support publicly the causes of the Dixicrats. And certainly they would have been socially and economically shunned by the Black community. Another factor that may have contributed to a dormant period of Black conservative politics was the emergence of widespread "massive resistance," associated with the Civil Rights Movement. Conservative forces in the African-American community were also discouraged from opposing the Civil Rights Movement because of the movement's religious tones and the conscious moral appeal to White America to correct social injustices inflicted on Southern Blacks. Although some Black ministers such as the Reverend J. H. Jackson, president of the Black National Baptist Convention, publicly denounced the sit-in movements and Martin Luther King, Jr.'s crusade of nonviolence for racial equality, and some like Schuyler opposed the Civil Rights Movement, most Black ministers were supportive of the movement.[5]

Black neoconservatives during the 1950s tended to support the national Republican Party, but with major qualifications. Most Black neoconservatives during this period probably found it politically unacceptable to support the "massive resistance" counterstrategy to desegration adopted by White conservatives. Some Republican leaders, such as U.S. Senator Barry Goldwater, opposed the Civil Rights Act of 1964 by insisting that this kind of legislation was an abridged and unwarranted intrusion on individual rights and a violation of states' rights. This position, however, forced some Black neoconservatives to support the national Democratic presidential candidates. As one Black Republican and conservative, Clarence Townes, Jr., explained, he was forced to support Lyndon Johnson for president because of Goldwater's position:

> For Virginia Negroes, the Republican National Convention in San Francisco held little hope. Senator Barry Goldwater, who had voted against the 1964 Civil Rights Bill, was nominated on the first ballot. Though his past civil rights record was creditable and he promised to uphold the law, Negroes looked upon him as against civil rights. Clarence Townes, Jr., a Richmond Negro representing the Virginia G.O.P. as an alternate delegate (a history-making precedent, as it is believed he was the first of his race to do so in either party since the turn of the century), openly stated that he could not follow his fellow delegates as they voted for Goldwater, 20 to 1.[6]

This suggests, however, that this earlier version of Black conservatism had a pragmatic and philosophical orientation that allowed its supporters to work with liberals.

The 1980s and New Challenges from the Right

Several factors contributed to the revival of Black conservative politics during the 1980s. A sense of crisis in national and local Black leadership did emerge as a result of a loss of charismatic leaders during the post-civil rights era. The deaths of Martin Luther King, Jr.,

Malcolm X, Fannie Lou Hamer, and others created a leadership vacuum. Additionally, Black leadership representing the liberal and Democratic Party section of the U.S. political spectrum found itself ineffective in responding to a plethora of social and economic problems. The failure of Black leaders to articulate a lucid agenda that included solutions for pressing problems such as crime in the African-American community, teen pregnancy, and the problems of poor people enabled Black neoconservatives to take advantage of the crisis and dominate Black political discourse on issues critical to African Americans.

Black Republicans who were also moderates and not hostile to the overall civil rights agenda and policies such as affirmative action, such as Edward Brooke, William Coleman, and Arthur Fletcher, were deposed and replaced by more stridently conservative individuals. This point is made by political scientists Robert Smith and Hanes Walton, Jr.:

> Many black traditional Republicans, while accepting in general the Party's conservative principles, worked hard to have it deal with the plight of African Americans. Senator Edward Brooke in his book *Challenge of Change* discusses his fidelity to traditional Republican conservatism but also how he and other black Republicans worked to have the Party use the powers of government to eradicate the problems facing blacks that grew out of racism and discrimination. Thus while the bashing of liberal leadership occurred, traditional black Republicans were for the most part also excluded from the administration.[7]

The exclusion of moderate Black Republicans and lack of access to an emergent right wing in the Republican Party accelerated the rise of more ideological Black neoconservatives and the demise of the traditional or pragmatic Black neoconservatives.

Still another related factor that led to the renaissance of Black conservative politics was the elections of Presidents Ronald Reagan and George Bush. The Reagan and Bush presidential elections enabled Black neoconservatives to gain access to the Oval Office and obtain political appointments to various federal departments and agencies. The Reagan/Bush appointees were able to solidify their power base and thus become the new Black "gatekeepers" in Washington, D.C. Moreover, these new appointees were constantly paraded over the airwaves spreading their conservative messages. The organic and neoconservative Black leaders were frequently sought after by most of the television talk shows and invited to air their conservative views.

In addition, public affair programs ensured that "new" Black neoconservative views were represented on most of their segments involving race, social welfare issues, and affirmative action. Black neoconservatives of the ideological bent, rather than the traditional pragmatists, were utilized by conservative news outlets but also liberal programs seeking to show "balance" in their reporting.

A shift in the voting electorate's political attitudes was another factor that revived Black conservatism. White voters began supporting and electing more ideologically conservative candidates in both parties. In some cases this resurgent conservatism was reflected in white support for a few Black neoconservatives. In Virginia, for example, there has been an increasing number of new Black neoconservatives entering the political arena. In 1983, Roy West, a staunch Black neoconservative, was elected to the city council of Richmond and subsequently to the post of mayor. West's election is significant because it led to the defeat of a liberal Black councilwoman, Willie Dell, and thus destabilized a growing African-American influence in the city council. West aligned with the White conservative city council members in return for their support to select him as mayor.

Once West was elected mayor, he consistently voted with the White minority against the Black majority. As mayor he undermined the Black voting bloc on the city council and along with White minority members reversed the direction of the city's economic development policies for Richmond.[8] Moreover, West received financial backing from a new political group in Richmond called the John Mercer Langston Fund, an organization mainly made up of young professional Black neoconservatives who support conservative candidates and causes.[9] The political implication of West's support was that it revealed the existence of a political coalition between Black neoconservatives and White Republicans.

This brief historical overview raises several questions. First, are Black neoconservative views consistent with the dominant White conservative views in America? Second, are African Americans who publicly espouse conservative views genuinely conservatives, or are they simply engaging in "clientele" politics? Third, are Black neoconservatives a viable political alternative force that can no longer be ignored by either White or Black liberals? Also, what are the potential long-term consequences of Black neoconservatism on the future direction of Black politics in a post-civil rights era? And, finally, what kinds of political responses, including coalitions among progressive sectors, can be generated to counter the influence and impact of Black neoconservatives?

Understanding the Limits of Black Neoconservatism

One major concern with Black neoconservatives today is that they have not offered coherent solutions to the problems that beset the African-American community. Additionally, their rhetoric and behavior are contradictory and hypocritical in some ways. For example, the Black neoconservative call for self-reliance is inconsistent with their extensive dependency on funding from White conservative sources.[10] Black neoconservatives reflect a heavy dependence on White conservative funds for research, book publications, and other enterprises. Very few Black neoconservatives have sought, or developed, careers and mobility on the basis of "self-help" or "self-reliance."[11]

If Black neoconservatives are opposed to race-based aid, and they are constantly preaching self-reliance and instructing African Americans to reject government handouts, then they should be challenged personally, and politically, to be consistent with their rhetoric. For example, Ward Connerly, a Black neoconservative businessman and a member of the University of California Board of Regents, is the initiator of the California initiative that was placed on the November 1996 ballot in California, as an amendment calling for the elimination of all affirmative action programs in the state of California. Moreover, Connerly, a longtime friend and political supporter of Republican Governor Pete Wilson, is one of the state's chief critics of affirmative action. However, Connerly forgot to inform Californians of one important detail about his business. Connerly's company received more than $1 million in contracts from the state's Department of Energy's weatherization program in 1989, 1992, and 1994 as a "minority" business qualifying for "set-aside" funding.[12] Will he give this money back since it is tinged as a product of affirmative action? No. Moreover, when the story was revealed in the *San Francisco Examiner,* he first denied it. When a follow-up story was published in the *Los Angeles Times*, Connerly stated that he "regretted" having to register with the state and participating in the "repugnant race-based program."[13] It appears that Connerly likes "talking the talk" but does not seem to enjoy "walking the walk."

There is another hypocrisy with this sector. If Black neoconservatives are going to chide the Black poor about their morality, or lack of it, then the messengers should lead by example. For instance, even though Glenn Loury claims that he is a born-again Christian, his chiding of the Black underclass about their dysfunctional behavior seems somewhat contradictory because Loury's "personal history includes fathering two out-of-wedlock children, a jailing for nonpayment of child support, and 1987 arrests for cocaine possession and for assaulting the young mistress he had established in a separate household."[14] Loury's excuse for his behavior: "I thought if I hung out in the community and engaged in certain kinds of social activities, in a way I was really being Black."[15] Loury's excuse is unacceptable.

The African-American middle class, furthermore, does not have a monopoly on appropriate behavior or morality. One only needs to carefully examine who the audience is and the economic standing of those Blacks who participate annually in the "Freakweek" festival that has been held in Virginia Beach and in Atlanta. Most of the participants in the annual event that has been marred by arrests for intoxication, drug use, and indecent exposure are Black middle-class college fraternity and sorority students. Therefore, if the Freakweek is any indication of middle-class behavior, the Black middle class should leave morality and soul saving to the Church. Hence, the Black middle class can best assist poor inner-city residents by spending money in those communities, and by volunteering to help strengthen those community institutions that are fighting several daily battles on many different fronts.

The arguments presented against policies such as affirmative action by Black neoconservatives are somewhat misleading because one must question if, based on their personal experiences, Black neoconservatives truly believe that race and gender biases will not influence promotion and hiring decisions. Even Justice Sandra Day O'Connor, an opponent of affirmative action and ardent conservative, stated in a 1995 Supreme Court decision that there is a need for using race as a factor when hiring in some instances.[16]

In terms of "self-esteem," when Stephen Carter and Clarence Thomas employ this line of reasoning to abolish affirmative action and other kinds of race-based programs, it appears that these individuals may be suffering from internalized racism. An illustration of this involves Clarence Thomas. Jane Mayer and Jill Abramson, in *Strange Justice: The Selling of Clarence Thomas*, provide an excellent account of how the scar of racism was internalized by Thomas during his undergraduate and law-student years at Holy Cross University and Yale University:

> [Thomas] saw himself stigmatized rather than helped by race-conscious aid, an analysis that no doubt reflected the emotional pain he felt but that again overlooked the advantages he had enjoyed – such as his admission to St. John Vianney, Immaculate Conception, and Holy Cross in the first place. The resentment that Thomas felt toward the helping hand he grasped

set him apart from a number of other minority students at the time – both at Holy Cross and Yale Law School – many of whom didn't care as much about others' perception of how they had gotten there. At Yale, which Thomas attended as an affirmative action student, he said later, his presence was so resented by the White professors and students that it was as if a monkey had jumped from the carved arches of the Gothic law school building onto his back. He never seemed to believe he had enough acceptance, which caused some friends to wonder if the problem wasn't more internal than external. . . . Lester Johnson, Thomas's friend since childhood, saw the problem as deep-seated. "It's hard to say whether Clarence ever truly had any real self-esteem – I'd have to say no," suggested Johnson.[17]

Obviously, Thomas suffered from low self-esteem, and he internalized the scars of racism. Moreover, Stephen Carter may have suffered from this same problem. For instance, Carter's explanation of the "best Black syndrome" implies that this syndrome can have a damaging impact on affirmative action hires in the long run because

to professionals who have worked hard to succeed, flattery of this kind carries an unsubtle insult, for we yearn to be called what our achievements often deserve: simply the best – no qualifiers needed! In this society, however, we sooner or later must accept that being viewed as the best Blacks is part of what has led us to where we are; and we must further accept that to some of our colleagues, Black as well as White, we will never be anything else.[18]

Thomas and Carter, and perhaps other conservative critics of affirmative action, may be suffering from a need to have "White validation" of their successes. The problem with Thomas and Carter is that both individuals have revealed that they have internalized Whites' negative perceptions of them and their abilities.

In summary of this point, the problem with Thomas and others like him who advocate the elimination of race-based programs is that they are actually attacking the programs that benefited them; further, because they cannot overcome their own internal problems with affirmative action, they have decided for altruistic reasons (i.e., the sake of the country) that affirmative action programs are morally wrong and that they should be terminated. The primary flaw with their argument is that it seems elitist, because if they were cognizant of these negative feelings when they were attending undergraduate and professional school, then why did it take both of them almost twenty years to publicly acknowledge them?

Black neoconservatives argue that the Republican Party should not establish any special outreach programs to attract African Americans. This particular position was articulated by Armstrong Williams on the Cal Thomas cable talk/interview show on WNBC in 1995.[19] This stance, however, contradicts the Republican Party's "Twenty Percent" solution program that was initiated by Bill Brock, chair of the Republican National Committee during the late 1970s and supported by Lee Atwater, who at the time was also the chair of the Republican National Committee.[20] Atwater supported this idea because he "contended that had Republicans won 20 percent of the Black vote in the 1986 midterm elections, they would not have lost control of the Senate."[21] In other words, Atwater inferred that if the Republicans had maintained their White voting base and picked up 20 percent of the Black vote, they could have become the majority party by the year 2000.[22] The implication of these contradictory signals is that Black neoconservatives seem to be more in agreement with White conservatives such as Pat Buchanan, who wrote a news column titled "GOP Vote Search Should Bypass Ghetto."[23] Therefore, if White and Black conservatives are saying that the Republican Party does not need to attract Black voters to win, and Republican pragmatic political leaders are saying the opposite, then one could understand Buchanan's motive, although one has to seriously question why Black conservatives oppose this strategy.

Do Black conservatives wish to keep the number of Blacks in the Republican Party small because they wish to be the new Black gatekeepers on the political block? The Booker T. Washington model, however, will not solve the current political and leadership crisis that confronts the African-American community. Millions of African Americans have worked hard, engaged in numerous self-help projects in their communities, and are law abiding, and to this day many of them may never be accepted as equals or treated as equal Americans in this society. African Americans must rely on government to protect their civil and human rights because, lest we forget, African Americans can find themselves in a new "Age of Conservatism" and victims of a much more severe oppression than that which was experienced by African Americans a hundred years ago.

Conclusion

As the American electorate continues in its rightward voting trend, political activists and leaders could thwart Black neoconservative challenges by employing certain strategies. First, Black progressive activists and leaders need to engage in honest and community-based dialogue about the state of African Americans. If Black liberal and progressive activists and leaders wish to regain control over the direction of political discourse in the African-American community, then they will have to demonstrate to the Black community how their agenda differs from that of the Black neoconservatives, and how it will benefit most Blacks.

Second, Black liberal and progressive activists and leaders should try to forge periodic political alliances with the more traditional Black conservatives, some of whom have rejected the rightwing stances of their colleagues. Some conservatives and Republicans like Arthur Fletcher and General Colin Powell, for example, support liberal positions such as set-aside programs and other kinds of affirmative action programs. Furthermore, except for Colin Powell, this sector of Black conservatives has been excluded from the inner workings of the Republican Party. According to Burrell Haseling, who spoke before the Black Republican Task Force on Civil Rights,

> Black Republicans must stop taking crumbs off the table. Black Republicans must let the Republican party know that it is a racist party and that it is wrong. The Republican party is racist because it has quotas! Black Republicans must pressure the Republican party to amend its charter to end quotas and include people of color. If they fail to act, then Black Republicans are wasting their time. As it stands now . . . we are not part of the Republican party because we are not part of the inner workings of the party decision-making process. If we are not part of the inner workings of the party, then we cannot do anything for Black people.[24]

Haseling's candid remarks on the current status of Black Republicans should convince some Black progressive activists and leaders that an alliance with these types of Black conservatives might be worth exploring. Moreover, an alliance between these Black groups is not unprecedented; according to Richard Hatcher, former mayor of Gary, Indiana, informal meetings between Black Democrats and Black moderate Republicans have occurred periodically in the past.[25] Although their relationship in the past may not have been perfect, future elections of national and local conservative candidates should provide ample incentive for both groups to at least explore the possibility of establishing some kind of political dialogue among themselves.

Third, progressive activists and leaders will have to address local concerns such as crime, violence in the Black communities, teen pregnancies, and the generation of viable Black enterprises. If Black liberals and progressive activists and leaders fail to respond to these needs with an effective program for the future for African Americans, then they might find themselves constantly reacting to someone else's agenda. Black liberal and progressive activists and leaders will have to provide an honest, and plausible, rationale for those African Americans who comprise the ranks of the apathetic Blacks who do not vote or participate in the political process. In essence, they must find an effective approach that convinces this population to become active participants in the process of their own empowerment.

Fourth, African-American liberals, progressive activists, and leaders should carefully consider forging political and/or economic alliances with other Third World groups in this country. Some of the problems that afflict African Americans also beset Latino Americans, Asian Americans, Native Americans, and the Caribbean population in the United States. Hence, what do liberals and progressive activists and leaders have to lose by coalition building?

Last, if Black liberal and progressive activists and leaders fail to provide a vision of the future for African Americans in a post-civil rights era, and if they continue their current strategies of relying on outdated ideas, methods, and old slogans to mobilize the Black population during an impending crisis period, Black liberals and progressive activists and leaders may find themselves in the minority and constantly reacting to a Black organic and neoconservative political, social, and economic agenda.

Notes

1. George S. Schuyler, *Black and Conservative: The Autobiography of George S. Schuyler* (New York: Arlington House Publishers, 1966), pp. 95–235, 341–52, and preface; also see Hanes Walton, Jr., "Blacks and Conservative Political Movements," *Quarterly Review of Higher Education among Negroes*, vol. 37, no. 4 (October 1969), p. 181.

2. Harold Cruse, *The Crisis of the Negro Intellectual* (New York: William Morrow, 1967), pp. 326–8.

3. Nancy J. Weiss, *Farewell to the Party of Lincoln: Black Politics in the Age of FDR* (Princeton, NJ: Princeton University Press, 1983), pp. 78–235. Also see Avon Drake, "Black Liberalism, Conservatism, and Social Democracy: The Social Policy Debate," *Western Journal of Black Studies*, vol. 14, no. 2 (1990), pp. 115–16.

4. Walton, "Blacks and Conservative Political Movements," p. 181.

5. Taylor Branch, *Parting the Waters* (New York: Simon & Schuster, 1988), pp. 372–3.

6. Andrew Buni, *The Negro in Virginia Politics: 1902–1965* (Charlottesville: University of Virginia Press, 1967), p. 219.

7. Robert C. Smith and Hanes Walton, Jr., "U-Turn: Martin Kilson and Black

Conservatives," *Transition*, no. 62 (1993), pp. 209–10; and Georgia Persons, "The Election of Gary Franks and the Ascendancy of the New Black Conservatives," in Georgia A. Persons, ed., *Dilemmas of Black Politics* (New York: HarperCollins College Publishers, 1993), pp. 200–2.

8. Lewis A. Randolph and Gayle T. Tate, "The Rise and Decline of African-American Political Power in Richmond: Race, Class, and Gender," in Judith A. Garber and Robyne S. Turner, eds., *Gender In Urban Research* (Thousand Oaks, CA: Sage Publications, 1995), p. 150.

9. Mercer interview, Richmond, Virginia (December 8,1992).

10. Deborah Toler, "Black Conservatives: Part Two," *The Public Eye Newsletter*, vol. 7, no. 4 (1993), pp. 4–5.

11. Ibid., pp. 4–6.

12. Suzanne Espinosa-Solis, "Affirmative Action Critic Used His Minority Status," *San Francisco Examiner* (May 8, 1995), p. A1.

13. Carl Ingram and Elaine Woo, "Affirmative Action FOE Widens Attack," *Los Angeles Times* (May 10, 1995), p. A3.

14. Toler, "Black Conservatives," p. 2.

15. Ibid.

16. *Adarand Construction Co. v. Pena*, 63 LW 4523 (June 12, 1995).

17. Jane Mayer and Jill Abramson, *Strange Justice: The Selling of Clarence Thomas* (Boston: Houghton Mifflin, 1994), p. 53.

18. Stephen L. Carter, *Reflections of an Affirmative Action Baby* (New York: Basic Books, 1991), p. 52.

19. Cable National Broadcasting Corporation, "Cal Thomas Show" (July 5, 1995).

20. Louis Bolce, Gerald De Maio, and Douglas Muzzio, "Blacks and the Republican Party: The 20 Percent Solution," *Political Science Quarterly,* vol. 107, no. 1 (1992), p. 63.

21. Ibid.

22. Ibid., pp. 63–79.

23. Toler, "Black Conservatives," p. 6.

24. Burrell Haseling, "Black Republican Civil Rights Task Force," sponsored by the National African-American Republican Council, C-SPAN (May 18, 1995).

25. Richard Hatcher interview, Memphis, Tennessee (August 19, 1995).

The Role of Political Racialization in the Neutralization of the Black Electorate

Farai Chideya

Few Americans would question the use of the term "Black issues" to describe any of a host of hot-button political topics including drugs, crime, welfare, and affirmative action. This is a significant claim because the classification of broad areas of political discourse by race has profound implications for the electorate. Americans vote their own interests, and if those interests diverge along racial lines, then so will voting patterns. As voting patterns diverge, so do the options for attaining political power available to the African-American community. For example, a community strongly identified with one political party (as African Americans are with the Democratic Party) arguably loses the political bargaining power available to constituencies utilizing a swing or bloc vote.

Racial polarization of the U.S. electorate is a fact: a study by the National Women's Political Caucus in 1995 found that the "race gap" – that is, the difference in the percentages of Blacks and Whites who voted for Democrats – was immense, and growing. In the 1994 elections, the race gap was 50 points, as compared to a "gender gap" of 11 points, a "geography gap" between urban and rural voters of 29 points, and a "religion gap" between Protestants and Jews of 38 points.[1] Just as the division between Black and White is the sharpest, so is the division of issues into "Black issues" and "mainstream" issues. But is the racial division of issues simply a reflection of demographic facts – or does it reflect stereotypic groupings by politicians and the media that in turn exacerbate polarizing trends? If so, who is responsible for the racial categorization of political issues, and who does the phenomenon benefit?

Perhaps the first question is what is it, exactly, that makes a "Black issue" Black? The very term indicates that a "Black issue" must have great import in shaping or influencing Black America. By connotation, such issues are less defining of the character or destiny of majority-White America, giving many White voters reason to believe that what falls under the rubric of a "Black issue" is something they can, or perhaps should, avoid. But the demographics do not add up – White America, and other non-Black constituencies, are deeply affected by the issues affecting the Black community, giving clear reasons to believe that much of the categorization of issues along racial lines is a result of stereotyping and political expediency. While certain government programs do affect proportionately more Blacks than Whites, the chief fallacy of the Black/mainstream issue dichotomy is that it erodes any sense of common self-interest between Blacks and Whites. And, of course, though this essay deals specifically with African Americans, racialization is not limited to Black issues alone. Much of the rhetoric surrounding California's anti-immigrant statute Proposition 187 (now under legal challenge) had a clear anti-Latino bent.

These common areas of self-interest between Blacks and Whites, and moreover between all races in American society, do exist. "Black issues," nevertheless, have much significance for the White electorate; for example, despite a disproportionate weighting toward African Americans, there are more White women receiving welfare than Black, and the majority of violent criminals are White.[2] Most disturbing, some issues identified with the African-American community, like drug use, also affect other communities equally. Thus, as more than 70 percent of America is White and 12 percent is Black, more than 70 percent of drug users are White, and 12 percent are Black.[3] Because the issues we think of as race-based are, at best, somewhat race-linked, what is going on is a "racialization" of political issues.

The current political climate is a harsh one for African Americans and other Americans of color, as bitter ideological wars in preparation for the past presidential campaign and future political battles have placed strong emphasis on the very issues that are consistently racialized in American politics. These ideological wars are being played out in various arenas. In the current political period drastic revisions in the welfare system have been approved by the U.S. Congress and President Bill Clinton, who promised during his 1992 campaign to "end welfare as we know it." Affirmative action is under challenge from both the U.S. Supreme Court and opponents in the

U.S. House and Senate, though no federal legislation dismantling affirmative action has yet been passed.

What is the danger of identifying issues with people of color, particularly African Americans? For much of White America the Black community in particular still embodies a sort of anti-American Dream. A study by the University of Chicago's National Opinion Research Center asked non-Black Americans what they thought of African Americans: 30.7 percent said Blacks were less intelligent than Whites; 53.7 percent said they were more violent; 46.6 percent said they were lazier; and 58.9 percent agreed that African Americans "preferred to live off of welfare."[4] Because of this continuing racial bias, any topic labeled as a "Black issue" is less likely to be embraced by Whites, making racialization a powerful political tool to maintain group divisions.

A 1995 poll found, for example, that more Americans supported affirmative action for women than disapproved of it; the reverse was true when respondents were asked about affirmative action for racial minorities.[5] Affirmative action, of course, does not only benefit African Americans (as suggested by some conservatives) but also other groups who experience workplace discrimination, including other Americans of color, women, and, in many instances, veterans. Given the power of race to shape political opinion, the question then becomes: is the racialization of affirmative action an unintended side effect of exploring the issue, or is it deliberately cultivated by opponents of the program? Unfortunately, there is much evidence for the latter. One of the most blatant examples (but not the first or only) occurred in 1991, when Senator Jesse Helms unabashedly exploited the use of race for electoral purposes. Running closely with African American Harvey Gantt, Helms broadcast a last-minute ad showing White hands holding a job rejection notice. A voice-over stated: "You needed that job, and you were the best qualified. But it had to go to a minority because of a racial quota." Many believe that as a result of this ad Helms won by a margin of 4 percent.[6]

California governor Pete Wilson, who briefly campaigned for the 1996 presidential race before withdrawing because of the lack of support and funds, also used the race card of affirmative action to boost his political profile. Wilson, once considered a strong civil rights supporter, backed affirmative action until 1994. By 1995, however, the dismantling of affirmative action had become his keynote issue, and he succeeded in ending the program at the prestigious University of California system, though the numbers of African Americans and Latinos enrolled were far below their proportion in the population.

Wilson's statement that affirmative action infects America with "the deadly virus of tribalism" was criticized as racially charged even by members of his own party.

Instead of educating the public about the historical and programmatic inaccuracies related to the racialization of affirmative action, the American news media have been participating in that trend. Terms like "racial preference program" and "quota system" are used interchangeably with "affirmative action" when they in fact are terms adopted by affirmative action opponents. "Racial preference program" is a clear racialization of the issue, as affirmative action does not apply on the basis of race alone; "quota system" ignores the fact that most affirmative action programs are not quotas, but less sharply defined recruitment, hiring, and retention efforts. To highlight the contrast, note that no major American newspaper has used terminology like "equal opportunity hiring effort" to substitute for "affirmative action."

The use of racially polarized terminology has a clear effect on public opinion. One poll asked young Americans if they supported giving "special consideration" to minorities in education and jobs, then asked the same question, substituting the phrase "special preference." The use of the word "preference" made negative reactions jump significantly – in Blacks as well as in Whites.[7] A 1992 poll found that most Americans did not support the media's use of polarized rhetoric; 70 percent approved the use of the term "affirmative action," while only 46 approved the term "racial preference program."[8]

The reporting treatment of African Americans by the criminal justice system illustrates yet another form of racialization: Black crime rates are easily presumed to be indicators of inherent racial propensities – and are thus exploited for political gain. The image of the Black criminal as bogeyman has proven political impact. A notable example is the 1988 presidential campaign. Supporters of George Bush, the victor, repeatedly ran ads showing a Black rapist and murderer named Willie Horton. As Bush's research director during the campaign said, "the more people who know who Willie Horton is, the better off we'll be."[9] Using African Americans as the foil for a get-tough-on-crime stance is not limited to conservatives alone. During his successful presidential campaign, then-Arkansas governor Bill Clinton executed Ricky Ray Rector, a Black murderer who, in a failed attempt to kill himself, became brain-damaged and profoundly retarded. At the time Clinton authorized his execution, Rector could not even understand that he was about to die.[10]

The idea that crime is inherently race-based is the underlying rationale for making an example of African Americans to appease White fears of crime. But that assumption bears more rigorous scrutiny. Take as your starting point the fact that because of poverty Blacks are more likely to commit certain types of crimes than Whites. Being Black becomes probable cause, so that a police officer who intimidates or arrests innocent Blacks as well as guilty ones is simply doing his job; the fact that African-American criminals get 50 percent more jail time on drug and weapons offenses than Whites who have committed the same crime is a regrettable cost of keeping the streets clean; and a justice system that is at least four times as likely to put an African American to death for the same offense that a White criminal has committed is actually fair and just, as implied by the U.S. Supreme Court.[11] In factoring socioeconomic status, however, one finds that Blacks and Whites of equal income levels have nearly identical crime rates. And once racial bias is factored in – and even a majority of judges surveyed admitted there was bias against African Americans in every step of the legal system, from arrests to time served – it is quite clear that African Americans are no more *inherently* prone to criminal behavior than Whites.[12]

The first effect of the racialization of crime is to justify racism in the criminal justice system, even those penalties that both blatantly and illogically target small-time African-American offenders over larger-scale White criminals. For example, five years is the penalty for possessing either 5 grams of crack cocaine or 500 (!) grams of powder cocaine. The first has a street value of $250, the second a street value of $40,000; the first is more often used by African Americans, the second by White Americans.[13] Anyone with a felony conviction will have a hard time finding work, closing off legitimate avenues of employment for criminals who want to go clean and often making a life of crime seem a necessary evil. Largely because of drug-possession arrests, an entire generation of Black men is growing up under the shadow of the criminal justice system – a third of Black men in their twenties are imprisoned, on probation, or on parole.[14]

Dinesh D'Souza's *The End of Racism*, a book funded by a conservative think tank and designed to provide fodder for the political savaging of the civil rights agenda, reinforces the idea of the innate Black criminal and even argues that Black intellectuals and activists are responsible for the perpetuation of "Black pathology." The author states, for example, that

> most African American scholars simply refuse to acknowledge the pathol-
> ogy of violence in the black underclass. . . . Activists recommend federal

job programs and recruitment into the private sector. Yet it seems
unrealistic, bordering on the surreal, to imagine underclass blacks with
their gold chains, limping walk, obscene language, and arsenal of
weapons doing nine-to-five jobs at Procter and Gamble or the State
Department.[15]

Here, the racial stereotype of the Black criminal is used as a trump
card in the political debate over equal opportunity. Instead of truly
addressing the interlocking issues of job opportunities and crime or
providing any socioeconomic analysis, the author finds it easier to
win his argument by conjuring up, again, the image of the Black
bogeyman.

Despite the fact that more women receiving AFDC are White than
Black, welfare is another racially charged issues. The vast majority of
the media's images of women on welfare are African Americans and,
beyond that, often fit the typical "welfare queen" image of women
with high numbers of children who have rarely, if ever, worked. That
is far from the reality: the majority of women on welfare have two
children and are on benefits for twenty-two months at a stretch, with
a total of five to eight years over their lifetime.[16] That portrait
illustrates the lives of women who want to work but are not able to
keep a steady job, primarily because of a lack of employment in their
community, child care and health care, or education and training. The
facts about welfare recipients indicate a group of individuals who
indeed want to work but have no choice but to drift in and out of the
American workforce. By contrast, the "welfare queen" stereotype is
based on the idea of women who do not want to work, begging
punitive political measures rather than any true assistance.

Although in 1992 President Clinton made welfare reform one of his
campaign pledges, it was the 104th Congress – the Newt Gingrich-led
"Republican Revolution" – that seized the issue as their own. The
U.S. House of Representatives passed a bill in the spring of 1995 that
would not so much have reformed welfare as dismantled it. Parts of
the House plan would have cut school lunches and benefits to disabled
children and teen mothers and their offspring. Those elements were
not realized – President Clinton vetoed the first Republican-crafted
welfare bill. But in August 1996, the president caved in to election-
year pressure and signed a welfare bill that included the most radical
of Republican "reforms" – ending the sixty-one-year guarantee of
assistance to poor children and their families. Adults in the welfare
program must begin working within two years of receiving benefits,
and the families cannot exceed five years' total in receiving welfare.

By many estimates the new welfare bill, which must be implemented by mid-1997, will throw one million more American children into poverty. In response to the perceived callousness of the bill (and Clinton's political expediency in signing it), several key Health and Human Services officials have resigned. Among them was Peter Edelman, the husband of Children's Defense Fund head Marion Wright Edelman, who organized a 1996 march for children's well-being titled the Stand for Children.[17]

When political issues such as welfare are given a racial spin, it erodes the possibility of mobilizing a multiracial constituency behind the issue and further isolates the Black community. With both welfare and affirmative action, women's groups have tried with varying degrees of both tenacity and success to "coidentify" with the Black community on the issues; very little multiracial support has otherwise materialized. Combined with continuing racial segregation, political racialization has the effect of making African-American concerns seem not only distant but distasteful to other members of the electorate.

A 1985 study of White voters by the Michigan Democratic Party found that blue-collar White voters "express a profound distaste for Blacks, a sentiment that pervades almost everything they think about government and politics. . . . Blacks constitute the explanation for their vulnerability and for almost everything that has gone wrong in their lives; not being Black is what constitutes being middle class; not living with Blacks is what makes a neighborhood a decent place to live."[18] This explanation of the role of race in politics indicates a seldom-talked-about side effect of racial polarization. The White electorate may be more complacent about their own socioeconomic and political situation – if they have a degraded image of Black America with which to compare their state. In a sense, the foil of the Black underclass keeps White working-class Americans from objectively judging their status and being too demanding of their political figureheads. As long as they do not sink to what they see as the level of Black America – and they never will because that view is largely subjective – White communities will feel less of a need to push for results on education, crime, and welfare from their politicians.

The political effects of segregation are inextricably entwined with the racialization of politics. As Douglas S. Massey and Nancy A. Denton point out in their book *American Apartheid*, no racial or ethnic group has experienced the degree of residential segregation that African Americans have: "Since no one except Blacks lived in the ghetto, no other ethnic group had a self-interest in seeing them

provided with public services or political patronage. . . . [B]ecause
patronage was the glue that held White political coalitions together,
resources to the ghetto automatically undermined the stability of the
pluralist machine." They continue to point out that the only basis for
Black–White cooperation, given these realities, is altruism, which is
"notoriously unreliable as a basis for political cooperation."[19] The
geographical overlap of ethnic neighborhoods and constituencies, in
contrast to the overwhelming isolation of Blacks, provides a basis for
political cooperation. If a jobs program or public works project in an
Italian neighborhood benefits the Chinese Americans who overlap in
the district, it creates a basis for cooperation between the two
constituencies. It also creates a basis for political leverage, if the
minority group within the constituency threaten to remove their
support from a candidate or project. By contrast, the African-
American community has little basis for such political leverage.

This can be illustrated in another crisis of altruism, occurring in
America's South, where White support for money to maintain public
schools in majority-Black areas is flagging. A 1995 school bond
measure in New Orleans was supported by 90 percent of voters in
majority-Black areas, and only a quarter of voters in majority-White
neighborhoods. Like many school districts, both southern and north-
ern, New Orleans's schools are overwhelmingly Black, as White
parents continue to put their children in private schools. Though the
city is 65 percent Black, the schools are 93 percent Black. Similar
schisms over funding schools have occurred in Mississippi and
Georgia.[20]

Racialization also narrows the range of acceptable discussion on
political issues, so fully supporting a pro-Black agenda seems unpal-
atable to politicians who must cling to the Right or the middle. In the
welfare debates, for example, the only options were centrist (President
Clinton), Right (the Senate) and far Right (the House). No strong
political leaders feel they have a chance of supporting an agenda that
would provide more money, not less, for jobs and training programs
for women in the main welfare program, Aid to Families with
Dependent Children. By extension, the racialization of political issues
narrows not only the band of acceptable debate, but the range of
acceptable candidates, since anyone supporting a pro-Black agenda is
seen as suspect by White America.

So what are the options open to the African-American community
in the face of the racial polarization of political issues? The first
imperative is to track the use of race to define political issues, and to
try to change the terms and context of the debate. In the welfare wars,

for example, far more Black experts than White ones – or even women's issues experts – are shown defending greater spending on the program. This puts African-American politicians and pundits in an awkward position. The constant identification of welfare as a "Black issue" is exacerbated by the very participation of Black experts in the debate. Yet it would be equally negative to forgo addressing an issue that does have a deep impact on the Black community. Perhaps the solution is for Black politicians and experts to be mindful of the fact that they will constantly have to frame issues like welfare and crime in a multiracial context since journalists and White political officials have no stake in doing so. Black officials and experts should know the statistics on the racial demographics of "Black issues," and be inclusive of White Americans in how they address the topics. One element of the battle may be purely semantic. "Black issues" tend to carry overwhelmingly negative connotations, just as most of America's media coverage of the Black community tends to be negative. For example, "poverty" and "joblessness" are words identified with Black America. (While a higher proportion of African Americans than Whites are poor, there are twice as many poor White families as Black ones – a perfect opportunity to "reinvest" the White electorate in discussing poverty.) The terms "jobs" and "the economy" have race-neutral connotations. African-American officials may find it useful to recast issues in race-neutral terms.

Recontextualizing "Black issues" as multiracial issues *of importance to the Black community* will by extension help achieve a second important goal: demonstrating that altruism is not the only reason for White Americans to support Black political interests. The need for jobs and training, and for a workable welfare system, should be an issue that all Americans can throw their support behind. Yet if they feel that only Black America has a stake in them, they will resist lending that support. The Black community must also reach out to other communities of color to build coalitions aimed at challenging the racialization of public issues. In many cities, including New York, San Francisco, and Los Angeles, a strong coalition of people of color could dictate the political agenda. Too often, however, these coalitions are left unexplored. Furthermore, African-American politicians – and indeed all politicians – need to speak openly and explicitly about what White America has to gain from a more racially inclusive society. If we cannot make the case for equal opportunity to White America, the cause is lost.

Finally, the most difficult task will be for African Americans to reconceptualize the Black community's place in the American political system. African Americans vote overwhelmingly for the Democratic Party, and with strong reason, as the Republican Party has shown little support for the civil rights agenda. But the strong party affiliation of African Americans necessarily limits political leverage. In races where the Democratic contender does not seem particularly appealing, many African Americans simply stay home. And in races where the Black community has contributed to a Democratic victory, it has rarely gotten credit. Blacks provided the margin of victory for President Clinton in 1992, as George Bush won 41 percent of the White vote, while Clinton won 39 percent. A similar situation occurred in 1976, when 47 percent of Whites voted for Jimmy Carter and 52 percent for Gerald Ford.[21] Yet Clinton's willingness and ability to fight for Black political interest has been limited by the fear that more of the White electorate will desert the Democrats – and by the idea that the Black vote is a "given."

The options open to the Black community include encouraging a swing vote – that is, supporting acceptable Republican candidates – and trying to form or support a third party. A 1992 poll by the Joint Center for Political and Economic Studies found that 23 percent of African Americans consider themselves independents.[22] Rev. Jesse Jackson has stated his support for a third party yet has not formally urged the creation of one. Billionaire Ross Perot, whose independent run for president in 1992 garnered 19 percent of the vote, has established a rather feeble third party, the Reform Party. Consumer crusader Ralph Nader, who talks tirelessly about the need to get big corporate donations out of politics, ran as the candidate of the Green Party. And third parties are emerging from the labor community. The New Party has attempted a grassroots organizing campaign focusing on building a progressive agenda.

The best hope for getting African Americans to vote Republican in the past presidential election would have been if retired General Colin Powell had chosen to run. At the time he declined, support for him was higher than for any other Republican who had expressed interest in running. Powell made it clear that if he had run, he would have done so as a Republican, though many of his positions on issues like civil rights are liberal. He "transcends" the stereotyping of race in many ways: his prominence as the leader of the military forces in the Gulf War gives him credentials with the conservatives; his status as the assimilated child of an immigrant family from Jamaica has also been seized upon, for both positive and negative reasons, as something that sets him aside from other African Americans.

It seems unlikely that large numbers of African Americans will begin to vote for the Republican Party until that party begins to address the issues of the Black community as a whole. A 1992 study of economic conditions and Black voting patterns found that, as opposed to wealthy Whites, even well-off African Americans tended to vote not based on their own finances but whether or not they felt the Black community as a whole was prospering or suffering. Those who believed conditions were improving for the Black community were much more likely to vote Republican. White Americans, by contrast, tended to base their choice on the economic status of their own families. The study's authors wonder if their "findings here mean that there is a potential for Republicans to make real inroads in the Black vote. Our answer is that it is possible, though not likely, given Republican policy stances."[23]

The most lasting solution to both the racialization of politics and the disenfranchisement of the Black electorate is to ameliorate the socioeconomic conditions of the African-American community. Studies of socioeconomic and voting patterns illustrate that political empowerment must go hand in hand with educational and economic empowerment. White Americans are more likely to vote than African Americans, but this reflects, to a certain extent, the lower socioeconomic status of the latter group. African Americans are twice as likely to be unemployed as Whites and are less likely to have a college education.[24] Voter participation varies significantly with job status and educational level, with employed Americans and college graduates the most likely to vote.[25]

It will be difficult to improve Black America's socioeconomic status, however, without simultaneously pushing to expand the Black voter base as well, leaving Black America with a chicken-and-egg conundrum – or, at least, a need to work on voter registration and economic enfranchisement simultaneously. The African-American community must find ways to get its members to the polls, even if the only choices fit the lesser-of-two-evils pattern. Groups like the Southern Christian Leadership Conference and the National Coalition on Black Voter Participation are determined to make large-scale Black voting a reality. Yet it seems unlikely that the cycle of racialization and disenfranchisement will be broken unless African Americans truly believe their participation in the political process will make a difference. At a time when few politicians – Democrat or Republican, liberal or conservative – realize that Black voters' concerns are issues of multiethnic importance, greater African-American turnout at the polls may prove a crucial first step to making those concerns a priority for all Americans.

Notes

1. Federal Document Clearing House/Political Transcripts, *News Conference on a New Study of Women and the Gender Gap* (August 24, 1995).

2. Bureau of Justice Statistics, *Sourcebook of Criminal Justice Statistics – 1992* (Washington, D.C.: Government Printing Office, 1993), pp. 46–7; and U.S. Department of Health and Human Services, *Characteristics and Financial Circumstances of AFDC Recipients: Fiscal Year 1992* (Washington, D.C.: Government Printing Office, 1994), pp. 1–4.

3. National Institute on Drug Abuse, *National Household Survey on Drug Abuse: Population Estimates 1991* (Rockville, MD: U.S. Department of Health and Human Services, n.3, 1992).

4. Robert C. Smith, *Racism in the Post-Civil Rights Era* (Albany, NY: State University of New York Press, 1995), p. 39.

5. Kevin Johnson and Desda Moss, "Affirmative Action Debate Skips Women," *USA Today* (February 28, 1995), p. 6A.

6. Priscilla Painton, "Quota Quagmire," *Time* (May 24, 1991), p. 20.

7. *Democracy's Next Generation II* (Washington, D.C.: People for the American Way, 1992).

8. Lionel McPherson, "Focus on Racism in the Media," *Extra!* (July/August 1992).

9. Sidney Blumenthal, "Willie Horton and the Making of a Campaign Issue," *Washington Post* (October 2, 1988).

10. Nat Hentoff, "The Race Game – Anyone Can Play," *The Village Voice* (October 26, 1993).

11. Seth Mydans, "The Courts on Trial," *New York Times* (April 8, 1993); and *McClesky v. Kemp,* 481 U.S. 279, 312 (1987).

12. E. F. Loftus and J. M. Doyle, "New Jersey Supreme Court Final Report of the Task Force on Minority Concerns," *New Jersey Law Journal* (August 10, 1993).

13. *Mandatory Minimum Penalties in the Federal Criminal Justice System* (Washington, D.C.: U.S. Sentencing Commission, 1991).

14. Fox Butterfield, "More Blacks in Their 20's Have Trouble with the Law," *New York Times* (October 5 1995).

15. Dinesh D'Souza, *The End of Racism* (New York: Free Press, 1995), p. 504.

16. U.S. Department of Health and Human Services, *Characteristics and Financial Circumstances of AFDC Recipients: Fiscal Year 1991*, pp. 1–4, 42; and *Fiscal Year 1992*, pp. 1–4 (Washington, D.C.: Government Printing Office, 1993 and 1994).

17. Elizabeth Shogren, "Clinton's Signature Launches Historic Overhaul of Welfare," *Los Angeles Times* (August 23, 1996), p. A-1.

18. Stanley B. Greenberg, *Report on Democratic Defection* (Washington, D.C.: Analysis Group, 1985), pp. 13–18, 28, cited in Douglas S. Massey and Nancy A. Denton, *American Apartheid* (Cambridge, MA: Harvard University Press, 1993), p. 94.

19. Massey and Denton, *American Apartheid*, pp. 154–155.

20. Curtis Wilkie, "Change in Southern Strategy Unfolds," *The Boston Globe* (August 7, 1995), p. 3.

21. Charles V. Hamilton, "Promoting Priorities: African-American Political Influence in the 1990s," in Billy J. Tidwell, ed., *The State of Black America 1993* (Washington, D.C.: Urban League Press, 1993).

22. E. J. Dionne, "In Poll, Blacks Defy Political Stereotyping" *Washington Post* (July 9, 1992).

23. Susan Welch and Lorn S. Foster, "The Impact of Economic Conditions on the Voting Behavior of Blacks," *Western Political Quarterly*, vol. 45 (March 1992), pp. 221–36.

24. U.S. Department of Commerce, *Money Income of Households, Families and*

Persons in the United States: 1992 (Washington, D.C.: Government Printing Office, 1993), pp. 12–14.

25. Harold W. Stanley and Richard G. Neimi, "Voting-Age Population Registered and Voting," *Vital Statistics on American Politics* (Washington, D.C.: Congressional Quarterly Press, 1994), table 3–1, pp. 87–8.

Responding to Racism and Crisis: Building Third Party Politics

James Jennings

Racial hierarchy, that is, a racial caste order, continues to be a fundamental and key feature of American society; this means that commentary and analysis regarding the future of American politics are incomplete without reference to the role and impact of race and evolving race relations between Whites and Blacks, as well as other communities of color.[1] Racial hierarchy, a concept differentiated from "race" and "racism," is reflected in the continuing racial gap between Blacks and Whites in income, poverty, unemployment, and health.[2] Note as one example of this continuing racial hierarchy, that in 1939 the proportion of Blacks in poverty was three times the proportion of Whites. In 1959 the Black poverty rate was still three times that of Whites. And in 1989, the Black poverty rate was still three times the White poverty rate. Thus, despite important changes in race relations in the United States, including the elimination of a multigenerational system of legally sanctioned political apartheid, society is still characterized by fundamental social and economic divisions along racial lines.

Neither the Democratic nor the Republican Party has offered policies that could eliminate racial hierarchy in the U.S. This is not to deny that some degree of racial progress has taken place in this country. Today, a Black "middle class" exists in part because of policies enacted by national administrations in the 1960s. Racial progress in the United States has been documented by several national reports, including the study sponsored by the National Academy of Science, *A Common Destiny*, and the series of volumes published under the title *Assessment of the Status of African Americans* by the William Monroe Trotter Institute in Boston.[3] The former study documents that the proportion of Black families earning incomes greater than $35,000 grew from 15.7 percent to 21.1 percent between 1970 and 1986.[4] But both these studies also document how the U.S. continues to be divided along racial lines in the 1990s. A racial chasm, reflected in the hierarchical ordering of race in the United States, is persisting and in some ways widening, according to these reports. America's racial gap apparently has not been impacted significantly by changing national administrations and regimes, changing family structure among Blacks, and increasing levels of schooling on the part of Blacks.

Despite the continuing existence of racial hierarchy, it is also true that class divisions are a fundamental feature of this society. Class divisions are based on the ownership, accumulation, and management of wealth. The public policies that are adopted and implemented generally tend to favor the social interests of those enjoying more wealth, as well as the needs of the corporate community. The Reagan policies in the 1980s, as a matter of fact, represented but an extreme version of class bias that is also reflected in Democratic/liberal national administrations.[5] And after a review of corporate donations to and influence on both major parties, political scientist Thomas Ferguson writes that "from the standpoint of social equity, it can scarcely be doubted that the Clinton final program differs drastically from anything ever contemplated by Presidents Reagan and Bush. Still, the notion that the plan amounts to class war is absurd on its face."[6]

Class divisions were exacerbated during the reign of the Republican Party in the 1980s. This period reflected a precipitous increase in the share of wealth held by the "superrich," the wealthiest 0.5 percent of U.S. households.[7] As a result of the kinds of social and economic development policies pursued by the Republican administration, the proportion of national income received by the first four quintiles of the U.S. population declined or remained the same between 1980 and 1988, while it increased for the highest quintile of the population during this period.[8] Under the current Democratic national administration, however, social welfare policy will continue to be limited and defined by the interests of the well-off, rather than for the benefit of working-class or poor people. Neither of the two major parties has offered national policy strategies to eliminate racial hierarchy, or pursue social welfare programs that might threaten the economic base of the well-off and corporate sectors.

By separating the concepts of race and class, I am not suggesting that the two major parties have the opportunity to resolve either one or the other. A challenge to eliminate racial hierarchy cannot be effective without also challenging the class interests of the corporate sector, and vice versa. C. L. R. James's observation in 1938 is still valid, that is, that race and class are intricately intertwined in the past, present, and future of U.S. and world politics.[9] I would add to this, however, that analysis of politics in the United States requires reference to the nature and distribution of *power*. This leads to the major argument in this essay. And this is that the history and current policies of the two major parties show that Democrats and Republicans will pursue policies to weaken racial and class hierarchies only if they are politically forced to do so. The evidence for this claim includes the history of actions (and inactions) of both the Democratic and Republican Parties regarding issues like racism; the fact that both parties have become the captives of corporate wealth and contributions; and the failure of the 1984 and 1988 Jesse Jackson movement to motivate Democratic Party leadership to pursue aggressive policies to eliminate racism and classism in the United States. Americans interested in seeing the major parties adopt more progressive stances in eliminating racial and class divisions, including poverty, should seek to support an independent front, or third party, that could at least influence the policies adopted by the Democrats and Republicans.

A third party encompassing independent politics at the local, state, and national level is essential in order to challenge effectively the philosophical and political tendencies of the Democratic and Republican Parties regarding social welfare, economic growth and development, and foreign affairs. Activists and intellectuals seeking to influence both major parties to pursue public policies more responsive to the needs of people, of the cities, of the working class and poor people must begin to build a national and democratically based third party. As stated by longtime advocate for independent Black politics Ron Daniels, a third party should be launched as "a massive human rights crusade to place America's injustices against African people, Native Americans, Latinos, Asian Americans, and poor and working people before the world. . . . Those who have been the historical victims of a racist and exploitive system must amass the power to govern and create a new society."[10] Under the framework of a third party based on progressive social change, the electoral arena is yet another space where large numbers of people can be organized and mobilized for political action. This is not to negate the critical importance of grassroots mobilization outside the electoral arena. Political activism directed at social change cannot be effective or long-ranging in terms of impact if it is confined by electoral institutions.

But grassroots mobilization directed at challenging structures of wealth and poverty could be more effective and far-reaching if it were complemented by electoral activism.

The following section examines in greater detail how both major parties have actually exploited and aggravated race and class divisions in the United States. This section is offered in order to illustrate that the Democrats and Republicans have no political reason to challenge these kinds of divisions. A third party, organized locally and nationally, could begin to extract from the major parties a political cost in continuing to ignore or exploit race and class hierarchies.

Race and the Major Parties

A recent report issued by the Milton Eisenhower Foundation reiterated the findings of the Kerner Commission of a quarter of a century ago regarding issues of race, poverty, and economic insecurity for masses of Americans.[11] Both these national reports, as well as the previously cited National Academy of Science's *A Common Destiny* and the Trotter Institute's *Assessment of the Status of African Americans*, conclude that race, race relations, and racism remain serious and systemic problems in the U.S.

At various times in our history, as well as in the current period, Republicans and Democrats have used, and manipulated, race symbols for political gain. This has had the effect of not only keeping the American public divided, but also neutralizing any kind of political or electoral base that could serve to push for social change and equality in this nation. In the book *Southern Politics*, political scientist V. O. Key described the history of the Democratic Party in the South in exploiting race in order to keep poor and working-class Whites focused on stopping the advancement of Blacks and, in the process, inhibiting their own social and economic advancement.[12]

In 1988, the Republicans used symbolism embodied in Willie Horton and quotas. And in 1992, the Democratic Party also used racial symbolism for political gain. In my opinion, the Sister Souljah incident, as well as Bill Clinton's highly publicized and carefully timed participation in the execution of a Black, mentally ill prisoner in the state of Arkansas, was an opportunity to get the same message to White voters regarding his political relationship with the Black community that George Bush delivered to many of these same White voters in 1988.

It is erroneous to assert that candidate Bill Clinton rose above racial politics; he merely adopted a different tactic from that used by Bush in reminding the electorate that he was primarily interested in the White middle-class and suburban vote. Furthermore, Clinton showed that he would go after this vote even if it meant marginalizing the most loyal bloc of voters in the Democratic Party in the past fifty years: Black voters.

This strategy was defended, even by some on the Left, by arguing that Clinton would have to do whatever it would take in order to win the White House. Thus, Black voters were asked, *again*, to mute their interests and concerns so that yet another White presidential candidate would not have to talk about their interests and thereby perhaps lose White votes. This was yet another instance of a national leader deciding that it is more politically expedient to ignore, or even to exploit, racial hierarchy in America rather than to challenge it. And, *by not challenging racial hierarchy*, as the work of V. O. Key and others show, *the saliency of populist and class-based demands are muted*.

Much of the Black elected and traditional civil rights leadership accepted this modern version of "The Atlanta Compromise" of 1895. Let me add that this was the same logic used by W. E. B. Du Bois and other Black leaders in arguing in 1912 that Blacks should support the segregationist Woodrow Wilson in order to help defeat candidates Theodore Roosevelt and William Taft. In one of his autobiographies, Du Bois quotes candidate Woodrow Wilson upon being asked if he would welcome Black voter support in the 1912 presidential election. Wilson assured Du Bois and other Black leaders of his earnest wish

> to see justice done the colored people in every matter; and not mere grudging justice, but justice executed with liberality and cordial good feeling. I want to assure them that should I become President of the United States they may count upon me for absolute fair dealing, for everything by which I could assist in advancing the interests of their race in the United States.[13]

Du Bois proceeds to conclude, despite this promise, that "we were cruelly disappointed when the Democratic party won and the next Congress met."[14]

In an article titled "Old Time New Democrats" political scientist Adolph Reed reminds us that this strategy has been especially prominent among liberal politicians in the South:

> When I was a kid and a young teenager, I remember quite vividly "liberal" candidates for office would approach the illegally limited Black electorate

for support by representing themselves as secret friends of Black interests:
Of course, I'll have to call you "niggers" when I'm campaigning in North
Louisiana . . . and other such places, the standard tale went, but you should
realize that I don't really mean it; I just have to do it to get elected.[15]

The politically and racially subordinate position of Blacks has been
defined by some in the Democratic Party as necessary for electoral
success.

The Republican Party has fared no better regarding this issue, of
course. While the Republican Party has attempted to keep Blacks off
the bus, the Democratic Party has insisted that victory requires that
Blacks sit in the back of the bus. Despite liberal rhetoric the
Democratic Party and liberal leadership have not committed themselves to significantly weakening racial hierarchy in America. Robert
S. Browne reminds us in *The American Prospect* that "with regard to
civil rights, the current discussion is grounded in the frank admission
that liberal Americans' commitment to just society is at best a fair-
weather commitment."[16] Neither of the major parties has sustained a
long-term challenge – whether on political or moral grounds – to the
existence of poverty and racial hierarchy in the United States.

Many of the victories of the Civil Rights Movement, as significant
as they have been for expanding political participation, did not change
the control or distribution of wealth or economic power in the United
States. The business sector came to realize after a short period that
some of the demands of the Civil Rights Movement, regardless of
how stridently they were presented, would not necessarily change
fundamentally the power or wealth status quo.[17] But despite this
realization, the major parties acquiesced to demands for greater
participation because of the pressure of grassroots movements that
flowered during the 1950s and 1960s. In the absence of a strong
Black grassroots social movement such as occurred during this period,
Black elected and civil rights leadership has not been able to pressure
the major parties to address effectively the social and economic
resources and needs of the Black community. A third party, founded
on the basis of eradicating racism and redistributing greater levels of
resources to the poor and working class, can continue to pressure the
major parties as did these earlier grassroots movements. A third party
that mobilizes voters effectively and runs independents for electoral
office can be, in effect, an important bargaining chip for poor and
working-class people, as well as for people of color.

Class, Social Welfare, and the Major Parties

There are similarities and differences between the Democratic and Republican Parties in the arena of social welfare and public policy. There are important differences, for instance, in how the two parties view the role of government. Generally, while the Republican Party theoretically favors less government and regulation, and more laissez-faire approaches to social welfare and economic growth and development, the Democratic Party under President Clinton has embarked, at least rhetorically, on a more aggressive posture regarding government activism as noted in the pursuit of national health care and international free trade.

This kind of philosophical difference should not be minimized. The legislative and policy consequences of these two different approaches are already evident in the passage of the Family Leave Act of 1993, heightened discussion about the appropriate governmental response to the health care fiscal crisis, and appointment of abortion rights and pro-choice governmental officials; and while the cabinet-level appointments certainly do not reflect *class* diversity, there was an attempt to have these appointments reflect *racial* diversity. These are positions that were not pursued, or that even were rejected, during twelve years of Reagan–Bush Republican politics.

While major differences between the Republican and Democratic Parties are acknowledged, however, it must be noted that the governmental activism of the Democratic Party is still quite timid compared to that of other nations with less economic resources. Both parties, as a matter of fact, are positioned at one end of the public policy spectrum regarding class and social welfare issues. Both parties support, albeit in different ways and degrees, what sociologist Nathan Glazer and others have referred to as the "incomplete welfare state."[18] Furthermore, it is a fact that both parties receive a major portion of their political contributions from large corporations. In an article titled "DLC – Democrats Looking for Cash," Joel Bleifuss points to a strong correlation between the one hundred congressional representatives who are members of the Democratic Party's Democratic Leadership Council and campaign and political contributions from the nation's top ten corporate lobbies.[19]

Some observers are proposing that the Democratic Party's push to the ideological center actually means movement toward and support of Republican-like policy positions. Even the conservative columnist George F. Will describes Bill Clinton's social welfare proposals as merely "year five of the Bush–Clinton era." As one example of the similarities in the area of social welfare, he points out that many of the programs Clinton has sought to increase actually started to grow during the Bush administration: funding for children's programs increased by 67 percent, education and training by 16 percent, aid to cities and states by 60 percent, nutrition programs by 72 percent, and monies for infrastructure by 32 percent.[20] This may illustrate that these major parties are not really very different in some areas, and that Democrats are not much more aggressive than Republicans when it comes to certain kinds of social welfare. Along this line of thought, it should be noted that as important as the passage of the Family Leave Act of 1993 is, for instance, the fact is that its provisions are very limited in scope: only 40 percent of all workers are eligible for family leaves because of a provision that businesses with less than 50 employees are exempted from the requirements of this Act; but it is in such businesses that most U.S. workers are found. This is one reason why David Moberg, a writer for *In These Times*, referred to the Family Leave Act as "chump change."[21] This legislation, as well as other, shows that Democrats may be as timid and limited as Republicans when it comes to social welfare in some areas.

Another instance of how the Democratic and Republican Parties share one end of the policy spectrum on issues of social welfare is public assistance and aid to cities. In a recent issue of *Poverty and Race*, Sean Gervasi claims that:

> It should now be clear that barring a basic change in policy, the new Administration in Washington is not going to address the major problems of America's cities, home for 58% of our African-American population and 52% of our Hispanic population. . . . While President Clinton has repeatedly stated that he intends to take the country in a "new direction" his recently announced plan represents little more than a minor correction in the course set by Presidents Reagan and Bush. The U.S. is again following the path of fiscal conservatism.[22]

To use Dolbeare's terminology again, Clinton's approach to national economic development may be but the gentler side of the "cowboy capitalism" that Americans experienced during the Reagan and Bush years. Basically, the two major parties protect the interests of wealth and merely debate the most effective policy approaches for preserving the basis of wealth. The debate regarding the national deficit, for instance, is pursued by both parties in ways that do not challenge basic assumptions that serve to preserve the economic and wealth status quo in this nation. Gervasi notes, for example, that neither of the two political parties is ready to propose a policy which would carry the country out of economic stagnation. A multi-year urban policy today – a policy aimed at truly rebuilding the cities of the U.S. and ending poverty – would cost hundreds of billions of dollars. Mesmerized, as they are meant to be, by the pseudo problem of the deficit, our political leaders lack the courage to go against the storm of propaganda from special interests which would greet any effort to rebuild the cities.[23]

In the area of public assistance and welfare reform the Clinton administration seems to be reemphasizing rather than questioning the assumptions about poverty and poor people entailed in the Family Support Act of 1988 passed under the administration of President Bush – and supported by many Democratic governors. Implicit in this legislation is a view of poor people and poverty as simply a problem of dependency and lack of human capital. Under the Family Support Act of 1988 the problem of persistent poverty is approached by requiring training, and providing day care, to prepare poor people for the workforce, as well as discouraging dependency on public welfare. Unfortunately, the Family Support Act of 1988 is a simplistic and narrow piece of legislation aimed at reducing dependency rather than poverty. The aim of this legislation, as are current efforts to abolish welfare "as we know it today," is simply to get people off the welfare rolls rather than to eliminate or reduce poverty through full employment, higher wages, and a redistribution of social and fiscal wealth. The current welfare reform discussions reflect, in part, the fact that poor persons have not developed a viable electoral mechanism that would represent their interests and points of view regarding public policy. This could be accomplished by a third party supported and organized by poor people and people of color.

The absence of a seriously organized and progressive third party today has allowed the Democratic Party leadership to backstep on progressive social welfare approaches. Even in the area of environmental politics today, all is not what seemed to be the case back in November 1992. For example, an editorial in the April 5, 1993 issue of *The Nation* reported:

A close look at the Clinton plan shows that, in the 1994 budget, spending for renewable energy and energy efficiency is low. The Administration promises these items will receive more money in 1995 and beyond, but talk – especially of future funding – is cheap. Environmentalists cheered Clinton's call for increased funding of mass transit. But now the Administration is considering no longer earmarking for that purpose a portion of the federal gasoline tax. Add the new mass transit funds, subtract the earmarked funds, and it's close to a wash.[24]

The backstepping of the Clinton administration has also been evident in foreign affairs, particularly regarding the case of Haitian refugees and Muslims in Bosnia. During the 1992 campaign, Clinton stated that these two issues represented moral outrages that required the U.S. to act ethically and forthrightly to correct these injustices; after that election, these same issues were redefined as "complex," requiring patience and cautionary nonaction. This kind of backstepping on the part of the Democratic Party occurs partially because of fear of a conservative backlash, as well as the absence of an independent, socially progressive, and nationally and locally organized political front. Such a front, in the form of a third party, could mobilize support for more progressive positions on a broad range of issues. A third party representing policies characteristic of economic democracy would at least be able to present alternative public policies to the electorate.

Towards a Third Party

The political stability and economic health of the U.S. require that our national leadership confront the issues of race and continuing racial hierarchy; it must also seek to ensure that every person in the United States has access to decent housing conditions, jobs with decent wages that keep people out of poverty, and a guarantee that adequate and quality health care is expanded and available for all people.

The people of the United States will not be able to move the two national parties toward a more progressive social welfare state, however, without breaking the "Republican–Democratic electoral lock" that political scientist E. E. Schattschneider made reference to in the 1960s.[25] The breaking of this electoral stranglehold on the part of the two major parties cannot happen through romanticized cheerleading on the Left for Bill Clinton to straighten things out, or by disgruntled Democrats threatening to join the Republican Party.

Noting how Jesse Jackson fared in the presidential race of 1992 compared to the 1988 race should serve as a reminder of the nature of national political power and what it would take to move people and interests who hold power. In 1988, Jackson led an organizing effort that produced one thousand delegates to the Democratic Party's national convention in Atlanta, Georgia. The leadership of the Democratic Party granted him some limited, and symbolic, victories only because of this delegate base. In 1992, rather than relying on a concrete delegate base that represented a certain, but limited, degree of power, Jackson used moral suasion to push his ideas and programs; as a result of this change in strategy, Clinton could politically afford to dismiss Jackson and the kind of politics he represents. Thus, it was Jackson's *independent* electoral base – albeit within the Democratic Party – that allowed a hearing of sorts for Jackson's positions. It was not moral suasion or the eloquence of Jackson's speeches, or his charisma but, rather, his base of delegates that guaranteed at least a hearing. The point here is *not* that Jackson should be followed around by political groupies as a way of pressuring the Democratic or Republican Parties, or that he gained major policy concessions by pursuing an inside-Democratic Party strategy in 1988. It is, however, to emphasize the observation that Jackson has been more of an influential player the more he has reflected organizational independence from the Democratic Party, and less influential the more his strategy reflected attempts to take over or change the policy orientation of this party from within its institutional boundaries.

The Jackson campaigns, in both 1984 and 1988, show that the idea of a third party – at least among Blacks – has gained saliency. Manning Marable is accurate in observing that in terms of national party politics, "throughout Black America, there is a sense that the political strategies, tactics and leadership are profoundly flawed."[26] Various surveys reflect some support for Black independent party strategies. The National Black Election Study found that in the early 1980s, 29 percent of Black respondents favored a Black political party. The Joint Center for Political and Economic Studies found that 18 percent of Blacks polled in 1986 would have supported Jesse Jackson as an independent candidate in 1988.[27]

There are many factors that encourage organization around a third party strategy at the national level. Political scientist Theodore J. Lowi wrote in the *New York Times Magazine* that "whatever the outcome of this year's Presidential race, historians will undoubtedly focus on 1992 as the beginning of the end of America's two-party system."[28] One factor supporting this possibility is the growing alienation of an increasing number of Americans, especially Blacks, from the two-party system. This alienation may be reflected in the fact that about 21 million voters turning out during the 1992 presidential election decided not to vote for either of the two major presidential candidates on the ballot. This, along with significant support for Ross Perot, shows that many Americans are becoming disillusioned with both the Democratic and Republican Parties. Perot received almost one-fifth (19 percent) of the popular vote as, in part, a candidate protesting the policies and influence of both major parties. Several important offices have been captured by individuals rejecting both major parties; these include Governor Lowell Weiker of Connecticut, Governor Walter Hickel of Alaska, and U.S. Representative Bernard Sanders of Vermont. Some of these efforts certainly are not calls for the adoption of progressive social welfare. But, as did the George Wallace campaign in 1968, these efforts show that the two major parties are vulnerable to electoral challenge. It seems that the right wing in this country has understood this far more effectively than the Left, which many times succumbs to a lesser-of-two-evils approach to the two major parties.

There are a number of broad issues that are justifiably raised regarding the efficacy of a third party strategy. Some observers have pointed out that in the current period it would be virtually impossible for a third party candidate to win national office. But the point of a third party does not have to be necessarily victory at the national level in a particular year. A well-organized third party could have far greater importance in pushing and pressuring the two national parties toward more enlightened and equitable social welfare. A broadly based and well-organized third party could also have many opportunities to win local and state races that in some instances are as important to the well-being of people as is the particular occupant in the White House.

Organizing a national and effective third party is extremely difficult. But there are several efforts already launched that are beginning to lay a potential organizational, if not yet philosophical, groundwork for a major third party at the national level. The more notable and recent efforts include the establishment of the Green Party USA, Labor Party Advocates, Project Tomorrow, the 21st Century Party, and the New Party.[29] One reason the New Alliance Party did relatively well in 1988 is that it tapped into voter and citizen dissatisfaction with the Democratic Party. Many of the people who voted for the New Alliance Party were those who understood that neither the Democratic Party nor the Republican Party could respond to their social needs, and they probably sought a mechanism for working this kind of statement rather than specifically supporting the program or leadership of the New Alliance Party. There is a significantly larger number of untapped voters in the U.S. electorate that could be potential targets for a third party built on the basis of progressive public and social welfare policies. And such a party would attract far more supporters than a Perot or a New Alliance Party effort.

The voter turnout in the 1992 presidential election was approximately 106 million voters, or 56 percent of the estimated 189 million persons of voting age in the U.S. There were 134 million registered voters in 1992; this means that *31 million* registered voters did not vote at all, and a total of *83 million* Americans of voting age did not register and/or did not vote.[30] The Rainbow Coalition had a major opportunity to emerge as a powerful and influential independent party after the 1988 election by organizing many of these alienated and traditional nonvoters, or what Jackson referred to as the "have-nots." Jackson decided, however, that organizing within the Democratic Party could result in fundamentally changing the philosophical basis of the party. This did not occur; indeed, the Democratic Party has actually moved toward the center of the political spectrum. What we do not yet have on the national scene, therefore, is a third party that could unify some of these nonvoters under a progressive and multiracial and multiethnic umbrella of social change and equality.

Another counterresponse to those calling for a major third party in the United States is the suggestion that the Democratic Party has been revitalized; that it has recaptured the center of the political spectrum; that it has brought back the Wallace and Reagan Democrats who left the party over the past quarter of a century. Electoral data on the 1992 presidential election, however, may not support this kind of optimism and romanticism about the Democratic Party. According to the Committee for the Study of the American Electorate, President Clinton received only 23 percent of the eligible adult vote in the United States. This is why journalist Thomas Oliphant quipped: "It is not at all clear that the election had very much to do with its winner, except to the extent that while many voters had doubts about Bill Clinton – in quite a few cases, substantial doubts – these were not serious enough to outweigh their far stronger desire to reject Bush's leadership and try something and somebody else."[31]

Blacks, as the most loyal and key bloc in the Democratic Party, are especially showing increasing disillusionment with and abandonment of this party. The proportion of the Black vote received by the Democratic Party presidential nominee in 1992 was low compared to many previous elections. In 1992 Clinton received a lesser proportion of the Black vote than did Michael Dukakis in 1988 in the states of Georgia, Illinois, Louisiana, Maryland, Mississippi, Missouri, Michigan, New York, Ohio, Texas, Virginia, Pennsylvania, and South Carolina. According to an analysis by Clarence Lusane of the Black vote in the Democratic primaries in 1988 and 1992, "In 14 states, where Jesse Jackson received 3.5 million Black votes in 1988, Clinton received only 1.6 million Black votes in those same states in 1992. While Jackson got between 88 and 96 percent of the vote, Clinton received between 49 and 80 percent."[32]

Candidate Bill Clinton won the general election in 1992 with 43 percent of the total votes cast; he received but 39 percent of all ballots cast by White voters. But he received about 82 percent of the Black vote, and 62 percent of the Latino vote. A switch of a few percentage points on the part of Blacks would have cost Clinton several states: he would have lost Illinois, Michigan, Ohio, and New Jersey with just a slightly lesser proportion of the Black vote than he received in these states. He could have also lost Louisiana and Mississippi, where Black votes formed a substantial majority of all votes cast in these states. Clinton, by the way, attained a majority of votes cast in only two places, Arkansas (53 percent) and the District of Columbia (85 percent). These figures indicate that the electoral base underlying Clinton's victory was quite fragile and open to political challenge. This presents an opportunity to those interested in moving the Democratic Party toward aggressive and progressive social welfare goals and progress.

Black Leadership and the Major Parties

The growing disaffection of the general electorate with both national parties, and that of Black voters with the Democratic Party, raises the question of how Black leadership, in particular, is responding to this development and opportunity. Unfortunately, much of Black elected leadership in the current period, as well as some who might be described as part of traditional civil rights leadership, have ignored the potential clout of an independent Black voting sector; some seem to have concluded that access to those in power is far more important for the well-being of the Black community than the development of an independent, and progressive, Black political base.[33]

Despite the fact that the Black vote is a critical factor in national elections, some Black leaders have passively acquiesced to the calculated marginalization of the Black electorate by the Democratic Party by arguing that Democrats must not openly address Black concerns lest they scare off White voters and thereby lose the White House. Additionally, some of these Black leaders have made very little attempt to reach out to other communities of color, instead choosing to play the traditional and divisive American political game of "ethnic leapfrogging." But for a third party to be successful as an effective agent of change in national politics Black grassroots activists must begin to challenge Black leadership to reach out to other groups facing depressed living conditions. Black leadership must also begin developing influence not on the basis of access to individuals or the party in power, but on the capability of pushing such individuals and parties toward support of policies that will mean a people-oriented, socially healthier, and economically productive society. This means that Black politics, Latino politics, Asian politics, labor politics, and so forth must move from operating within a conceptual framework that emphasizes a politics of access, or a politics of the lesser of two evils, as represented by the boundaries of two-major-party-only politics, to a politics of power. At this point in the social and economic development of the United States, only an independent, third party force on the national and local political landscape, which pushes a progressive social welfare agenda, can make this happen.

Notes

1. This article is based on a presentation to "Future Directions for American Politics and Public Policy," seminar at Harvard University, Kennedy School of Government (May 6, 1993). Special appreciation is due to Gemima Remy for editorial and research assistance in completing this article, as well as to the editor and anonymous readers for *New Political Science*.

2. See James Jennings, "The Foundation of American Racism: Defining Bigotry, Racism, and Racial Hierarchy," *Trotter Review*, vol. 4, no. 3 (Fall 1990).

3. Gerald David Jaynes and Robin M. Williams, Jr., eds., *A Common Destiny: Blacks and American Society* (Washington, D.C.: National Academy Press, 1989); Wornie L. Reed, ed., *Assessment of the Status of African Americans*, vols. 1–5 (Boston: William Monroe Trotter Institute at the University of Massachusetts, 1990).

4. Jaynes and Williams, *A Common Destiny*, p. 275.

5. Kenneth M. Dolbeare, *Democracy at Risk: The Politics of Economic Renewal* (Chatham, NJ: Chatham House, 1986).

6. Thomas Ferguson, "Organized Capitalism, Fiscal Policy, and the 1992 Democratic Campaign," in Lawrence Dodd and Calvin Jillson, eds., *New Perspectives on American Politics* (Washington, D.C.: Congressional Quarterly Press, 1993).

7. Kevin Phillips, *The Politics of Rich and Poor: Wealth and the American Electorate in the Reagan Aftermath* (New York: Random House, 1990), p. 241.

8. Ibid., p. 13.

9. C. L. R. James, *The Black Jacobins: Toussaint L'Ouverture and the San Domingo Revolution* (New York: Vintage, 1963), p. 283.

10. Ron Daniels, speech made in Cleveland, Ohio (October 14, 1991).

11. *Investing in Children and Youth: Reconstructing Our Cities* (Washington, D.C.: Milton S. Eisenhower Foundation, 1993).

12. V. O. Key, *Southern Politics* (New York: Alfred A. Knopf, 1940).

13. *The Autobiography of W. E .B. Du Bois* (New York: International Publishers, 1973), p. 264.

14. Ibid.

15. Adolph Reed, "Old Time New Democrats" *The Progressive*, vol. 57, no. 4 (April 1993), p. 16.

16. Robert S. Browne, "The Road to Rectification," *The American Prospect*, no. 10 (Summer 1992), p. 93.

17. See Manning Marable, *Race, Reform and Rebellion: The Second Reconstruction in Black America, 1945–1982* (Jackson: University of Mississippi Press, 1984), p. 95.

18. Nathan Glazer, *The Limits of Social Policy* (Cambridge, MA: Harvard University Press, 1988).

19. Joel Bleifuss, "DLC–Democrats Looking for Cash," *In These Times*, (April 5, 1993).

20. George F. Will, "Clinton's Phony Dazzle," *Boston Globe* (April 4, 1993).

21. David Moberg, "All in the Family," *In These Times*, vol. 17, no. 7 (February 1993), pp. 18–20.

22. Sean Gervasi, *Poverty and Race*, vol. 2, no. 2 (March 1993), p. 1.

23. Ibid., p. 8.

24. Editorial, *The Nation* (April 5, 1993), p. 436.

25. E. E. Schattschneider, *The Semi-Sovereign People: A Realist's View of Democracy in America* (New York: Holt, Rinehart & Winston, 1960).

26. Manning Marable, "At the End of the Rainbow," *Race and Class*, vol. 34, no. 2 (October–December 1992), p. 75.

27. I have provided several examples of Blacks pursuing independent electoral strategies across the U.S. in *The Politics of Black Empowerment: Transformation of Black Activism in Urban America* (Detroit: Wayne State University Press, 1992), pp. 64–73.

28. Theodore J. Lowi, "The Party Crasher," *New York Times Magazine* (August 23, 1992), p. 28.

29. For a historical overview of third party strategies in the Black community, see Hanes Walton, Jr., in *The Negro in Third Party Politics* (Philadelphia: Dorrance, 1969).

30. These figures are rounded; see Kimball W. Brace, *The Election Data Book: A Statistical Portrait of Voting in America, 1992* (Lanham, MD: Berman Press, 1993).

31. Thomas Oliphant, *Boston Globe* (November 8, 1992).

32. Clarence Lusane, "New Beginnings and a Cautious Celebration: African Americans and the 1992 Election," Occasional Paper No. 26 (Boston: William Monroe Trotter Institute, 1993), p. 18.

33. I explain these "two faces" of Black politics in *The Politics of Black Empowerment*, especially the chapter "Race and the Failure of Political Managerialism"; also see James Jennings and Mel King, *From Access to Power: Black Politics in Boston* (Cambridge, MA: Schenkman Books, 1985).

About the Contributors

TONY AFFIGNE is a scholar and activist who teaches political science at Providence College and serves as acting director of the Program in Black Studies. In 1995 he was founding cochair of the American Political Science Association's organized section on Race, Ethnicity and Politics and he is a member of the Association's Committee on the Status of "Latinos y Latinas." He is coauthor of the forthcoming *Race and Politics in the Americas: The Rise and Fall of the American Racial Empire*. He was a founder of Rhode Island's Puerto Rican Political Action Committee and the first Latino candidate for governor of that state in 1986. He cofounded the Green Party of Rhode Island and was honored in 1994 as the *padrino* of the state's Puerto Rican Parade.

JOHN J. BETANCUR is Assistant Professor at the Urban Planning and Policy Program of the University of Illinois at Chicago. A former professor in Colombia, he has been closely associated with community-based organizations and other efforts in minority communities in Chicago. His main field of research and professional work in the United States is on economic development, particularly as it relates to communities of color. His academic publications include articles and chapters on Latinos, settlement patterns of Latinos, race and class in economic development, community development organizations, manufacturing displacement, and squatter settlements.

RODERICK BUSH is Assistant Professor of African-American Studies at Seton Hall University. He was a member of the Congress of African People, the Student Organization for Black Unity, the Youth Organization for Black Unity, and the African Liberation Support Committee. He was associate director of *Contemporary Marxism*, editor of *The New Black Vote: Politics and Power in Four American Cities*, and a member of the research and editorial board of the Institute for the Study of Labor and Economic Crisis. He is currently completing a book titled *Black Power and Social Transformation: Race, Class, and Social Movements in the 20th Century United States.*

FARAI CHIDEYA is a CNN political analyst and a freelance journalist. She is the author of *Don't Believe the Hype: Fighting Cultural Misinformation about African Americans.* She is currently working on a book titled *The Color of America: How the Nation's Most Diverse Generation Is Reshaping American Culture.* Chideya was a fall 1996 Research Fellow at the Freedom Forum Media Studies Center in New York City, where she analyzed issues related to youth and the news media. She has won several awards, including a National Education Reporting Award and a Unity Award in Media.

DOUGLAS C. GILLS is Assistant Professor of Urban Planning and Policy, and Assistant Research Professor in the Center for Urban Economic Development at the University of Illinois at Chicago. He is a scholar and activist. His current research interests are in the areas of urban and international community development practices, new forms of progressive democratic practices, the impact of technological developments on social movements, and coalition politics.

CYNTHIA HAMILTON currently serves as Director of African and African-American Studies at the University of Rhode Island. She has taught for more than twenty years at universities across the country. In addition to being a teacher, she has been involved extensively in community-based organizing for economic development.

JAMES JENNINGS is Professor of Political Science and Director of the William Monroe Trotter Institute, University of Massachusetts Boston. His books include *Understanding the Nature of Poverty in Urban America*, *The Politics of Black Empowerment*, and *Race, Politics, and Economic Development: Community Perspectives.* He has edited *Blacks, Latinos, and Asians in Urban America: Status and Prospects for Politics and Activism.* He is also involved in a broad range of civic and neighborhood activism in Black and Puerto Rican communities in the United States.

LOUIS KUSHNICK is Vice Chair of the Institute of Race Relations and has been editor of *Sage Race Relations Abstracts* since 1980. He has written extensively on race and class in Britain, the United States, and Western Europe. He is currently cowriting, *The Race Card: Race and Politics in Post-War Britain* with Huw Beynon. He is also a Research Associate of the William Monroe Trotter Institute at the University of Massachusetts Boston.

CLARENCE LUSANE is the author of several books, including *African Americans at the Crossroads*. He is completing his doctorate in Political Science at Howard University and teaches at Columbia University in New York City through the Institute for Research in African-American Studies.

LEWIS A. RANDOLPH is Assistant Professor in the Political Science Department/Public Administration Program at Ohio University. His areas of interests include urban development and politics, Black politics, social movements, and ideology. He is coauthor of *African-American Officials and the Future of Progressive Political Movements* and *Rise and Decline of African-American Political Power in Richmond: Race, Class, and Gender*.

DAVID B. REYNOLDS is Professor of Political Science at Wayne State University, where he teaches Labor Studies. He has worked as a union organizer and participated in progressive electoral and community politics for many years. His most recent book, *Democracy Unbound: Progressive Grassroots Challenges to the Two Party System*, examines current efforts to build a progressive political movement.

WILLIAM W. SALES, JR. is Associate Professor and Chairperson of the Department of African-American Studies at Seton Hall University. He is also an activist whose community organizing in Harlem earned him one of Columbia University's prestigious Revson Fellowships. A student of Black nationalism, Sales is the author of *From Civil Rights to Black Liberation: Malcolm X and the Organization of Afro-American Unity*. He is also the author of *Southern Africa/Black America: Same Struggle, Same Fight*. A founding member of the Malcolm X Work Group, Sales was coconvener of the first international conference on Malcolm X held in New York City in the fall of 1990.

JAMES STEELE is Executive Director of Breakthrough Political Consulting Service. He is the author of *Freedom's River: The African-American Contribution to Democracy*, and numerous articles on electoral politics and legislative issues. Until recently, he served as Deputy District Director for Organization for Congressman Major R. Owens. He was a founder of the Center for African-American Studies at Ohio State University, where he also taught courses on African-American history and politics.

Index

THE HAYMARKET SERIES

Recent and forthcoming titles

THE INVENTION OF THE WHITE RACE, Volume I: Racial Oppression and Social Control *by Theodore Allen*

LABOR AND THE COURSE OF AMERICAN DEMOCRACY: US History in Latin American Perspective *by Charles Bergquist*

PUBLIC ACCESS: Literary Theory and American Cultural Politics *by Michael Bérubé*

MARXISM IN THE USA: Remapping the History of the American Left *by Paul Buhle*

FIRE IN THE AMERICAS: Forging a Revolutionary Agenda *by Roger Burbach and Orlando Núñez*

THE FINAL FRONTIER: The Rise and Fall of the American Rocket State *by Dale Carter*

CORRUPTIONS OF EMPIRE: Life Studies and the Reagan Era *by Alexander Cockburn*

THE SOCIAL ORIGINS OF PRIVATE LIFE: A History of American Families, 1600–1900 *by Stephanie Coontz*

ROLL OVER CHE GUEVARA: Travels of a Radical Reporter *by Marc Cooper*

SHADES OF NOIR: A Reader *by Joan Copjec*

BUILDING THE WORKINGMAN'S PARADISE: The Design of American Company Towns *by Margaret Crawford*

WAR AND TELEVISION *by Bruce Cumings*

IT'S NOT ABOUT A SALARY: Rap, Race and Resistance in Los Angeles *by Brian Cross, with additional texts by Reagan Kelly and T-Love*

CITY OF QUARTZ: EXCAVATING THE FUTURE IN LOS ANGELES *by Mike Davis*

PRISONERS OF THE AMERICAN DREAM: Politics and Economy in the History of the US Working Class *by Mike Davis*

THE CULTURAL FRONT: The Laboring of American Culture in the Twentieth Century *by Michael Denning*

MECHANIC ACCENTS: Dime Novels and Working-Class Culture in America *by Michael Denning*

THE ASSASSINATION OF NEW YORK *by Robert Fitch*

No Crystal Stair: African Americans in the City of Angels *by Lynell George*

Where the Boys Are: Cuba, Cold War America and the Making of a New Left *by Van Gosse*

Power Misses: Essays Across (Un)Popular Culture *by David E. James*

Race, Politics and Economic Development: Community Perspectives *edited by James Jennings*

Postmodernism and Its Discontents: Theories, Practices *edited by E. Ann Kaplan*

White Savages in the South Seas *by Mel Kernahan*

Seven Minutes: The Life and Death of the American Animated Cartoon *by Norman M. Klein*

The History of Forgetting: Los Angeles and the Erasure of Memory *by Norman M. Klein*

Rank-and-File Rebellion: Teamsters for a Democratic Union *by Dan La Botz*

Imagining Home: Class, Culture and Nationalism in the African Diaspora *edited by Sidney Lemelle and Robin D.G. Kelley*

Twice the Work of Free Labor: The Political Economy of Convict Labor in the New South *by Alex Lichtenstein*

Dangerous Crossroads: Popular Music, Postmodernism and the Poetics of Place *by George Lipsitz*

Black American Politics: From the Washington Marches to Jesse Jackson *by Manning Marable*

The Other Side: Los Angeles from Both Sides of the Border *by Rubén Martinez*

An Injury to All: The Decline of American Unionism *by Kim Moody*

Youth, Identity, Power: The Chicano Movement *by Carlos Muñoz, Jr.*

Selling Culture: Magazines, Markets, and Class at the Turn of the Century *by Richard Ohmann*

Red Dirt: Growing Up Okie *by Roxanne Dunbar Ortiz*

ANOTHER TALE TO TELL: Politics and Narrative in Postmodern Culture *by Fred Pfeil*

WHITE GUYS: Studies in Postmodern Domination and Difference *by Fred Pfeil*

THEY MUST BE REPRESENTED: The Politics of Documentary *by Paula Rabinowitz*

THE WAGES OF WHITENESS: Race and the Making of the American Working Class *by David R. Roediger*

TOWARDS THE ABOLITION OF WHITENESS: Essays on Race, Politics and Working-Class History *by David R. Roediger*

OUR OWN TIME: A History of American Labor and the Working Day *by David R. Roediger and Philip S. Foner*

THE CHICAGO GANGSTER THEORY OF LIFE: Nature's Debt to Society *by Andrew Ross*

STRANGE WEATHER: Culture, Science and Technology in the Age of Limits *by Andrew Ross*

CIRCUS AMERICANUS: *by Ralph Rugoff*

IMAGINEERING ATLANTA: The Politics of Place in the City of Dreams *by Charles Rutheiser*

THE RISE AND FALL OF THE WHITE REPUBLIC: Class Politics and Mass Culture in Nineteenth-Century America *by Alexander Saxton*

MILLENNIAL DREAMS: Contemporary Culture and Capital in the North *by Paul Smith*

UNFINISHED BUSINESS: Twenty Years of Socialist Review *edited by the Socialist Review collective*

WRITING FROM THE LEFT: New Essays on Radical Culture and Politics *by Alan M. Wald*

BLACK MACHO AND THE MYTH OF SUPERWOMAN *by Michele Wallace*

INVISIBILITY BLUES: From Pop to Theory *by Michele Wallace*

PROFESSORS, POLITICS AND POP *by Jon Wiener*

THE LEFT AND THE DEMOCRATS *The Year Left 1*

TOWARDS A RAINBOW SOCIALISM *The Year Left 2*